1863

Republic in the Balance
A Year of Slaughter and Hope

Nick Patz

ISBN: 979-8-218-73788-7

TABLE OF CONTENTS

Author's Note

There have been many years in the history of the United States of America that were consequential to the formation of our great democratic republic. I was drawn to write about the year 1863, not solely because of its consequential turning points for American history, but also by its human weight. The sacrifice was almost too much to comprehend. It was a year of incredible human toll, great ferocity, intense sorrow, patriotism, and even at times a little compassion. Amongst all of that there was a ray of hope outside of the constant despair. As I researched the battles, the politics, the geography, and the people, it occurred to me that this single year revealed more about the American character than perhaps any other.

This book is not meant to settle debates or glorify the immense struggle. I have a hope that it brings readers closer to understanding the people who lived through the war, presidents and generals, soldiers and nurses, rioters and writers, the newly freed, as well as white families from either side of the conflict. Their words, their choices, and their silences echo through our history.

In telling these stories, I hope to remind us all of what was risked, and what was made possible, in the firelight of 1863.

Introduction

The year 1863 lingers in the shadow of horrifying sorrow brought on by savage destruction. The scale of bloodshed strains the imagination, and no simple tally can capture the depth of grief that bled through homes on both sides of the war.

Most of the generals of the Civil War had graduated from West Point, where they studied the war tactics of Napoleon. These tactics included frontal assaults in line formations, with emphasis on taking high ground. They centered around, speed, quick decisions and using a combination of arms. Napoleon used flanking maneuvers, with infantry using bayonet charges, calvary, and artillery combined to take on his enemy. Use of these tactics naturally inflicted a lot of casualties.

On the battlefields of the war between the states, men died not so much as names but merely as bodies, piled in tangled rows, faceless and forgotten, trodden underfoot by comrades urged forward into the same storm of musket shot and cannon fire. When the volleys ceased, the burial parties dug wide trenches and laid their comrades down, one atop another, without ceremony or farewell and sometimes without recording their names.

Repeatedly, when a battle line was shattered in the grass, a general's command summoned another line. Those men often had to step over the dead and the dying and into the enemy fire themselves, very often to meet the same consequence as those before them. Looking back now, the strategy seems almost deranged in its repetition, a machinery of sacrifice cloaked in the illusion of valor. There was no glory in it, there was only the brutality of a war fought to save the idea of a nation, and in an extraordinary contradiction, the idea to end brutality of one race toward another.

By 1863, the nation had been torn and nearly devastated by three years of civil war. It stood at its most fragile point since the signing of the Declaration of Independence. The nation teetered on the edge of transformation and separation; with no certainty of which direction we would fall. The battles of Gettysburg, Vicksburg and Chattanooga would help give a preferential direction of the possibility of the end of the Civil War, but in certainty, there was nothing definitive. The Emancipation Proclamation, issued at the year's onset began to redefine the very soul of the nation creating more of a moral stance to obtaining victory for the North.

Cities trembled, some with riots, others with cannon fire. On both sides, soldiers deserted their armies by the tens of thousands. And in some very real way, the war entered every home in every state of the Union and the Confederacy. In quiet towns across the land, removed from the actual battles, families opened letters bearing unthinkable news.

It was a year when the future of the United States truly hung in the balance, a balance of a republic as had been imagined by the founding fathers after the revolutionary war, or two distinct nations and two distinct philosophies on what is right, moral and just.

This book is not merely a record of battlefield triumphs or presidential decisions. It is an attempt to capture the texture of a year, its politics and proclamations, its music and mourning, its military ignorance and brilliance, as well as its courage and death. From the booming cannons along the Mississippi River to the bravery of newly freed men joining the Union cause, from Lincoln's private doubts and incredible patience to the public fury over the nation's first military draft, this is a story of transformation, both national and deeply personal.

1863 was not the beginning of the war, nor was it the end. But it was the pivot, the year when America's identity was recast in fire, blood, freedom and resolve.

We begin not with a battle, but with a question, What kind of nation was struggling to be born in the fires of 1863?

This book seeks to explore that answer.

PART I: A NATION ON THE BRINK

CHAPTER 1
A NATION DIVIDED, THE ROAD TO 1863

The United States of America, forged in revolution and loosely bound by a fragile Constitution, found itself at a crossroads as it entered the third year of civil war. The extensive carnage of the war was brutal on a daily basis, it took a dramatic toll in terms of the lives lost and lives mutilated, as well as the psyche of the common citizenry on both sides. The war had begun in 1861 as a political dispute over many aspects of the United States Constitution, including the expansion of states' rights. But the cornerstone of the separation between the North and South had been the insistence on the part of the South for the absolute legalization of slavery as a right, due to the supremacy of the white race. By 1863 the war had evolved into an existential struggle over the very nature of the Union, and whether it could survive the weight of the contradictions amongst the states of the north and the south.

For decades leading up to the war, a series of uneasy political compromises had held the Union together, albeit barely. The Missouri Compromise of 1820, crafted by Henry Clay, a Kentucky Congressman and Speaker of the House, sought to balance the number of slave and free states. Maine was entering the United States at the same time as Missouri. Maine wanted to enter as a free state, but Missouri wanted to enter as a slave state. The compromise drew an arbitrary line at latitude 36°30' designating all future states above that line would be admitted as free (except for Missouri). This temporarily cooled tempers but did nothing to resolve the deeper ideological divide.

The Compromise of 1850 was another attempt to calm increasing tensions between the states that was largely sparked by the Federal territorial acquisitions following the Mexican-American War. The Compromise was actually five separate bills that had been passed by Congress, combined to form the agreement. These legislations were also primarily negotiated by Henry Clay in concert with Stephen Douglas, Senator from Illinois and antagonist of future President Lincoln. The Compromise of 1850 was centered on how to handle the idea of slavery in the new territories accumulated from victory in the Mexican-American War.

The provisions of the Compromise included that California and New Mexico were admitted to the Union as a free states, and it banned slave trade in Washington (but slavery was still allowed), defined the borders of Texas, and established a territorial government in Utah. But the Fugitive Slave Act was also a part of the Compromise package.

The Fugitive Slave Act was passed to appease the South, but it also managed to absolutely outrage the North. The legislation required the return of escaped slaves, even from free states, and penalized those who aided them. That penalty would be mostly in substantial fines. The result of the Fugitive Slave Act was a larger and ever-growing divide between free and slave states. Moral lines were being drawn with increasing clarity. The act was favorably received in the South, but in the North, it drove many moderates toward abolition. The resolve on both sides deepened. The Compromise of 1850 was successful to a certain point, in that it did delay for a time, a civil war.

The Compromise was followed by the Kansas-Nebraska Act of 1854. This act overturned the Missouri Compromise by allowing settlers in those territories to decide the question of slavery by popular sovereignty. This led to violent clashes known as "Bleeding Kansas," as pro- and anti-slavery factions fought for control of the new territories until the start of the Civil War in 1861. Over 200 persons were killed during these clashes between pro- and anti-slavery individuals One such clash involved John Brown and a seven supporters, six of whom were family, who killed five pro-slavery settlers. They were dragged from their sleep, and hacked to death with broadswords. Nobody from Brown's group was arrested. The era of compromise was ending, not with debate, but with bloodshed.

There was no single issue more consequential to become a driving force in dividing the nation than the decision of the Supreme Court in the case of Dred Scott v. Sandford (1857).

Dred Scott was a slave whose owner had taken him from Missouri (a slave state) into Illinois (a free state) where slavery was illegal. His owner was an Army doctor who had been reassigned. The doctor then was again reassigned to

Missouri. Scott tried to legally obtain his freedom when back in Missouri. He first tried to buy freedom for himself and his family, but his owner refused. Then he decided to go through the legal channels. Scott and his wife received financial assistance from a previous owner and used those funds to sue for their freedom claiming that because he was taken to a free state and resided there for a time, he was a free man. There was substantial recent legal precedence for the suit to be easily won.

Dred Scott would soon be introduced to a legal system that was not always fair. The initial suit was filed and tried in Missouri, where the court ruled that he was still a slave. The case received the same result from an appellate court in Missouri. He then took the case to a U.S federal court in Missouri where they upheld the lower Missouri court decisions. So, then the appeal all the way to the United States Supreme Court.

The case was initially before the Court in February 1856 and was reargued in My and December of that year. Finally on March 6, 1857, the Supreme Court issued a decision, by a 7-2 vote, that declared that African Americans were not citizens and could expect no protection from the Federal government or the courts, and that Congress had no power to ban slavery in any territory. The decision of the Court was likely significantly influenced by President Buchannan who was seeking a second term. He lobbied justices with mild anti-slavery preferences to join those with Southern pro-slavery preferences. Buchannan was fully aware of the Court's decision and how the Chief Justice would address it, before the decision was made public. Chief Justice Roger Tanney wrote the majority opinion, which in part stated: that people of African descent *"are not included, and were not intended to be included, under the word 'citizens' in the Constitution, and can therefore claim none of the rights and privileges which that instrument provides for and secures to citizens of the United States."*

Dred Scott and his family eventually obtained their freedom later in 1857. Scott's owner had married an abolitionist congressman, who faced great scrutiny from his constituents for holding a slave, although it was his brother that held ownership to the Scott family. The congressman executed a deed to transfer Scott and his family to Henry Blow, the son of Scott's former owner, both of whom had donated to Scott's defense fund. Taylor Blow then filed the appropriate papers to free the family on May 26, 1857.

The Supreme Court's decision over Dred Scott was a devastating blow to abolitionists and moderate Northerners alike, radicalizing many who had once sought reconciliation between the states.

Another spark in what was soon to soon become the raging fire of secession came in October 1859. Radical abolitionist, John Brown led an assault with 17 whites and five free blacks, to capture the federal arsenal at Harpers Ferry, Virginia (now West Virginia). He was hoping to ignite a slave uprising, by distributing the arms he planned to capture at the arsenal to African Americans who would then fight to free those enslaved.

The raid was put down rapidly by U.S. Marines stationed at Harpers Ferry who were under the leadership of Colonel Robert E. Lee. Ten of the 17 raiders were killed by the Marines protecting the arsenal, including two sons of John Brown. Two civilians and five Marines were also killed in the raid. Brown himself was wounded and badly beaten before his arrest. For their efforts Brown and six of his followers were hung. Brown's execution made him a martyr in the North and a symbol of terror in the South. Mr. John Wilkes Booth was in the vast crowd of about 2500 onlookers at the execution of Brown and the other six assailants.

Despite the raid's failure, John Brown's actions, especially his dignified conduct at trial, intensified sectional tensions. Abraham Lincoln would later say that Brown's raid *"initiated the war that ended American slavery."*

The 1860 Election

If the John Brown raid was the actual spark that simmered the fire of separation of the South from the Union, the election of Abraham Lincoln in 1860 ignited that fire into a soaring blaze. That election was more than the South was willing to endure. Upon Lincoln's election the United States almost immediately fell apart as a whole.

The 1860 Republican National Convention was held in Chicago from May 16 to 18. It was a hugely pivotal moment in American political history. Initially, Senator William Seward of New York was widely considered the frontrunner for the Republican presidential nomination. However, concerns about his perceived radicalism as an abolitionist and opposition to nativism led delegates to seek a more moderate candidate.

Abraham Lincoln of Illinois, though less nationally known had gained prominence through his debates with Stephen A. Douglas, which demonstrated his moderate stance on slavery. He was seen as more of a unifying figure. Lincoln's supporters skillfully positioned him as the second choice for many delegates. Seward won the first tally by gathering 173 ½ votes to 102 for Lincoln. None of the other candidates had as many as 51 votes. After the second ballot Lincoln was only 3 ½ votes behind Seward. Lincoln secured the majority on his third try and became his party's nominee. Senator Hannibal Hamlin of Maine, whom Lincoln had never met, was chosen as the vice-presidential nominee to balance the ticket geographically and politically.

The Democratic Party was significantly split into Northern and Southern factions. The Southern faction demanded a platform that supported federal protection of slavery. The North preferred the idea of each state deciding slavery for itself. 50 Southern delegates forced a close of the convention by walking out. The convention reconvened in Baltimore where many Southerners again walked out but this time there were enough delegates left to reach a consensus. On the second ballot the democrats nominated a long-time Lincoln rival in Stephen A. Douglas with his running mate John C. Breckinridge.

Additionally, there was a third-party, the Constitutional Union Party, which nominated John Bell from Tennessee. The party had a platform that proved to be too vague to garner substantial support

The general election on November 6, 1860, featured a deeply divided political landscape. Lincoln ended up winning the presidency with approximately 40% of the popular vote, carrying all the free Northern states and securing 180 electoral votes. His victory was achieved without any electoral support from the Southern states.

Lincoln, representing the newly-formed Republican Party, opposed the expansion of slavery into new territories. He pledged not to interfere with slavery where it already existed. However, southern leaders saw his election as a direct threat to their way of life and economic foundation. Within weeks of Lincoln being elected, South Carolina seceded from the Union.

By the time of Lincoln's inauguration, six other states had seceded and had joined to form the Confederate States of America, claiming the United States Constitution gave them the right to secede. Those states included: South Carolina, Mississippi, Florida, Alabama, Georgia, Louisiana, and Texas. Jefferson Davis was appointed by the Congress of the Confederate States of America to be President. There was no general election. He was inaugurated to the presidency on February 18, 1861, to lead the new nation. Lincoln's inauguration did not take place until March 4.

On April 12, 1861, Confederate forces unloaded an attack on the Union held Fort Sumter, marking the official beginning of the Civil War. Fort Sumter was the North's only remaining military position in the South. The fort was low on supplies and effectively surrounded by forces led by General P.G.T Beauregard. Before dawn on April 12, the Confederate force began its bombardment, which continued for 34 hours. On April 13, with the fort in flames, Major Robert Anderson surrendered to the invaders. During the bombardment there was no loss of life. But the war had begun in earnest. Four more states seceded shortly thereafter Virginia, Arkansas, North Carolina, and Tennessee.

The First Years of the War

Each side was overly confident in its ultimate victory, initially believing the war would be very short-lived. There appeared to be some good reasons on the side of the North for this overconfidence. The North held overwhelming advantages in manpower, industry, and transportation. They were not at all well prepared for an extended conflict. Many in the North thought their chances of quick victory were very good: Senator James Grimes (Iowa), May 1861. *"The war will not be a long one. I expect it will be over in sixty days."* New York Tribune editorial, April 1861. *"Forward to Richmond! Forward to Richmond! The Rebel Congress must not be allowed to meet there on the 20th of July. By that date the place must be held by the national army!"* Congressman Albert Riddle of Ohio: *"There is no doubt but that Jeff Davis will be swinging from the battlements of Washington in less than a month."*

But there was also great confidence in the Confederacy's chances to win the war quickly. In the South, they believed their society produced a better soldier, as well as a better military leader. They mistakenly thought that their vast cotton resources would provide economic leverage over France and England, forcing those countries to support the war by trade and by recognition. The South recognized that they were fighting for *"The Cause,"* a way of life that included slavery. The North was not in total unity, especially a unity that would be willing to fight a prolonged war.

"One of our companies can whip a regiment of Yankees," wrote a soldier just before the start of the war. James Chesnutt, Confederate aide (and former U.S. Senator) wrote *"We will welcome the Yankees with bloody hands and hospitable graves."*

Richmond Examiner, May 1861 reported *"The idea of invading Virginia with such a force is simply ridiculous. They will be driven back like sheep."* Major General Robert Toombs of Georgia wrote *"We could whip the Yankees with cornstalks."* As would soon be proven, comments by Northerners and Southerners were mostly born in ignorance.

Southerners prided themselves on a culture steeped in honor, chivalry, and military tradition. Many Southern men were raised with firearms, rode horses from a young age, and had attended military academies. This bred a belief that Southern soldiers were naturally superior, more rugged, and better prepared for war than their Northern counterparts, whom they often viewed as soft or industrialized. The South believed that it only had to defend its territory, not conquer the North. This defensive stance was seen by many as easier and less costly. They viewed the war as one of independence, not conquest, so if they could simply resist long enough, they believed the Union would give up.

When the war began, tens of thousands of Southern men volunteered to fight, convinced they would be celebrating their victory by Christmas. Newspapers on both sides fanned the flames of patriotic fervor, often painting a romanticized image of war that quickly clashed with the brutal reality of sustained 19th century conflict.

For the North, early defeats, including the first battle of Bull Run (Manassas) and the failed Peninsula Campaign, sobered public expectations. The immense casualties at Antietam (1862) where there were 12,400 Union troop casualties and 10,320 Confederate casualties in a single day of battle shocked the nation, even though the battle was labeled a Union strategic victory.

In the South, initial battle successes bolstered their over-confidence. However, as the ensuing battle victories were traded between the two sides, over confidence soon led to despair and a depletion of morale.

The Confederacy had significant victories at Bull Run, Chancellorsville, and Fredericksburg. These wins were celebrated because they were seen as an indication of the future war, recognition from Britain or France was imminent. Such recognition, even if it did not include military support, would greatly increase the coffers of the South, through trade, allowing them to fight the war on a much higher level. Yet under the surface, the war was taking its toll. Certainty of victory was fading from most minds. The Union blockade was strangling Southern ports, causing massive inflation, food shortages, and near starvation. As the death toll rose, the romanticism of *"The Cause"* gave way to hardship and sacrifice among the citizenry.

Despite commanding a vast and resource-rich army, Lincoln's greatest challenge in the early years of the war was not necessarily just the Confederate army, it was his own generals. The Union's high command was plagued by indecision, personal ambition, and political rivalry. For these reasons and more Union leadership repeatedly squandered opportunities for early victories, perhaps even ending the war.

General George McClellan, who twice led the Army of the Potomac, was beloved by his men but maddeningly cautious, often overestimating enemy strength and refusing to press a battle when he had a decided advantage. His failure to pursue Lee's retreating army after the battle of Antietam drove Lincoln to exasperation. *"If General McClellan does not want to use the army,"* Lincoln famously said, *"I would like to borrow it for a time."*

Other generals would fare no better. Ambrose Burnside's ill-conceived frontal assault at Fredericksburg resulted in a bloodbath, while Joseph Hooker, who succeeded him, was routed at Chancellorsville despite having twice the number of troops as Lee. Lincoln, who had very little formal military training, was forced to learn strategy on the job while searching tirelessly for a commander who would both fight and win. It would not be until the arrival of Ulysses S. Grant, a quiet and unrelenting general from the Western Theater, that Lincoln would finally find a man whose vision for total war matched the scale of the conflict.

Lincoln's Moral Evolution and Emancipation

"My paramount object in this struggle is to save the Union and is not either to save or to destroy slavery. If I could save the Union without freeing any slave, I would do it... and if I could save it by freeing all the slaves I would do it." Abraham Lincoln, August 22, 1862

"Fondly do we hope, fervently do we pray, that this mighty scourge of war may speedily pass away. Yet, if God wills that it continue... until every drop of blood drawn with the lash shall be paid by another drawn with the sword... still it must be said 'the judgments of the Lord are true and righteous altogether... With malice toward none, with charity for all, with firmness in the right as God gives us to see the right, let us strive on to finish the work we are in... to do all which may achieve and cherish a just and lasting peace among ourselves and with all nations." - Abraham Lincoln, Second Inaugural Address

Abraham Lincoln did not begin his presidency as a radical abolitionist. His primary goal in 1861 was to preserve the Union, not to dismantle slavery. Though personally opposed to the institution of slavery, he believed the Constitution protected it where it already existed. Early in the war, he reassured border states and moderate Northerners that the conflict was not about emancipation, but about national survival. Yet as the war dragged on, Lincoln's views began to evolve, shaped by military necessity, moral conviction, and the persistent advocacy of abolitionists and Black leaders like Frederick Douglass. Lincoln came to see emancipation not just as a moral imperative, but as a strategic weapon. Striking at slavery would undermine the Southern economy, deprive the Confederacy of labor, and add strength to the Union cause.

In July 1862, Lincoln drafted the Emancipation Proclamation but waited for a military victory before its announcement. As he explained to his Cabinet, *"I must save the Union in the shortest way under the Constitution."* Privately, Lincoln believed slavery must die so that the nation might live. After the bloody battle of Antietam, he delivered the preliminary proclamation, declaring that as of January 1, 1863, all slaves in Confederate-held territory would be free. It was a bold and unprecedented move. While limited in immediate practical effect, it transformed the war into a fight for human liberty. It also opened the door to the recruitment of Black soldiers, who would go on to serve with distinction in the Union army.

By 1863, Lincoln was no longer simply the preserver of the Union, he had become its moral compass. *"The dogmas of the quiet past are inadequate to the stormy present,"* he would later say. *"As our case is new, so we must think anew, and act anew."* The Emancipation Proclamation gave the war a higher purpose. In reshaping the aims of the conflict, Lincoln reshaped the nation itself.

Southern Politics and Confederate Vision

The Confederate States of America were founded not merely in reaction to perceived Northern aggression over slavery, but with a political ideology rooted in the preservation of slavery and the assertion of white supremacy.

On February 9, 1861, Jefferson Davis was selected as the provisional president of the Confederacy by a constitutional convention that included delegates from six former states. It was for a six-year term. He was hoping for a military assignment but agreed to accept the presidency. Davis was a graduate of the U.S. Military Academy at West Point and a veteran of the Mexican-American War. He served as Secretary of War under Franklin Pierce and was a longtime

U.S. senator from Mississippi. His first wife, Sarah Knox, was the daughter of President Zachary Taylor. He was a strong advocate of states' rights but often tried to temper the antagonism between North and South. By 1860 Jefferson Davis owned 113 slaves. When Mississippi seceded from the Union in January 1861, Davis left the Senate and joined the Confederacy.

Alexander Stephens had been appointed Vice President of the Confederacy to serve alongside Jefferson Davis. Stephens gave a speech on March 21, 1861, to delineate the differences between the United States Constitution and that of the newly formed, seven state, confederacy. The Confederate Constitution had been adopted by its Congress on March 11. The Confederate constitution enshrined slavery as a protected institution, banning any law that would interfere with *"the right of property in negro slaves."* Unlike the U.S. Constitution, it left no ambiguity about the role of slavery in its new government.

Stephen's speech was labeled *"The Cornerstone Speech"* and was given in front of a large audience at the Savannah Athenaeum, a public lecture hall. Jefferson Davis, though a staunch defender of slavery, preferred to frame the Confederacy's cause in terms of states' rights and constitutional liberty, which he hoped would resonate more favorably with foreign governments, particularly Britain and France. Stephens' open declaration that slavery was the *"cornerstone"* of the new government risked undermining those diplomatic efforts.

In his speech Stephens explicitly stated that the Confederate government was founded on the principle of white supremacy and the enslavement of African Americans, which he declared was the *"natural and normal condition"* of Black people. There were many topics explored in the speech, but the topic most remembered is about slavery.

"The new constitution has put at rest, forever, all the agitating questions relating to our peculiar institution African slavery as it exists amongst us the proper status of the negro in our form of civilization. This was the immediate cause of the late rupture and present revolution. Jefferson in his forecast, had anticipated this, as the "rock upon which the old Union would split." He was right. What was conjecture with him, is now a realized fact… The prevailing ideas entertained by him and most of the leading statesmen at the time of the formation of the old constitution, were that the enslavement of the African was in violation of the laws of nature; that it was wrong in principle, socially, morally, and politically. It was an evil they knew not well how to deal with, but the general opinion of the men of that day was that, somehow or other in the order of Providence, the institution would be evanescent and pass away. This idea, though

not incorporated in the constitution, was the prevailing idea at that time. The constitution, it is true, secured every essential guarantee to the institution while it should last, and hence no argument can be justly urged against the constitutional guarantees thus secured, because of the common sentiment of the day. Those ideas, however, were fundamentally wrong. They rested upon the assumption of the equality of races. This was an error. It was a sandy foundation, and the government built upon it fell when the "storm came and the wind blew.""

    "Our new government is founded upon exactly the opposite idea [of racial equality]; its foundations are laid, its cornerstone rests upon the great truth that the negro is not equal to the white man; that slavery, subordination to the superior race, is his natural and normal condition."

On April 12, 1861, three weeks after Stephen's speech, the Confederate navy began their assault on Fort Sumter, to initiate the Civil War.

Southern politics during the war were often dominated by internal contradictions. While fighting for a decentralized system based on states' rights, the Confederate government was forced to centralize power to manage the war effort, introducing taxes, conscription, and even confiscation of goods as well as slaves into the war effort. These policies were met with resistance from local leaders and ordinary citizens, revealing the underlying fragility of the Confederate political experiment.

Though Jefferson Davis attempted to present a united front to the rest of the world, cracks within the Confederacy were deepening as the war lingered. There was no true political party system in the South. Davis was elected to a six-year term, not by the people but by its legislators. Davis governed through a tenuous network of allies and rivals. State governors, especially in Georgia and North Carolina, resisted directives from Richmond. The illusion of Southern unity was just that, an illusion, papered over by battlefield victories and patriotic rhetoric.

As hardship mounted in 1863, dissent grew louder. The Union was blockading southern ports. Food for the citizenry as well as the army was at times hard to come by. Riots broke out, desertions increased, and ordinary Southerners began to question whether the sacrifices demanded were worth the cost. Even the Confederate Congress debated whether to arm enslaved men, an idea that Davis eventually supported. But that support came too late and too reluctantly for it to have meaningful effect.

The American Mindset in 1863

Americans on both sides of the conflict faced the sobering truth that this war was lasting much longer than originally thought and would not end anytime soon, not without fundamental change. In the North, public opinion was divided. War Democrats and Republicans mostly supported Lincoln's efforts, while Peace Democrats ("Copperheads") called for an immediate armistice and negotiation with the Confederacy. Opposition to the enacted draft erupted into violent protests irrespective of politics. Lincoln, though politically embattled, remained steadfast. With the Emancipation Proclamation now in effect, the war had a moral dimension that galvanized many in the abolitionist movement and laid the groundwork for the eventual enlistment of Black troops.

In the South, wealthy plantation owners and their sons avoided military service because of the number of slaves they owned, leading to resentment among poorer whites. The slogan *"a rich man's war and a poor man's fight"* captured the growing discontent among the non-gentry. There was hyperinflation, significant food shortages, and in April 1863 the famous Richmond Bread Riots, when hundreds of women looted bakeries and stores solely to feed their families. Army desertion was becoming common place. There was even open political criticism of their military and political leaders. Slaves, sensing the shifting winds of history, began to escape in larger numbers, and some openly resisted. Confederate authorities were forced to divert troops to guard against slave uprisings and control the enslaved population, particularly in areas near Union lines.

1863 stood like a gateway between two Americas: one side clinging to its fractured past, and the other struggling to define a new identity. The war had exposed the contradictions at the heart of the republic, freedom in a land of bondage, unity in a land torn apart. And so, the stage was set for the events that would define the year such as the epic confrontations at Gettysburg, Chancellorsville, Vicksburg, and Chickamauga, the enlistment of the United States Colored Troops, Lincoln's immortal Gettysburg Address, and the growing realization that America would emerge from this war forever changed, if it was able to emerge at all.

CHAPTER 2
LINCOLN AND CONGRESS DEFINING FEDERAL POWER

The presidency of Abraham Lincoln in 1863 was marked by extraordinary pressure, political polarization, and transformative decisions that reshaped the meaning of the war as well as the much of the role of the federal government. It was a year in which Lincoln's leadership was both severely tested and ultimately vindicated, but vindication would not be swift in coming. The third year of the war was far from a time of clarity for what the future might become. The presidency of the North in 1863 must be understood through a combination of wartime governance, acute political maneuvering, moral leadership, and personal burden.

In 1863, Abraham Lincoln's relationship with the Constitution was defined by the extraordinary demands of civil war. Lincoln saw the Constitution not as a rigid document, but as a living framework designed to preserve the Union, which he believed was more sacred than any individual state or administration. Lincoln saw the Declaration of Independence as the guiding document for the country, and the Constitution as a way to run it. His presidency that year tested the boundaries of executive power in ways never before imagined, raising both admiration and alarm over how far a president could go in time of national crisis. The North was fractured and bloodied and could not afford caution. It needed action and quickly. Politics as normal was very tedious and could not be implemented nearly quickly enough, so powers were assumed until Congress saw fit to codify them.

On one hand, Lincoln held the reins of a rapidly expanding presidential powers by suspending habeas corpus, silencing and imprisoning dissenters, and signing executive orders that reshaped American life. On the other hand, Congress pressed forward with its own revolution of legislation, drafting poor men into military service, taxing the wealthy to pay for war, and centralizing a chaotic banking system into a cohesive national economy. Together, sometimes in tandem, often in tension, Lincoln and the wartime Congress remade the government of the Republic. What began as a war to restore the Union, had in many ways become a war to redefine it.

Lincoln believed the Civil War was not just a rebellion to divide a nation. It was a test of the Constitution itself. If the Union could be lawfully dissolved by secession, then the constitutional government had no authority to defend itself. He framed the war as a fight to preserve the constitutional republic. In a message to Congress in July 1863 Lincoln said, *"We cannot have free government without elections; and if the rebellion could force us to forego, or postpone, a national election, it might fairly claim to have already conquered and ruined us."* He held that secession was unconstitutional, and the southern rebellion was not a legitimate revolution, but an insurrection that must be quelled. This position justified his use of wartime powers that often were extreme and stretched the constitutional limits of the presidency.

The year 1863 not only became a turning point on the battlefield, but it was also a year that the federal government further expanded its control over states and personal rights. It was a year when the Founders' blueprints were stretched, reinterpreted, and, some opponents said, broken. But it was also the year when the America of the northern states learned what it meant to have a government powerful enough to fight for its own survival and ultimately, to fight for the freedom of all its citizenry.

At the onset of the war, Lincoln assumed the presidency with little executive experience and even less inclination toward sweeping authority. He had very limited military experience. In 1832, he had volunteered for military service and was elected captain by the other volunteers of his unit. His unit was formed to engage in the Black Hawk War, a brief war between the United States and a band of Sauk and Fox Indians, led by Chief Black Hawk. The Chief led an effort to resettle his tribes on their own formal tribal lands in Illinois. Lincoln was 23 years old. He saw no military action during the engagement. *"I had a good many bloody struggles with the mosquitoes"* he reported later. That was the end of Lincoln's military career.

As Confederate forces seized federal arsenals and railroads and greatly shook the arrogance and somewhat the resolve of the North, Lincoln took unprecedented steps that were not normal executive action for previous presidencies Without waiting for Congress to act on his behalf, he expanded defense spending for the army and navy, called for volunteers to fill their ranks, and declared a blockade of Southern ports. He would later retroactively ask

Congress to approve his actions (and they did). This was a pattern that would define much of his approach toward management of the war, act and then seek permission from Congress.

Nowhere was Lincoln's boldness more controversial than his suspension of the writ of habeas corpus (a legal action that allows a court to review the legality of a person's detention). John Merryman of Maryland was arrested and jailed without due process. His arrest led to Chief Justice Roger Taney's famous rebuke in ex parte Merryman, declaring the suspension of habeas corpus was unconstitutional. Merryman was a southern sympathizer who owned a plantation in Maryland and was a member of the state militia. He was arrested for destroying railroad bridges that had been carrying Union troops. He was held prisoner and was kept inaccessible to the judiciary. Chief Justice Taney wrote that the suspension of habeas corpus lies only with Congress. Lincoln ignored the ruling, which was issued only by Taney, it was not a Supreme Court decision. But a decision of Taney as a circuit judge. In a July 4 address to Congress, Lincoln asked rhetorically: *"Are all the laws but one to go unexecuted, and the government itself go to pieces, lest that one be violated?"*

The lines between civil liberty and national security were blurred. Lincoln authorized military arrests of civilians suspected of disloyalty, suppressed anti-war newspapers, and detained political figures like Congressman Clement Vallandigham, who vocally opposed the draft. While critics cried tyranny, supporters argued Lincoln was preserving the very Constitution his detractors claimed he was defying. During the suspension of habeas corpus thousands of people were detained, including Confederate sympathizers, suspected spies, draft resisters, and newspaper editors, all without formal charges. By 1863, with Congress's passage of the Habeas Corpus Suspension Act, his actions gained legislative backing.

Lincoln justified these actions by pointing to Article I, Section 9 of the Constitution, which allows suspension of habeas corpus *"when in cases of rebellion or invasion the public safety may require it."* Traditionally, as pointed out by Taney, this was viewed as a congressional power, but Lincoln, as commander-in-chief, believed he could act when Congress was not in session or unable to respond quickly.

The Emancipation Proclamation of January 1, 1863, further demonstrated Lincoln's evolving view of executive power. Justified as a *"military necessity,"* the proclamation freed slaves only in rebellious states. It was not legislation, Congress had passed no such law, but the Proclamation transformed the war's moral landscape and tethered Union victory to the cause of human freedom.

The Union Congress

While Lincoln and Secretary of War, Seward commanded generals to action on the battlefield, Congress worked to rewire the economic and political structure of the Union. In March 1863, the Enrollment Act introduced the first federal draft of young men to military service in American history. The law required all male citizens (and immigrants intending to naturalize) between the ages of 20 and 45 to register for the draft. It included a controversial provision where men could pay $300 or hire a substitute to avoid service. To working-class Northerners, especially to the many poor Irish immigrants, the law screamed injustice. The backlash would explode in the New York City Draft Riots just a few months later.

At the same time, Congress passed the Revenue Act of 1863, introducing a graduated income tax, mostly on the middle class and rich, and expanding duties on luxury goods. This, combined with massive war bond campaigns created a foundation for modern federal revenue. Posters and newspapers hailed bond buyers as patriots. It was not only a war of armies, but of economics and Congress was arming the Treasury to fund the war.

The National Banking Act, passed in the same month, aimed to bring order to a fractured financial system. Before the war, thousands of state-chartered banks issued their own unreliable currencies. The new law established a system of nationally chartered banks and a uniform paper currency backed by federal bonds. It centralized economic power in Washington and planted the seeds of the Federal Reserve System to come (in 1913).

Amidst these economic reforms, early ideas of federal responsibility for the formerly enslaved were beginning to circulate. While the Freedmen's Bureau wouldn't be created until 1865, the notion of using federal authority to educate, employ, and protect freed men gained traction in 1863. Radical Republicans like Senator Charles Sumner (who is most famous for having been physically beaten on the Senate floor by Preston Brooks in 1856 for giving an anti-slavery speech) and Congressman Thaddeus Stevens (who later organized the impeachment of President Andrew Johnson) began to argue that victory would be meaningless unless accompanied by social justice.

The year 1863 marked a pivotal chapter in the working relationship between President Abraham Lincoln and congress. It was a year shaped by both shared purpose and growing friction. While united by the overarching goal of preserving the Union, Lincoln and his congressional counterparts often diverged over questions of civil liberties, military policy, emancipation, and the very structure of reconstruction. Some measures passed with firm executive support; others came only after hard bargaining or open conflict. Still others never came at all, delayed or derailed by suspicion, ideology, or the immense pressures of civil war.

Despite their different spheres, Lincoln and Congress were often interdependent. They pushed each other forward, sometimes contentiously. Congress pressured Lincoln to go further on emancipation, while Lincoln tempered radical impulses with political pragmatism. Disagreements arose over arrests of civilians, the role of military governance in loyal states, and the treatment of Southern Unionists. But the overarching theme was collaboration under stress. As Lincoln expanded presidential authority, Congress legitimized many of those actions retroactively. They were bound by necessity, not ideology: a wartime government improvising a new way to survive.

Where Lincoln and Congress most often clashed was over the pace and scope of emancipation and reconstruction. Though Radical Republicans in Congress supported the Emancipation Proclamation, many believed Lincoln remained too cautious, too slow to recognize the revolutionary implications of Black freedom. They pressed for equal treatment of Black soldiers, land redistribution, and punishment of Confederate leaders, while Lincoln urged moderation and national reconciliation. When he unveiled his Proclamation of Amnesty and Reconstruction in December 1863, offering reentry to Southern states if just ten percent of their 1860 electorate swore loyalty and accepted emancipation, many in Congress saw it as executive overreach. Reconstruction, they believed, was a legislative responsibility.

The presidency and the legislature were learning how to share the enormous burden of civil war. In many ways, it was a year of testing, of principles, of tempers, and of the capacity of a republican government to endure a national trauma. That it did endure is a testament to the fragile but functional working relationship between Abraham Lincoln and his Congress.

The year marked a fundamental shift in American governance. What had begun in 1861 as a war to preserve the Union had, by 1863, evolved into something far larger: a contest over the very meaning of the American republic, the scope of federal power, and the future of democracy. In this cauldron of national crisis, were the institutions of American government, the presidency, Congress, military, and civil society. These were reformed largely because of the tensions of being involved in a war. It was not only the battlefield that turned that year; the political and constitutional order did as well.

At the center of this transformation stood the President, whose decisions in 1863 redefined the role of the executive branch. With the Emancipation Proclamation, issued on January 1, Lincoln expanded the moral and constitutional purpose of the war. Though justified as a wartime measure under his authority as commander-in-chief, the proclamation was revolutionary in scope. It declared the freedom of millions of enslaved persons and altered the constitutional balance by making human liberty a core aim of the government. Never had the presidency exercised such moral authority on such a scale. Lincoln did not wait for Congress to act. He used the powers of his office to change the nature of the nation itself.

At the same time, Lincoln was walking a constitutional tightrope. His suspension of habeas corpus, authorization of military arrests, and censorship of dissenting newspapers all expanded executive authority in ways that would have been unthinkable in peacetime. In 1863, Congress both challenged and legitimized many of these moves. The Habeas Corpus Suspension Act of March 1863 ratified the president's earlier unilateral decisions, setting a precedent for broad federal power in emergencies. The Enrollment Act, passed the same month, established the first national military draft, bringing the lives of ordinary citizens into direct contact with federal authority.

This growing federal reach was not without consequence. The New York City Draft Riots in July began as protests against conscription and then soon exploded into a violent and deadly uprising. Importantly. The riots demonstrated how profoundly the federal government had come to shape daily life and how deeply contested that authority remained. For many in the North, particularly the working poor, the notion that the war had become a rich man's war but a poor man's fight, pointed to a broader anxiety about government favoritism, inequality, and the erosion of civil liberties. Lincoln and Congress pressed on, determined that the machinery of national governance must be strong enough to preserve the Union and finish the war.

Meanwhile, Congress itself also evolved. While legislative debates remained bitter and partisan, particularly between Republicans and Peace Democrats, the wartime Congress undertook sweeping measures that would permanently alter the federal landscape. The establishment of the national banking system, the issuance of greenbacks, the Homestead Act (passed the previous year but implemented throughout 1863), and the continued expansion of the railroad system all pointed toward a centralized vision of governance. Even as the war raged, the federal government was laying the foundations for a modern industrial state.

Governance also shifted in its relationship to the people. The very concept of citizenship began to change. With the enlistment of Black troops following emancipation, and the increasing political activism of African Americans and abolitionists in the North, a new vision of participatory democracy began to emerge. This reimagining of citizenship, as something inclusive of race and rooted in freedom, was still incomplete, but the foundations were laid in 1863.

The year also tested the capacity of democratic governance to survive internal revolt. The Union held elections in the fall, amid rebellion, conscription, and civil strife, was itself a declaration of confidence in republican government. Lincoln, ever mindful of the fragility of the American experiment, understood this deeply. He wrote, *"We cannot have free government without elections,"* and insisted on preserving the outward forms of democracy even as he stretched its institutions to their limits.

1863 was a turning point not simply in the conflict of the war, but in American governance. It marked the emergence of a stronger, more centralized federal state, one that could wage total war, reshape the Constitution by executive action, and redefine the relationship between government and the governed. These changes, born of necessity, would outlast the war itself and become permanent features of the American political system. What had begun as a republic of limited powers in the federal and state governments, by the end of 1863, become a nation of consolidated authority, capable of both destruction and renewal.

Lincoln's Cabinet: Conflict with Common Purpose

The Civil War demanded a new type of leadership, not only on the battlefield but within the very heart of government. Abraham Lincoln, once dismissed as an inexperienced country lawyer (which was mostly true), faced the challenge of holding together, not only a fractured nation, but a cabinet as politically combustible as any in American history. In 1863, the men seated at Lincoln's conference table were as divided in temperament and ambition as the Union was by geography and morality. And yet, under Lincoln's quiet manner, they functioned, not always harmoniously, but mostly effectively.

Each cabinet member brought a distinct background and a unique orbit of influence. Their disagreements were often as intense as their devotion to the preservation of the Union. Lincoln, fully aware of their rivalries, deliberately chose strong men with independent followings. He believed in surrounding himself with capable individuals who would challenge him and each other. With that advice Lincoln, would make an independent decision, whether that decision agreed with the consensus of his cabinet or not.

William H. Seward, Secretary of State, had once expected to be the president. A former governor and senator from New York, he had been the presumed front-runner for the 1860 Republican nomination. After defeat, he accepted the foreign policy post when Lincoln offered with some expectation that he would be the true power in the administration. But Lincoln's administration of his authority soon earned Seward's respect, and a genuine partnership emerged. Seward's brilliance shone most clearly in 1863 as he worked to keep Britain and France neutral. With the Emancipation Proclamation in effect, Seward emphasized that any recognition of the Confederacy would now be an endorsement of slavery. He often used subtle statecraft, and he sometimes used a hammer, and both helped prevent diplomatic disaster.

In contrast, **Salmon P. Chase**, Secretary of the Treasury, never gave up his dream of replacing Lincoln. A devout abolitionist and Free Soil advocate from Ohio, Chase viewed himself as the moral backbone of the administration. He presided over the financing of the war, creating the national banking system and introducing paper currency that would help fund the Union cause. But Chase was more than a financier; he positioned himself as a rival to Lincoln. He routinely lobbied against Lincoln behind the scenes, cultivated the Radical Republicans, and saw himself as a purer vessel from which to promote the Union's cause. Lincoln, fully aware of Chase's maneuverings, nevertheless retained him, choosing competence and continuity over political security.

If Chase symbolized ambition, **Edwin M. Stanton,** Secretary of War, embodied intensity. Stanton had often initially mocked Lincoln in private correspondence. In 1855 the two men were set to work with each other in a patent case. Lincoln was brought in as local counsel. But Stanton refused to work with him, referring to Lincoln as *"a long-armed ape"* and he didn't want to work with *"such a damned gawky specimen."* Amazingly, Lincoln never held a grudge. By 1863, Stanton had become one of Lincoln's most loyal and essential lieutenants. Gruff, exacting, and tireless, Stanton brought discipline to the War Department. He micromanaged details, demanded results, and drove the Union war machine forward at an unrelenting pace. Lincoln, in turn, gave Stanton near-total freedom, only stepping in when judgment or mercy required the president's hand.

Gideon Welles, Secretary of the Navy, operated more quietly. A Connecticut newspaperman and former Democrat, he had basically no political experience. Lincoln wanted a cabinet represented by a broad coalition of individuals, and Welles fit that narrative. Welles expanded the Navy from a modest peacetime fleet to a dominant wartime force. Under his guidance, the Union blockade of Southern ports began to strangle the Confederacy's commerce. Though not a central political figure, Welles earned Lincoln's enduring trust. His diary would later become one of the most valuable firsthand accounts of the administration.

Montgomery Blair, the Postmaster General, was from a politically powerful family with ties to both the North as well as the border states. As a moderate conservative, Blair supported the Union cause but initially favored colonization as a solution to slavery (resettling of freed African Americans outside the United States), an idea Lincoln had once entertained. Blair's influence lay in his understanding of the fragile loyalty of border states like Maryland and Missouri. Though increasingly out of step with Radical Republicans, Blair gave Lincoln a vital channel to conservative and Democratic constituencies.

The Department of the Interior saw a transition just before 1863. Caleb Smith, who had served since Lincoln's inauguration, resigned in late 1862 and was replaced by **John P. Usher,** a loyal Lincoln ally from Indiana. Usher, though not a political heavyweight, oversaw a wide portfolio that included federal land policy, public infrastructure, territorial governance, patents, and the administration of Indian affairs. Though far from the spotlight, his department was vital in shaping the American West at a time when the Union was fighting not only to preserve itself but to define its future geography. Usher's office was responsible for managing treaty negotiations, overseeing Indian agents, and administering the flawed and often brutal reservation system.

Edward Bates, the Attorney General, brought a voice of elder statesmanship to the cabinet. He was a respected jurist from Missouri and one of Lincoln's rivals in the campaign for the Republican nomination in 1860. Bates was conservative by temperament. He supported the Union but remained uneasy about emancipation and military overreach. As the war intensified and the administration embraced bolder measures, Bates became increasingly marginalized. Yet Lincoln kept him on, respecting both his integrity and his regional influence.

The cabinet in 1863 was not a council of friends. Chase resented Seward; Stanton ignored Blair; Bates was often out of step with everyone. And yet, under Lincoln's patient leadership, these men served the administration very well. Lincoln listened to them, disagreed with them, and, when needed, overruled them. They, in turn, saw what many others did not yet recognize: that behind Lincoln's informal manner lay a will of iron. When the decision of the cabinet was against his intentions Lincoln would say *"Seven nays and one aye; the ayes have it."*

In the crucible of war, Lincoln's cabinet was not a model of harmony, but it was a reflection of the Union itself: diverse, divided, often contentious, and yet still committed to the cause of survival.

Key Cabinet Successes of 1863

Emancipation Proclamation Implemented and Defended

The Emancipation Proclamation had gone into effect on January 1, 1863, and while Lincoln had issued it, the Cabinet was deeply involved in its development and implementation. Seward had suggested delaying the notice of the proclamation until after a military victory (which came at the Battle of Antietam in late 1862). Lincoln had agreed. Stanton prepared the military for its upcoming struggles, including allowing African Americans to enlist in the Union Army. Blair reluctantly supported it, fearing border state backlash, but stayed in the Cabinet to avoid a deeper political fracture. The Proclamation did not have the full force of the law. But it had the desired result as it went into effect on the first day of the year.

Keeping Foreign Powers Neutral

William Seward – Secretary of State - Seward was the most critical individual insuring that foreign powers did not recognize the legitimacy of the South as a separate country. From the earliest days of the rebellion, Seward understood that the Civil War was not merely a domestic crisis, it was watched keenly by Britain and France, both of whom had the economic ties of their huge textile economies to Southern cotton. The Confederacy wagered heavily that its cotton would prove king in London and Paris, pressing those countries to recognize its independence. Seward, however, moved swiftly to douse any such ambitions.

His message to European governments was recognition of the Confederacy would be seen as an act of war. Through a network of Union diplomats, in London, Seward made clear that the United States considered the Confederacy a rebellion that was to be handled internally. The South did not have the right of independence. Seward's diplomacy walked a line between dignity and deterrence, preserving peace while defending principle.

A significant test of that balancing act came in late 1861 with the Trent Affair. A Union warship intercepted a British mail steamer and seized two Confederate envoys in-route to London. British outrage was immediate. The threat of a Union war with Britain seemed it could be very near. Such a conflict with Britain while conducting the war between the states would be untenable. Seward's handling of the crisis was a masterstroke of diplomacy. He agreed to release the envoys to Britain, averting conflict, yet couched the decision in legal reasoning that avoided apology. By doing so, he preserved Union honor while cooling tempers across the Atlantic.

With the Emancipation Proclamation, the war's meaning shifted in the minds of foreign nations. Slavery now stood at the center of the conflict between the states and Seward seized that moment. With polished subtlety, he reminded European powers that the United States was now engaged in a struggle not just for union, but for freedom of all its citizens. European nations had already rejected slavery; this made it increasingly untenable for any government to openly support the Confederacy.

No European power ever recognized the Confederacy. No foreign armies landed in Southern ports. And though few headlines celebrated him, Seward kept the Union from fighting a war on two fronts. In the end, it was said of Seward that he practiced diplomacy *with a dagger under his cloak but a smile on his lips.* In a war that threatened the soul of the Republic, it was precisely what was needed.

Stabilizing the Union Economy and War Financing

Salmon P. Chase – Secretary of the Treasury - The man entrusted with managing the economy of the North was Salmon Chase. He was a lifelong abolitionist and former Ohio governor. Chase viewed the war as not only a battle for the Union, but a moral crusade to end slavery. It fell to him to keep the government solvent, as it fought the most expensive war in American history up to that time. When Chase took office in 1861, the federal government was financially unprepared for war. The national debt stood at $65 million, and the Treasury's ability to raise funds was limited by the absence of a central banking authority. As the war escalated, expenses mounted astronomically, at times exceeding $2 million per day. Chase's challenge was daunting: he had to fund the war, manage inflation, and maintain the public's confidence in a currency no longer backed by gold.

Chase pursued a multi-pronged strategy, pioneering financial reforms that would reshape the nation's economic structure and far outlive the war. First, Chase turned to borrowing. He initiated massive bond drives, appealing to the patriotism of Northern citizens to lend their savings to the government. Chase launched a nationwide campaign that turned bond buying into an act of civic duty and patriotism. Small investors such as schoolteachers and farmers, began purchasing bonds. By 1863, these efforts had brought in hundreds of millions of dollars, helping keep the Union armies in the field and the federal government afloat.

In 1862, with Congress's authorization, Chase oversaw the introduction of a new national paper currency. These notes were not backed by gold but were legal tender for all debts except tariffs and interest on federal bonds. It was a radical move. For the first time, the U.S. government was directly printing money to finance its operations. These notes allowed the government to pay soldiers, contractors, and suppliers without draining its limited reserves.

Perhaps Chase's most enduring legacy came through the National Banking Acts of 1863 and 1864. These laws established a system of federally chartered banks and a uniform national currency, replacing the chaotic patchwork of state banknotes that had flooded the economy. National banks were required to purchase U.S. bonds, tying their existence directly to the government's financial success. In return, they could issue national bank notes, which were backed by those bonds and regulated by the federal government. This system both stabilized the currency and created a reliable market for Union debt, knitting together the government's borrowing needs with the banking infrastructure of the North.

For Chase, these efforts were not just fiscal, they were moral and ideological. He believed a strong national government, guided by righteous principles, required strong financial institutions. A war fought to free enslaved people deserved to be financed in a way that expanded federal power, increased economic opportunity, and reflected the seriousness of the Union cause. Chase helped keep the Union alive in its most vulnerable years. As one wartime editor wrote, *"The men in blue fight the war. Chase funds it."*

Military Reforms and Mobilization

<u>Edwin Stanton – Secretary of War</u> . Stanton managed the engine that kept the North's armies moving. A man of uncompromising intensity, sharp intellect, and boundless energy, Stanton assumed the office in January 1862 amid widespread disarray in the War Department. Within months he had transformed it from a sluggish and corrupt bureaucracy into a disciplined machine of mobilization and supply. Stanton did not court popularity. He barked orders, accepted no delay, and dismissed incompetence. He had once called Lincoln a *"gorilla,"* but the president, knowing talent when he saw it, brought him into the cabinet. But soon Stanton came to be one of Lincoln's most trusted and loyal lieutenants.

The early months of the war had seen military contracts handed out without oversight, army logistics snarled by confusion, and volunteer units mustered with little accountability. Stanton responded with a sweeping program of military reform. He centralized control of military logistics and tightened contracting procedures, rooting out corrupt suppliers and enforcing stricter standards on arms procurement and provisioning. He introduced standardized record-keeping, so the War Department could track troop movements, supply flows, and battlefield reports with precision. He relied on the growing power of telegraph lines, establishing the War Department's own military telegraph corps to ensure direct communication with field commanders.

As the war dragged on, the need for manpower grew ever more dire. The initial wave of patriotic enlistments had dwindled, and by 1863, the Union turned to drafting men into service. It was an unpopular but necessary step. Stanton oversaw the implementation of the Enrollment Act. He expanded federal authority, sent troops to quell riots, and reaffirmed the government's right to enforce the draft. Under his watch, the Union would eventually mobilize over two million soldiers, the largest army in American history to that point.

Stanton's tenure was marked by tense relationships with some of the Union's top generals. He clashed with George McClellan, whom he found slow and arrogant, and did not hesitate to support Lincoln in removing commanders who failed to deliver expected results. When Ulysses S. Grant emerged as a general capable of delivering consistent victories, Stanton gave him wide latitude and support without interference, a rare and welcome gesture from a man known for his tight grip.

Stanton visited battlefields, inspected hospitals, and made unscheduled visits to rail yards and armories. He often worked through the night. It was said that his office light never dimmed. Stanton reimagined the War Department not as a passive support body, but as the nerve center of a nation at war. Under his leadership, the Union became capable of fighting a modern, multi-front war. While he inspired fear among subordinates and venom among opponents, his results were undeniable. *"If Stanton were in the field, he would be a tyrant,"* one officer wrote. *"But from Washington, he made us a force of iron."*

Naval Superiority and Riverine Warfare

Gideon Welles – Secretary of the Navy - was not a military man, he was a journalist. He worked for the Jacksonian Democrat, then turned into a Republican. Once in office, he steered the Navy with administrative brilliance and strategic insight. When Welles took office in March 1861, the U.S. Navy was woefully unprepared for any conflict. The entire force numbered just 42 usable ships, many scattered around the globe, with barely enough sailors to crew them. If the Union was to win, it needed to dominate the sea and diminish or eliminate the South's ability to exports and import goods. The South had an extremely limited naval presence, that was exasperated by their inability to fund the construction of new ships.

Welles threw himself into organizing the Union blockade, the first step in General Winfield Scott's "Anaconda Plan" to surround and squeeze the South economically. Welles expanded the Navy with astonishing speed. By war's end, his miniscule fleet had grown to over 600 ships, including steam-powered ironclads, gunboats, and converted merchant vessels. Naval shipyards operated at full operational speed, and private yards were enlisted to help meet demand. Welles used the Navy not just to blockade Confederate ports, but to seize and control river systems, especially the Mississippi River and its tributaries.

Over time the blockade succeeded in crippling the Southern economy, choking off cotton exports, limiting imports of guns and supplies, and forcing the Confederacy into financial collapse as well as a citizenry approaching starvation. European powers, once tempted to support the South, found it harder to justify recognition of a rebellion so thoroughly isolated.

Welles was also a key architect of the Navy's inland operations. He supported the development of the *"brown-water navy,"* armored gunboats designed to patrol rivers, especially in the Western Theater. These vessels assisted in the capture of Forts Henry and Donelson, helping Grant open Tennessee to Union forces. They played a decisive role in the victory at Vicksburg, helping Grant control the Mississippi River cutting the Confederacy in half. This innovation in joint Army-Navy operations was unprecedented and a precursor to modern amphibious warfare.

Under Welles' leadership, the Navy embraced radical new technology, most famously in the form of the ironclad warship. Welles continued to support innovations, including torpedo boats, mines, and advanced propulsion systems. He ran the Navy Department with efficiency and integrity, resisting corruption and bureaucratic inertia. He maintained detailed diaries that remain invaluable to historians. And while the war consumed most naval attention, Welles ensured a continued global naval presence, projecting American power and safeguarding trade routes.

Gideon Welles contributions were strategic, structural, and enduring. He built the Navy that sealed off the Confederacy, split it with riverine power, and ushered in the modern age of naval warfare. Lincoln called him *"the quiet pillar,"* and indeed he was. While others spoke louder or rode horses into battle, Welles reshaped the Navy in the image of the Union's resolve: expanding, unrelenting, and inevitable.

Legislative Coordination and Border State Management

Edward Bates (Attorney General) - In a cabinet of outsized personalities, the figure of Edward Bates offered a kind of sober, measured calm. A respected jurist from Missouri and the first cabinet member from west of the Mississippi, Bates brought to Lincoln's inner circle a voice of legal tradition, border state sensibility, and cautious unionism. His role was neither as dynamic as Stanton's nor as visionary as Chase's, but in the machinery of wartime governance, Bates functioned as an essential gear, quietly coordinating law with policy, and helping hold the fragile loyalty of the border states.

As Attorney General, Bates was charged with interpreting the law in a time when the Constitution itself seemed stretched to its limits. In the opening years of the war, Lincoln faced criticism for actions taken under emergency powers, suspending habeas corpus, calling up militias without congressional approval, and arresting suspected traitors. Bates's opinions often provided the legal cover for these decisions, offering the administration a shield of legitimacy.

One of his most notable legal contributions came in 1862, when Bates issued an opinion affirming that Black men born in the United States were citizens, a statement with major implications for freed men and the future of civil rights. Though his views on race remained cautious compared to those of Radical Republicans, this decision was a clear step away from the Dred Scott ruling and toward a more expansive understanding of citizenship.

Bates played a behind-the-scenes role in shaping legislation consistent with wartime needs. He consulted with members of Congress on legal frameworks for emancipation, especially as they related to confiscated property as well as questions surrounding martial law, military commissions, and the legal treatment of captured Confederate soldiers. He helped settle issues of loyalty oaths and disenfranchisement of Confederate sympathizers, walking a delicate line between punishment and reconciliation. His legal opinions helped navigate the Union through a minefield of wartime statutes, keeping executive authority on something resembling constitutional footing even as it expanded rapidly.

Perhaps Bates's most unique and subtle contribution came in his symbolic and practical role as a liaison to the border states, particularly Missouri and Kentucky. These states were crucial to the Union's war strategy, geographically, politically, and ideologically. Holding them required delicate persuasion, not heavy-handed compulsion.

Bates was a conservative Republican by temperament and a Unionist who opposed slavery, but not a confirmed emancipationist. This made him a credible figure to the cautious, slaveholding elites of the border states who feared federal overreach but loathed secession. His presence in the cabinet was part of Lincoln's broader effort to show that the war was not about abolition alone, but the preservation of the Union. When emancipation did come, Bates accepted it as a military necessity and moved with the rest of the cabinet in defending it as constitutional under the war powers of the president.

Though he would resign in late 1864, frustrated by the shifting tides of politics and the rise of more radical figures within the administration, Bates had helped the government walk a critical tightrope. He had kept the legal framework of war intact, defended the government's extraordinary actions, and helped maintain loyalty in a region where it might have crumbled.

Department of the Interior

John P Usher - Appointed Secretary of the Interior on January 1,1863, Usher took charge of a sprawling portfolio that included federal lands, Native American affairs, the Patent Office, and the fledgling system of national resources. Prior to this appointment he had served as Assistant Secretary of the Interior under Caleb Smith. Though his office was not at the center of war strategy, it was at the core of national infrastructure, and Usher understood that the business of government could not be suspended in the face of civil war.

Usher's most critical responsibility was the management of western territories, many of which were undergoing rapid population growth, as war raged in the east. He oversaw the distribution of land grants, the settlement of homesteaders, and the operation of territorial governments. These duties became more complex as the war disrupted normal administration and increased demands for western resources. Usher helped implement parts of the Homestead Act of 1862, encouraging westward migration and reinforcing Union control over the frontier.

Usher also had oversight of the Bureau of Indian Affairs, which during the war was frequently embroiled in conflict. The war drained military forces away from the frontier, leading to increased tensions and violence between settlers and Native tribes.

The Department of the Interior also supported the war effort in more indirect ways. Usher oversaw the Patent Office, which during the war became a hive of activity. Innovations in weaponry, railways, telegraph systems, and agricultural machinery poured in, many of them used to improve battlefield efficiency or sustain the Northern economy. He was also responsible for managing federal mines and mineral lands, particularly in the West. With the war placing new demands on coal, copper, and iron, the Interior Department's role in regulating these resources gained significance.

Usher's greatest value to Lincoln may have been his loyalty and competence. He supported the administration's policies without seeking the spotlight, and he shared Lincoln's pragmatic approach to governance. His correspondence with the president reveals a man deeply respectful of Lincoln's burdens and eager to ease them where he could. He resigned in May 1865, shortly after Lincoln's assassination, returning to private life without controversy.

John P. Usher left no sweeping reforms or landmark legislation behind him. But he helped keep the machinery of government running during a very difficult time. His work in managing western expansion, natural resources, and civil administration ensured that the United States did not lose its internal cohesion even as it fought to preserve its national identity. As one postwar observer noted, *"He served in quiet, and left a house in order."*

Managing Unity in Diversity

<u>Abraham Lincoln - President </u>- In 1860, Lincoln deliberately chose to form what historian Doris Kearns Goodwin later called a *"team of rivals."* Obviously, Lincoln did not seek docile yes-men. He chose men of ability and experience, then let them argue, sometimes furiously, before making his own quiet decision. Abraham Lincoln's cabinet looked like a recipe for dysfunction. It was composed of powerful, willful men, two who had run against him for the presidency, and none of whom seemed especially eager to take orders from a country lawyer with only a single term in Congress experience. Lincoln transformed that volatile collection of individuals into a functioning wartime government, not by force of personality, but by an extraordinary sense of timing, patience, and political insight.

Lincoln had an extraordinary capacity to listen to the grievances, ideas, and egos of his cabinet members. He met regularly with each of them, heard their disputes, allowed them to vent, and absorbed their views. But once he had listened, he made up his mind with clarity, often surprising those who thought they had steered him in their direction.

When Seward offered to assume control of policy at the war's outset, Lincoln firmly rejected it, asserting his own authority. When Chase attempted to outmaneuver rivals or shape policy from the Treasury, Lincoln indulged him, until he didn't. When Stanton barked, Lincoln bore it with wry amusement and turned the War Department into a powerful engine of mobilization with Stanton at the helm, but always under presidential direction. Lincoln allowed each man to shine on his own, but he never relinquished the role of final arbiter.

Few could have maintained unity among such ambitious personalities. Chase and Seward clashed. Stanton and Blair had frequent disagreements. Bates, the elder jurist, occasionally found himself adrift amid the personalities. Lincoln kept them working together, often through a kind of political judo, deflecting force rather than confronting it head-on. He would calm tempers with humor, defuse tensions with carefully chosen words, and allow arguments to burn themselves out before issuing his decision. It was said by some that Lincoln moved too slowly, but often his delay was deliberate calculation, not indecision. He gave room for consensus to form, or for opposition to collapse under its own weight.

Lincoln's cabinet was not a harmonious chorus, but a political mosaic, and Lincoln was its quiet composer. He understood that a nation at war required strong voices and divergent perspectives, but only if they moved in the end toward a common goal. He tolerated dissent but never lost sight of direction. In the end, perhaps his greatest political skill lay not in any single appointment or policy, but in his ability to hold together a cabinet, a party, and a fractured nation, long enough to see it begin to heal.

The Cabinet members did not always like one another. They often did not like Lincoln. But they followed him. By 1863, Lincoln had transformed not just the presidency, but the role of executive leadership. He had shown how debate could forge unity, and how humility could command strength.

"With malice toward none, with charity for all..." he would later say. That spirit was forged in the entirety of these meetings with his advisers, where conviction met compromise, and America's fate was redefined.

CHAPTER 3
FREEDOM RINGS - THE EMANCIPATION PROCLAMATION

By 1863 advanced western nations had long ago abolished slavery. It was abolished from the British Empire in 1833 and from France and its colonies in 1848. To the south Mexico had abolished slavery in 1829. And by 1863 enslaved persons from the South were flocking to the North in larger and larger numbers in a quest to find freedom.

Early in the war, Union General Benjamin Butler refused to return escaped slaves to Confederate owners, arguing they were *"contraband of war"* property being used to support the rebellion. This label offered them a kind of protection from re-enslavement, but it did not confer freedom, citizenship, or full rights. *"These men are property, and if the rebels use them to support the war, I will not return them,"* Butler famously declared in 1861. Many were hired or impressed into labor supporting Union forces digging trenches, building fortifications, cooking, driving wagons, serving as scouts or guides, and doing laundry. Much of this labor was unpaid or poorly paid, and conditions were often harsh and dangerous. Their presence was essential in supporting Union logistics, especially in the Southern theater.

Abraham Lincoln had always regarded slavery as a moral wrong. As early as the 1850s, he described it as a *"monstrous injustice."* He initially did not see the abolishment of slavery as a particular desired end of the war. He was intent on saving the Union, not abolishing slavery. In 1862 Lincoln wrote a letter to Horace Greely stating, *"My paramount object in this struggle is to save the Union and is not either to save or to destroy slavery."* Even with that statement in August, Lincoln had presented the idea of a proclamation of emancipation to his cabinet on July 22, 1862.

As the war progressed and casualties mounted in significant numbers, Lincoln came to see emancipation of Blacks as a strategic weapon. Slavery was greatly helping the Confederacy in their war effort; enslaved labor supported the Southern economy and freed up white men to fight. Striking at slavery, therefore, would weaken the South's war effort. It would also further encourage enslaved people to flee, rebel, or join the Union side. When reaching this way of thinking, Lincoln concluded that his emancipation proclamation could be justified as a war measure under his powers as commander-in-chief. This gave him legal ground to act, despite the constitutional limits on federal authority over slavery in peacetime.

The Emancipation Proclamation was not born of sudden inspiration. It emerged gradually, shaped by military necessity, political caution, moral conviction, and relentless calculation and recalculation. Abraham Lincoln's journey from cautious anti-slavery advocate to emancipator of millions of enslaved persons reflected the shifting ground of war as well as politics in 1862 and 1863. The Proclamation was not only a moral turning point, but also a brilliant exercise in strategic governance, diplomacy, and political orchestration.

Before the Emancipation Proclamation, Abraham Lincoln's thoughts on slavery were shaped as much by political necessity as by personal conviction. Personally, Lincoln found slavery morally repugnant. Even as he condemned slavery in moral terms, he was deeply cautious in his approach as a statesman. His primary aim was always preserving the Union, and he tread carefully to avoid alienating border states or provoking further secession.

During his early presidency, Lincoln maintained that he had no intention, nor constitutional authority, to interfere with slavery where it already existed. His inaugural address in 1861 affirmed this, and he supported the proposed Corwin Amendment, which would have constitutionally protected slavery in the states where it was already legal. He believed that containing the spread of slavery would lead to its eventual extinction, a moderate stance that he hoped would hold the fragile Union together. But as the war progressed and especially as enslaved people themselves began fleeing to Union lines in large numbers, Lincoln came to see emancipation not only as a moral imperative but also as a military necessity. This evolution laid the groundwork for the Emancipation Proclamation, which would fundamentally alter both the character of the war and the legacy of the nation.

When the Civil War began in 1861, Lincoln feared that immediate action against slavery might drive the border states, Kentucky, Missouri, Maryland, and Delaware, into the Confederacy, potentially dooming the Union cause. In his First Inaugural Address, he had even stated explicitly that he had no intention to interfere with slavery where it already existed.

Even in these early months, Lincoln was exploring the edges of what was possible. He supported the Confiscation Acts, which allowed Union forces to seize enslaved people being used to support the Confederate war effort. He also backed compensated emancipation in the border states, though this proposal failed to gain traction. Compensated emancipation was a policy idea in which slaveholders would be paid by the government in exchange for freeing their enslaved people. The idea had been used successfully in the British Empire when it abolished slavery back in 1833.

He proposed the idea of compensated emancipation multiple times, particularly to the border states, such as Kentucky, Missouri, Maryland, and Delaware, where slavery still existed but loyalty to the Union remained. In 1862, he presented a plan to Congress for compensated emancipation in the District of Columbia, which was passed. He hoped this success would encourage other states to voluntarily adopt similar measures.

However, most slaveholding states rejected the idea outright. Many southern leaders saw slavery not just as an economic institution but as a way of life that couldn't be bought out, while others believed the government had no right to interfere at all. The failure of these efforts, along with the growing urgency of the war and the increasing number of enslaved people fleeing to Union lines, ultimately led Lincoln to embrace immediate emancipation as a war measure without compensation, as embodied in the Emancipation Proclamation.

Gradually, he began to see that the war could not be won without confronting slavery head-on, not only as a moral blight, but as the foundation of the Confederate economy and military.

General Fremont's Early Proclamation

The idea of an Emancipation Proclamation had already been instituted, although illegally and without a lot of forethought in Missouri by General John C. Fremont, who gave his order on August 39, 1861. He had no authorization to do so. Fremont announced martial law and declared *"The property, real and personal, of all persons in the State of Missouri who shall take up arms against the United States... is declared to be confiscated... and their slaves, if any they have, are hereby declared free men."*

The enigmatic and sometimes contentious and irresponsible General John Fremont had been an active commander in the west, first by securing California shortly after the territory had briefly called itself an independent country. With this maneuver he went from conducting cartographic assignments in the mountains of California to eliminating innocent peace-loving Indian populations on his march to the Pacific Coast. This, to a certain extent garnered him positive press in Washington. He was temporarily named as the Military Governor of California before his next promotion. Lincoln appointed Fremont to become a Major General and gave him command of The Department of the West, which he administered out of Saint Louis.

Though energetic, Frémont governed with imperiousness. He surrounded himself with a lavish court of foreign advisers, spent extravagantly, and awarded contracts and commissions recklessly. His military competence was also questioned, his field campaigns were sluggish, and he failed to intercept Confederate forces under Sterling Price during the Missouri Campaign of 1861. But the most dramatic moment came in August 1861, when Fremont declared martial law in Missouri and issued his emancipation order, freeing the slaves of all Missourians who supported the rebellion. The move shocked the country. Fremont had taken the bold step of making the war about slavery, long before Lincoln was ready to do so publicly. It was not a politicly-made strategic order.

Fremont had a clear reason for issuing his emancipation order. He intended to strike a blow against Confederate sympathizers and guerrilla warfare in a deeply divided border state, while also asserting bold leadership in a moment of uncertainty. Missouri was teetering between Union and Confederate control, and Fremont believed that a decisive statement could suppress rebellion and solidify Union authority.

His order was the first emancipation of its kind and marked a radical departure from Lincoln's more cautious approach. Fremont was a presidential candidate in 1856 and ardent anti-slavery man. He likely saw the order as both a moral imperative and a strategic weapon of war.

However, the political fallout was swift. Lincoln, still trying to keep the fragile coalition of Union states together, especially in the slaveholding border states, was alarmed. He asked Fremont to modify the order to conform to federal law, which still protected slavery where it legally existed. When Fremont refused, Lincoln revoked the order himself on September 11, 1861. The incident highlighted the deep tensions between abolitionist generals and the president's carefully calibrated wartime strategy, and it foreshadowed future conflicts between military initiative and executive authority.

Though radical Republicans praised Fremont, the more reasonable were upset for a multitude of reasons. Border states particularly Kentucky, threatened to secede if emancipation became Union policy. The political situation in the Union was not yet ready to initiate emancipation.

Drafting and Issuing Lincoln's Proclamation

In the summer of 1862, Abraham Lincoln, with the aid of his cabinet, drafted a preliminary emancipation order. Secretary of State William Seward supported the policy but counseled delay. Issuing such a proclamation after a string of Union defeats, he warned, would appear to the world like *"the last measure of an exhausted government."* Seward suggested that Lincoln wait for a military victory, so that the move could appear from a position of strength. Lincoln agreed and pocketed the draft.

The Cabinet members agreed on the text on July 22. That much-needed Union victory came at Antietam in September 1862. Though tactically inconclusive, the battle halted Lee's advance into Maryland and gave Lincoln the moment he needed to release the document. On September 22, 1862, Lincoln issued the Preliminary Emancipation Proclamation. It declared that if the rebellious states did not lay down their arms by January 1, 1863, he would proclaim the freedom of their slaves.

It was a bold move, the war was not going as well as the public, the press, nor the government had anticipated, and the nation was deeply divided, not only between north and south, but within the north as well. As written, Lincon's proclamation would declare all enslaved people in Confederate-held territory to be free, changing the character of the war from one of uniting the stats to one of liberation of the enslaved.

The reaction around the country was immediate and sometimes fierce. Abolitionists celebrated cautiously. Frederick Douglass praised the shift but worried that implementation might fall short. Conservatives, especially in the border states, were alarmed. Northern Democrats attacked Lincoln mercilessly, accusing him of turning the war into a crusade for racial equality. Newspapers warned of racial unrest and political upheaval.

Within the Republican Party, divisions emerged. Radical Republicans wanted more immediate and universal emancipation, without conditions. Moderates and border state representatives were deeply uneasy about the effect of such a proclamation would have. Yet Lincoln stood firm. He met with leaders from various constituencies, listened patiently, but did not waver from the direction he had chosen.

Privately, Lincoln made clear that his motivations were layered. He wrote in a letter to Horace Greeley in August 1862, just weeks before issuing the preliminary proclamation, *"If I could save the Union without freeing any slave I would do it... and if I could save it by freeing all the slaves I would do it... I intend no modification of my oft-expressed personal wish that all men everywhere could be free."* It was not a confession of indifference; it was a declaration of realism. He was governing a divided country in the midst of civil war, and he knew that timing and framing were as important as principle.

As January 1 approached, Lincoln had refined the language of the proclamation. He consulted with legal advisors and worked closely with Secretary of War Edwin Stanton and Attorney General Edward Bates. He deliberately limited its reach: it applied only to states *"in rebellion,"* and not to the border states or areas of the Confederacy already under Union control. This narrow scope was both a legal necessity and a political compromise, it allowed Lincoln to act under his constitutional authority as commander-in-chief, and it helped hold the fragile Union coalition together. The entire proclamation was only 720 words, and the language was formal and legalistic.

In the morning of New Year's Day 1863, Lincoln, after spending hours shaking hands at the White House New Year's reception, retreated to his office and signed the final Emancipation Proclamation document. His hand was tired, his signature shaky, but his resolve was clear. *"If my name ever goes into history,"* he said, *"it will be for this act, and my whole soul is in it."*

The preliminary proclamation gave the Confederacy 100 days to lay down arms or face a decree of emancipation of their slaves. They did not lay down their arms and on the first day of the new year, Lincoln had followed through with his promise.

Critics called the proclamation a symbolic gesture. But for the enslaved people of the South, the symbolism was extremely powerful. Word of the proclamation spread quickly. It was carried by Union soldiers, escaped slaves, and Northern newspapers. Where Union troops advanced, freedom of the enslaved followed. Lincoln acknowledged the proclamation's limits, but he believed its power lay in what it symbolized. It declared that the end of slavery was a central aim of the war. It reframed the conflict before the world so that it was no longer just a civil war, it was a war against human bondage.

European powers, particularly Britain and France, were less inclined to recognize the Confederacy, now that it was known for certainty that the Confederate States of America stood explicitly for slavery.

Beyond its moral and diplomatic impact, the proclamation had tangible military consequences. It authorized the recruitment of Black men into the Union Army and Navy. By the war's end, nearly 200,000 African American soldiers and sailors had served the war effort. Their valor and determination in combat not only strengthened the Union war effort but challenged racist assumptions in the North and South alike. Black regiments like the 54th Massachusetts would become symbols of courage and resolve. Frederick Douglass, once critical of Lincoln's caution, now championed the President's action: *"The proclamation is the trumpet that called us to arms and liberty."*

In the North, the Emancipation Proclamation sparked a wide range of responses, from jubilation to outrage. Radical Republicans in Congress and abolitionists like William Lloyd Garrison hailed it as a long-overdue strike against an immoral institution. Frederick Douglass called it a *"moral torch"* and encouraged Black men to enlist in the Union Army, stating, *"Who would be free themselves must strike the blow."*

New York Tribune, January 2, 1863: *"It is the beginning of a new era. The President has struck at the root of the rebellion. Henceforth, the war is for liberty as well as Union."* Yet not all Northern voices were supportive. Many moderate Republicans and nearly all Democrats condemned the proclamation. Peace Democrats argued that Lincoln had overstepped his constitutional authority and feared that freeing slaves would provoke unrest and competition for jobs in the North. The 38th Congress became a battleground over the future of emancipation, with fierce debates about whether the war's focus should remain on restoring the Union or extend to ending slavery.

Chicago Times, January 3, 1863: *"The Proclamation is not law. It is only a piece of paper, worth as much as the paper on which it is written. Mr. Lincoln has proclaimed the freedom of people over whom he has no control."*

In the South, the response was swift and defiant. Southern newspapers denounced the proclamation as an incitement to servile insurrection. Confederate President Jefferson Davis issued a proclamation declaring that any Black Union soldier captured in battle would not be treated as a prisoner of war, but as a criminal inciting rebellion. White officers leading Black troops faced threats of execution. The Richmond Examiner, January 5, 1863, reported: *"Lincoln's proclamation is the most monstrous political crime known in the history of civilized nations. It is a proposal for the butchery of women and children."*

The Confederate Congress, in an act of bitter resistance, passed resolutions denouncing the proclamation and solidifying their commitment to slavery as central to their cause. Far from encouraging Southern states to rejoin the Union, Lincoln's action deepened the Confederacy's resolve to fight on. In many areas, the proclamation was seen not only as a threat to the institution of slavery but as an existential challenge to Southern society itself.

Despite the hostile reactions, the proclamation had the intended effect of shifting the moral ground of the war.

In countless Black churches across the North and in Southern communities where Union soldiers had begun to arrive, ministers read the text of the proclamation aloud as if it were a holy writ. Congregations wept, shouted, and sang. The words on the page offered no guarantees, but they carried the force of prophecy, and a glimmer of hope for living a freed life.

Frederick Douglass, the nation's most famous Black voice, was both jubilant and impatient. He recognized the document as a moral milestone, but also as a call to action. *"Let the Black man get upon his person the brass letters U.S.,"* he declared*, "and a musket on his shoulder, and bullets in his pocket, and there is no power on earth or under the earth which can deny that he has earned the right to citizenship."* Douglass understood that freedom without service might be ignored. But freedom earned by fighting against slavery could never be denied.

By May, the Bureau of Colored Troops was established, and recruitment offices were opened in the North and along parts of the Southern coast where Union forces held territory. Black men came forward by the thousands, former slaves seeking to claim their manhood, and free men eager to transform their dignity into something the law could no longer overlook.

But their path into the blue uniform was neither smooth nor fair. White officers, even those sympathetic to the cause of emancipation, often recoiled at the thought of serving in regiments with Black soldiers. Some officers refused such assignments altogether. Equipment issued to these new Black recruits was most often second-rate: old weapons, mismatched uniforms and, in some cases, defective supplies. Possibly worst of all, the federal government offered Black soldiers lower pay: ten dollars per month, with three of those dollars deducted from that salary to cover the cost of clothing. White soldiers received thirteen dollars with no deductions for clothing. The insult was palpable and protests soon followed. This payroll system had been initiated by an act of Congress that was signed by the President and was finalized by General Order 143 which came from the Secretary of War Stanton. Congress eventually corrected this wrong by passing a new law in June 1864 which granted equal pay and was retroactive to January 1, 1864.

Still, despite the voiced prejudices of the officers in the military and the government they fought to serve they enrolled in the military as soon as they were allowed. A volunteer from Pennsylvania wrote to his sister, *"I know not if I shall live or die, but if I die, it shall be as a man and not as a slave."*

In communities across the North, especially in cities like Boston and Philadelphia, the response to the Emancipation Proclamation was mostly jubilant. There were prayer meetings and torchlit processions, bells ringing from church towers, and women draping their homes in red, white, and blue bunting. But beneath the public celebration was private worry. Many Black families were about to have sons heading off to war with substandard equipment, pay, and recognition. In the South, where the reach of federal authority was uncertain, the news of freedom moved slowly, and often met with violent backlash from the white enslavers.

Black newspapers, long the voices of free African American communities, became critical conduits for both celebration and skepticism. The Christian Recorder, published in Philadelphia, urged its readers to see in Lincoln's words the hand of Providence. At the same time, editorials reminded readers that freedom required vigilance. *"The death of slavery,"* one article presciently warned, *"does not guarantee the birth of equality."*

No one understood this better than Douglass. Tireless in his speeches and writings, he continued to press the Lincoln administration to do more. He demanded equal pay, fair treatment for Black troops, and above all, the right for them to serve as commissioned officers. He met with President Lincoln in the White House, and while he came away impressed by Lincoln's intellect and temperament, he remained uneasy. *"I never doubted the president's heart,"* Douglass said, *"but I sometimes feared the caution of his head."* That fear would wane over time, but it never fully vanished.

One of the most profound expressions of Black courage in 1863 came from the 54th Massachusetts Infantry Regiment. The regiment was raised in Boston and commanded by Colonel Robert Gould Shaw. It was composed entirely of free Black men from the North, many of whom came from well-educated families. But all the officers in the regiment were white. The 54th trained under the glare of public scrutiny, with detractors certain they would collapse under fire and supporters desperate for them to prove otherwise.

The regiment got its chance to prove its capabilities in July, when they were ordered to participate in the assault on Fort Wagner, a Confederate stronghold near Charleston, South Carolina. The attack was a near-suicidal mission, it had almost no chance of success. It was not fought by the 54th alone, but they were to lead the charge. The courage and discipline of the 54th was evident in that battle, and the news of their deeds reverberated across the North. Newspapers that had once scoffed at the idea of Black men in uniform now praised their valor. Their example helped spur additional enlistment and began to chip away at the deeply held prejudice that had long insisted Black men lacked the bravery and discipline for war.

By the end of 1863, nearly 100,000 African American men had enlisted in the Union army and navy. Their service was reshaping the public imagination of the war and of America itself. In camps, on battlefields, and in letters home, they declared that the struggle for freedom was no longer a white man's war, but a national rebirth, with Black Americans at the center of its moral heart. Freedom, for so long denied, was now being claimed as a right paid in blood.

The Emancipation Proclamation did not free all slaves. It did not end racism or even guarantee permanent freedom. But it changed the purpose of the war, the composition of the Union Army, and the place of African Americans in the national narrative. *"In giving freedom to the slave, we assure freedom to the free,"* Lincoln had told Congress in 1862 *"We shall nobly save, or meanly lose, the last best hope of earth."*

The Emancipation Proclamation had expanded the scope and stakes of the war, turning it into a conflict not just to preserve the Union, but to end slavery. With this shift came questions about how to treat the enslaved in occupied territories, how to respond to Confederate guerrilla tactics, and how to deal with loyalty and rebellion. The Lieber Code answered many of these questions by affirming that slaves were to be considered free persons when encountered by Union troops. Reprisals and retaliation were governed by strict moral and military considerations. War could be cruel, but it must be bounded by law and conscience.

The Lieber Code, Law and War

In the spring of 1863, as the nation was engulfed in the bloodiest conflict it had ever known, a quietly revolutionary document emerged from the War Department in Washington. It was General Orders No. 100, more commonly known as the Lieber Code. Signed by President Abraham Lincoln and issued on April 24, 1863, the code laid out, for the first time in American history, a formalized set of rules governing the conduct of war. It was a landmark in the evolution of both military and international law, and its author was an unlikely but extraordinary figure: Francis Lieber.

Francis Lieber was born in Prussia in 1800. He was a scholar, soldier, and political exile who had fled the repressive regimes of Europe for the freer air of America. He fought briefly against France in the Napoleonic Wars as a teenager. He was wounded and imprisoned by the French. After immigrating to the United States, he became a noted professor of political science and international law, eventually teaching at Columbia College in New York. Though a committed Unionist, Lieber had three sons who fought in the Civil War, two for the North, and one who chose the South and was killed in action. His personal grief gave his scholarly work a tragic moral urgency.

Lieber was deeply concerned with the question of how war could be conducted within the bounds of civilization. In an age when war often descended into butchery and retribution, he believed it was possible, even necessary, to impose moral constraints on military action. In 1862, at the request of General Henry Halleck, the general-in-chief of the Union Army, Lieber drafted a code of conduct for Union troops. It was not merely a list of dos and don'ts. It was a sweeping philosophical and legal framework rooted in history, ethics, and practicality.

The Lieber Code consisted of 157 articles, written in plain but forceful language. It addressed a wide array of military situations: the treatment of prisoners of war, civilians, deserters, spies, property, and the use of force. It prohibited torture, collective punishment, and wanton destruction. It emphasized the distinction between combatants and noncombatants, and recognized that even in total war, there must be limits.

One of the Code's most radical provisions was its recognition of enslaved people in the Confederate states. Article 42 declared that all persons in an enemy's country are liable to be treated as enemies but went on to specify that the United States does not recognize slavery as a legal institution. Enslaved people who were found within Union-occupied territory were not to be returned to their masters but treated as free individuals. In effect, the Code formalized the policy of emancipation as an element of military strategy and moral obligation.

Equally important was the Code's defense of military necessity, tempered by humanity. Lieber wrote that military necessity *"consists in the necessity of those measures which are indispensable for securing the ends of the war, and which are lawful according to the modern law and usages of war."* Yet he added that necessity must never justify cruelty for its own sake.

The Code was not merely aspirational. It was enforced. Union officers received printed copies. Courts-martial referred to its articles. Commanders such as Grant and Sherman were known to consult it during campaigns. It gave legitimacy to the destruction of military resources in the South, while prohibiting wanton pillage. It also offered a legal shield for the treatment of Black soldiers and civilians, who were increasingly vulnerable as the war turned into a revolution of liberation.

Francis Lieber saw the Code not as a relic of abstract theory, but as a living guide for a new kind of war, one in which modern armies would be bound by something more than instinct and vengeance. He viewed war as inevitable in human affairs, but not beyond the reach of law and conscience.

The influence of the Lieber Code did not end with the Civil War. It became the foundation for later international conventions, including the Hague Regulations of 1899 and 1907, and the Geneva Conventions of the 20th century. In that sense, Lieber's work transcended his own time. His Code marked the moment when the United States took a leading role in the effort to humanize warfare, not through weakness, but through principle.

For a nation torn apart by fratricide, the Lieber Code stood as a quiet testament to civilization amid chaos. It told soldiers and generals alike that even in the most desperate hour, there remained a difference between justice and cruelty, between force and savagery. In doing so, it helped shape the very meaning of honorable conduct in war.

PART 2: COMMANDERS

CHAPTER 4
ROBERT E. LEE, DUTY OR STATE ALLEGIANCE

At the outbreak of the Civil War, Robert E. Lee was a respected colonel in the United States Army, known for his distinguished service in the Mexican-American War and as the superintendent of West Point. He excelled in civil engineering. When Southern states began seceding, Lee's choice of loyalty was seen as a bellwether decision. President Lincoln, through General Winfield Scott, offered Lee command of all Union forces on April 18, 1861, seven days after the war began at Fort Sumter. Scott said that if one man were to lead the defense of the country, *"I would say with my dying breath, let it be Robert E. Lee."*

For a time, many in Washington believed Lee might accept. Instead, Lee declined the offer and, within days, resigned his commission, writing to Scott: *"Save in defense of my native State, I never desire again to draw my sword."*

His resignation shocked the capital. In the North, where many still hoped the South's rebellion could be peacefully resolved, Lee's decision to join the Confederacy, especially as he had long served under the flag of the United States, was viewed by many as a deep personal betrayal. A correspondent for the New York Evening Post called Lee's resignation *"a grievous wound to the army and a sorrowful blow to the Union cause."* Others were less diplomatic. One Pennsylvania congressman denounced him as a traitor who had *"spurned the flag under which he rose to honor."*

Northern newspapers reflected this mixed sense of personal loss and growing rage. The Chicago Tribune published an editorial lamenting that *"the finest soldier in America has turned his back on his country."* In concert, the New York

Times called Lee's decision *"a man's fall from principle, no different than Benedict Arnold's, and perhaps worse, for it lends the gloss of honor to rebellion."*

In his contradictory mindset Lee wrote to a friend. *"I look upon secession as anarchy, If I owned all the slaves in the South, I would give them up to save the Union."*

Lee had graduated second in the West Point class of 1829 from a class of 45. He spent four years of cadet study without any demerits. He was one of only five to do so. He was initially commissioned a second Lieutenant in the Corps of Engineers. His first assignment was to build a fort on an island in the Savannah River. He was not promoted to a first lieutenant until 1836, still functioning as a civil works engineer. His first military experience was in the Mexican-American War, and while there he was quickly promoted to major after battle success. Following that war, he spent three years teaching at West Point, when his son was serving as a cadet. At the time Lee had been promoted to a brevet Colonel. In 1860 Lee became a Lieutenant Colonel and was stationed in Texas. In March 1861 Lee was appointed be in command of the 1st U.S. Calvary Regiment of Texas. He was working from Washington and living at his Arlington House in Virginia. The promotion was signed by Abraham Lincoln.

Lee wrote: *"The South, in my opinion, has been aggrieved by the acts of the North, as you say. I feel the aggression and am willing to take every proper step for redress. It is the principle I contend for, not individual or private benefit. As an American citizen, I take great pride in my country, her prosperity and institutions, and would defend any State if her rights were invaded. But I can anticipate no greater calamity for the country than a dissolution of the Union. It would be an accumulation of all the evils we complain of, and I am willing to sacrifice everything but honor for its preservation. I hope, therefore, that all constitutional means will be exhausted before there is a resort to force. Secession is nothing but revolution. The framers of our Constitution never exhausted so much labor, wisdom, and forbearance in its formation, and surrounded it with so many guards and securities, if it was intended to be broken by every member of the Confederacy at will. It was intended for "perpetual union", so expressed in the preamble, and for the establishment of a government, not a compact, which can only be dissolved by revolution, or the consent of all the people in convention assembled."*

When Virginia seceded on April 17, his course was set. On April 20, Lee resigned his commission in the U.S. Army. *"I cannot raise my hand against my birthplace, my home, my children,"* he wrote to Scott. *"Save in defense of my native State, I hope I may never be called upon to draw my sword."* It was a decision of heartbreak and conflicted honor. Unlike the radical secessionists of the South, Lee had never embraced secession or slavery with zeal. But to him, Virginia was sacred ground and as Virgina goes so goes Lee. The notion of fighting against it, even for a government he had served for over three decades, was personally intolerable.

On April 23, 1861, Lee assumed command of the forces of North Virginia (not all the Armies of the Confederacy) as a Major General. He was soon credited with wining significant victories in 1862, such as at Second Bull Run and Fredericksburg

The tone in the Northern press grew more hostile toward him. Lee was no longer described as a noble Virginian following his conscience, but as the most dangerous general of the rebellion. Even then, a reluctant respect often lingered. The Chicago Tribune lamented that *"the finest soldier in America has turned his back on his country,"* a line that captured the sense of both admiration and betrayal many Northerners felt.

The North's reaction to Lee's decision evolved from sorrow and surprise to resentment and strategic urgency. What had begun as a painful loss became, over time, a confrontation with a man who personified the Southern cause. For many in the Union, Robert E. Lee had not just joined the enemy, he had become the soul of the enemy.

Virginia joined the Confederacy in May 1861, Lee was commissioned as a full general, but rather than taking a field army into battle, he initially served as a senior military advisor to President Davis. In these early months, the Confederate military effort was fragmented, with different armies scattered across the South, each responding to threats in their own region. There was no single "main" Confederate army.

It was not until the spring of 1862, following the Union's advance on Richmond during the Peninsula Campaign, that circumstances changed dramatically. On May 31, 1862, at the Battle of Seven Pines, Confederate General Joseph E. Johnston was seriously wounded. Two days later, on June 1, President Davis appointed Lee to command Johnston's army. This force, soon to be formally designated the Army of Northern Virginia, would become the Confederacy's principal fighting force. Under Lee's leadership, the army would be molded into an instrument of remarkable discipline, endurance, and aggression. From the Seven Days Battles through Gettysburg and ultimately to the trenches of Petersburg and the surrender at Appomattox, the Army of Northern Virginia carried the burden of the South's hopes. It was the largest Confederate army and the one most closely identified with the Confederacy's fate, largely due to Lee's commanding presence and reputation for audacious strategy.

By early1863, Robert E. Lee had fully emerged as the military and symbolic heart of the Confederate cause. His leadership was characterized by a boldness that inspired reverence among his men and fear among his enemies. That year, Lee stood at the height of his influence, respected across the South, admired even by some in the North, and entrusted with the Confederacy's most important military campaigns. 1863 would also test the limits of his judgment and the resilience of the army he had so carefully molded.

At the start of the year, Lee was basking in the glow of a string of remarkable victories. His twin triumphs at Fredericksburg in December 1862 and Chancellorsville in May 1863 stunned the Union and galvanized Southern morale. At Chancellorsville, he displayed one of the most daring maneuvers of the war by dividing his already outnumbered forces in the face of a larger enemy and launching a surprise flank attack led by General Thomas "Stonewall" Jackson. The result was a crushing Union defeat.

Lee's conduct at Chancellorsville revealed much about his leadership style. He was a commander who trusted his subordinates, favored rapid movement over defensive entrenchment, and sought to always maintain the initiative. He placed a high premium on audacity, believing that bold action could compensate for the South's numerical inferiority. His soldiers revered him, not only for his tactical genius but for his personal humility and deeply religious character.

Following Chancellorsville, Lee made his most ambitious move yet with an invasion of the North. In June 1863, he led his army across the Potomac River and into Pennsylvania, aiming to shift the theater of war out of Virginia, disrupt Union logistics, gather supplies, and potentially force a political crisis in the North. It was a calculated gamble, rooted in the belief that another Southern victory on Northern soil might lead to recognition by a foreign nation or increased pressure on Lincoln to negotiate peace.

At Gettysburg in July, his fortunes turned. Lee had crossed into Pennsylvania, believing a bold strike on Union soil might break northern morale. But his army met disaster on Cemetery Ridge. With his orders of a major charge up a hill, his forces were eliminated in a disastrous storm of cannon and musket fire. Gettysburg marked the first major defeat of Lee's military career and a turning point in the war. Though his retreat was orderly, and his army remained a potent force, the campaign's failure shattered the myth of Confederate invincibility. Lee accepted full responsibility for the defeat. The day after the defeat, Lee offered to resign. *"I am truly grateful for the kind expressions of your letter,"* he wrote to Jefferson Davis in response. *"But I am the more distressed at the result of the recent operations. I cannot even accomplish what I myself desire. I, therefore, respectfully tender the resignation of my commission…"* Davis refused.

Later in the fall, at Bristoe Station and Mine Run, Lee again attempted to turn the tide. But the campaigns brought little gain and only deepened the winter gloom. Supplies were running low. Many of his men were barefoot. And Lee, once called the *"Marble Man"* for his calm, was aging rapidly under the weight of it all.

By December 1863, General Lee was no longer the portrait of serene command. In the flickering candlelight of his headquarters tent near Orange, Virginia, he sat exhausted. The year had begun with triumph but ended somewhere in the shadows. At Chancellorsville in May, Lee's most trusted General, Stonewall Jackson, was killed by friendly fire. Lee was devastated. *"I have lost my right arm,"* he said, tears welling in his eyes. *"But I thank God for having given me such a man."* There simply was no reasonable way to replace General Jackson. With the loss of Jackson, the war took a very serious turn.

Lee's Leadership Style and Temperament

Throughout 1863, Lee also took on broader responsibilities beyond the battlefield. He advised Davis on military policy, coordinated with other Confederate commanders, and expressed concern about declining morale and desertion rates. He was not a political figure by nature, but his stature drew him into the broader debates about Confederate strategy and national survival.

In the eyes of many Southerners, Lee remained a paragon of leadership. He was calm in crisis, pious in purpose, and unwavering in loyalty. For all his brilliance and resolve, the events of 1863 revealed the limitations of even the most gifted general. The Confederate cause could not be won through tactical daring alone. The losses at Gettysburg and the near simultaneous Union victory at Vicksburg marked a significant turning point of the war. The South was still far from defeated, but its best general had suffered his first real reversal. For Lee, the war would go on, but never again with the same momentum or promise of triumph as he had held in the first half of that fateful year.

Lee's leadership style was aristocratic, yet humble. He seldom raised his voice, but his presence commanded immediate respect. To his officers he extended great trust, sometimes too much. He expected them to exercise initiative, and when they failed, he bore the blame himself. He dressed simply, but regally. He avoided profanity. Soldiers noted that he often passed through camp silently, tipping his hat to privates and asking about their health. He inspired almost mystical loyalty. *"We could follow General Lee into hell,"* one soldier wrote. *"And if he turned to us and said, 'Men, this is the right road,' we'd believe him."*

Lee's often used delegation of authority came with risks. At Gettysburg, his failure to control General Ewell or override Longstreet's hesitations contributed to the Confederate defeat. His greatest victories often came through bold maneuvers that exposed his army to enormous risk.

When Robert E. Lee assumed command of the Army of Northern Virginia in June 1862, few could have predicted that he would hold that position for the remainder of the war, or that he would come to embody the entire Confederate cause, both in its hopes and its ultimate downfall.

What made Lee so exceptional and so enduring was not just his military talent but the fact that he never lost the confidence of his superiors, his men, or the Southern public. In a Confederate government often beset by infighting and regional distrust, Lee became a unifying figure. Lee's greatest protection against challenge was the near-mythic status he had attained by 1863. He was often referred to as *"the marble man,"* and the Southern press treated him with deference, portraying him as virtuous, almost beyond reproach. This aura made it politically dangerous for anyone to criticize him publicly, especially while the war was ongoing, and morale was fragile.

Even after defeats, his soldiers remained fiercely loyal. Letters from the ranks suggest that men in the Army of Northern Virginia consistently blamed others, often Longstreet, for setbacks, while continuing to venerate Lee as a flawless commander.

Jefferson Davis trusted him completely. The two men shared similar views on honor, hierarchy, and the sacredness of the Southern cause. Davis gave Lee more autonomy than perhaps any general in American history. His soldiers revered him. Though aloof and formal in demeanor, Lee's bravery and calm under fire won the affection of his troops. They called him *"Marse Robert"* and would follow him into near-impossible situations. He worked harmoniously with subordinates. While some generals ruled by fear or rigidity, Lee fostered a culture of trust. He gave his corps commanders, especially Stonewall Jackson and James Longstreet, broad freedom, expecting them to act with initiative. When they did, as at Chancellorsville, the results could be spectacular.

Lee's leadership was not without flaws. His aggressive nature, most notably at Gettysburg, where he ordered Pickett's Charge, sometimes led to devastating losses. He could also be too deferential to states' rights in matters of supply and logistics, allowing critical resources to fall into disrepair. But his command was never seriously challenged, even in the darkest months of the war.

By 1863, Lee's status had grown beyond mere command. He was the living symbol of Confederate resolve, the embodiment of gallantry, Christian duty, and the belief that the Southern way of life could be defended with dignity. The contrast between his consistency and the Union's many missteps in leadership only heightened his legend. Foreign observers marveled at him. Southern newspapers revered him. Even many in the North respected him, grudgingly or otherwise. He became, in the minds of many, the last best hope for the South and the only man capable of holding back the tide of Northern manpower and industry.

That symbolic role may have contributed to the Confederacy's strategic blindness. As long as Lee and his army remained in the field, many Southerners believed the cause still had a chance, even as cities burned and supplies vanished. His refusal to abandon the fight, even in early 1865, spoke to his sense of duty but also prolonged a war that had, by then, become unwinnable.

While Lee's decisions were questioned in private and grumbled about in political circles, particularly after the setback at Gettysburg or the increasingly dire state of the Confederate war effort, there was never a formal or public challenge to his command. His resignation offer had been declined. His critics held their tongues. His soldiers followed him with devotion. In the eyes of the Confederacy, Robert E. Lee was the war's indispensable man and that perception, whether justified or not, protected him from replacement until the very end.

Lee remained in command until the final day on April 9, 1865, when he met Ulysses S. Grant at Appomattox and surrendered. His army was starving, encircled, and exhausted. Yet even in defeat, Lee preserved the dignity of his men and insisted on honor rather than bitterness. Few military leaders in history have held power so long, with so little opposition, and in such trying circumstances. Lee's leadership was not merely military, it was moral, political, and deeply personal. His strengths and his flaws were both magnified by the war. In the story of the Civil War, Lee was not just a commander he was the Confederacy itself.

Lee and Slavery, Not So Complicated

Contrary to the *Lost Cause* mythology that justified Confederate defeat by downplaying slavery and highlighting honor and states' rights, Lee was not an abolitionist. He inherited slaves from his father-in-law and managed them with an air of distant obligation. He reportedly believed slavery was morally wrong, but also that it was *"a greater evil to the white man than to the black race."* In 1856, Lee wrote: *"Slavery as an institution is a moral and political evil. But it is useless to expatiate on its disadvantages. The painful discipline they are undergoing is necessary for their instruction as a race."*

After the war, Lee opposed granting voting rights to freed men and resisted radical Reconstruction. While he urged reconciliation, he did not embrace equality. In public, he remained guarded. In private, his letters show a man bound by a caste worldview, unable or unwilling to envision a nation where Black Americans stood as equals.

In the spring of 1859, three young, enslaved people, Wesley Norris, his sister Mary, and a cousin, made a desperate bid for freedom from Arlington Plantation, the grand estate managed by Lee. The Custis will, which governed Arlington's enslaved population, had promised their freedom within five years of George Washington Parke Custis's death. But Lee, who had inherited not only the land but also its debts, postponed the emancipation, forcing the men, women, and children on the estate into continued bondage.

Faced with the crushing realization that their promised freedom was being denied, the Norris siblings and their cousin took what must have been an agonizing risk. They fled, hoping to reach Pennsylvania and liberty. They made it only a few miles from the estate before they were captured and dragged back to Arlington in chains.

What followed was an act of cruelty that would haunt Lee's legacy. According to Wesley Norris's detailed account, published after the war, Lee personally ordered their punishment. He instructed his overseer to have them whipped, and when the man showed hesitation at striking with force, Lee demanded the lash fall harder. Stripped and tied to a post, Wesley, Mary, and their cousin were beaten viciously, 50 lashes for each of the men and 20 for

Mary. After the lashing, saltwater was poured into their open wounds to wash the wounds, which created unbearable pain. Norris recalled that Lee stood by, coldly overseeing the ordeal, ensuring that the price for seeking freedom was made unbearable.

Defenders of Lee in later years would claim that he was a man trapped by circumstance, that he detested slavery as an institution. But in the moment that truly mattered, Lee chose to wield the whip rather than show mercy. The episode at Arlington strips away the comforting myths of reluctant loyalty and reveals a man who, whatever private doubts he may have harbored, enforced human bondage with deliberate violence.

By the time the war began, most of the enslaved people from Arlington were finally freed, but their freedom came only after years of betrayal, broken promises, and brutality. For Wesley Norris and those who bore the scars, the truth of Robert E. Lee was not carved into statues or softened by lost-cause mythology, it was written into their very flesh.

Lee's decision to join the Confederacy was born of loyalty to Virginia, to tradition, to an ideal of duty. Yet the war he helped lead brought untold suffering. And by 1863, the consequences were plain even to him. The cause he served was crumbling.

CHAPTER 5
FRUSTRATIONS OF UNION COMMAND

The South had an amazingly stable command structure, that carried it from the near beginning of the war until it's very end. The command of the South nearly carried it to ultimate victory. The North, which was clearly superior in man-power, financials, and natural resources, was not nearly as fortunate with their command structure.

From the very outset of the Civil War, the Union faced a problem that would haunt the war effort throughout the first three and a half years. Lincoln himself had no real military experience, and he struggled greatly to find a competent general who possessed all the skills and aptitude that could win the war. The South's president had significant military experience, and his Confederate states rallied around the magnetic leadership of the exceptional Robert E. Lee. The North cycled through one commanding general after another, each was ushered in with great hope and political fanfare, and each, with few exceptions, were ultimately dismissed in failure and frustration.

Some of these men were brave soldiers, others were seasoned officers, and one was predominately a political appointee with more influence than talent. But whatever their backgrounds, they shared a common fate, struggling to grasp the scope and brutality of a war. Hesitancy, bad decisions, unreadiness, were common traits of the men assigned to lead the military effort of the Northern Armies.

President Lincoln, though not a soldier himself, grew into his role as commander-in-chief with a sharper eye and a keener strategic military mind than many of his generals. He watched in anguish and frustration as his armies suffered from cautious hesitations. Those hesitations sometimes grew into absolute paralysis, outright insubordination, missed opportunities, and utter blunders. He replaced one general after another, seeking not perfection, but decisiveness and vision. In the process, Lincoln became not just the nation's political leader, but one of its sharpest military minds as well, and a sharp critic.

The following section explores the men who held the reins of Union military power at different points during the war. Men who led armies, shaped battles, and in some cases cost countless lives through incompetence or ego. Some, like Irvin McDowell and Ambrose Burnside, were overmatched and incompetent as battlefield commanders, and they knew it but served in the post as required. Others, like Joseph Hooker and George Meade, flashed potential but failed to deliver at the most crucial of times. And then came Ulysses S. Grant, a general forged in war, whose understanding of the totality of war finally aligned with Lincoln's unwavering resolve.

Before Grant, however, came a catalogue full of commanders whose stories are filled with over confidence and great arrogance. Both of which masked the worst of their military flaws. These were the men who stumbled through the war without expressing a strategic end to the war, or even seldom planned a strategic end to many of their battles. Their stories reflect not only the chaos of war and their lack of understanding it, but Lincoln's desperate urgency to save a nation in crisis, always searching for a leader who could turn the tide. It is difficult to imagine how the North survived the war at all before the arrival of its final and only totally competent commander.

Irvin McDowell at Bull Run

In the opening months of the Civil War, the Union found itself woefully unprepared for the scale and ferocity of the conflict that was about to unfold. It was unprepared for any kind of military conflict. Politicians and periodicals in Washington, still gripped by the illusion that the rebellion of the South could be swiftly quelled, pressed President Lincoln to take immediate military action with a miserably under prepared military.

Caught between public impatience and the lack of a seasoned command structure. Lincoln and the existing head of the army Winfield Scott had considered Robert E. Lee as their first choice to lead the Union Army, but Lee turned them down. Their second and third choices, Albert Johnson and Joseph Mansfield also turned down the position. Finally, they turned to a career officer not known for battlefield prowess but for his administrative competence, Major Irvin McDowell.

McDowell was a methodical man, a product of West Point's Class of 1838, who had spent most of his career in administrative staff positions. He had seen service in the Mexican-American War, but not in the kind of frontline combat that would test a general's mettle. When The Civil War broke out in 1861, he was working in Washington providing his expertise in organizing troop movements and managing supply lines not in commanding an army. But he was well known to Treasury Secretary Salmon Chase, a fellow Ohioan, who advocated for his promotion. Despite his own protests, acknowledging that he lacked the experience for such responsibility, McDowell was placed in command of the newly formed Army of Northeastern Virginia.

His orders were to advance on the Confederate forces gathering near Manassas Junction, just twenty-five miles southwest of Washington, and put an end to this uprising. But the army under his command was barely an army at all. It was a loose collection of some 35,000 raw recruits, most had only been enlisted for ninety days or less, and their limited training had been substandard. They and their commander were wholly unprepared for the rigors or complexities of battle. McDowell's plans involved a complicated flanking maneuver intended to strike the Confederate left and roll up their line. Days of hesitation allowed Confederate commanders Beauregard and Johnston to consolidate their positions, aided by the timely arrival of reinforcements by rail, the first such use of a railroad in warfare.

On the morning of July 21, 1861, McDowell's forces launched their assault in earnest, and for a brief time victory seemed within reach. Union troops pushed back the Confederate line and advanced on the enemy. Shortly thereafter came the turning point. General Thomas Jackson held firm in the face of repeated assaults, and a Confederate officer is said to have shouted, *"There stands Jackson like a stone wall!"* a moment that not only saved the Confederate line but immortalized Jackson's name in military legend.

The Union assault faltered in the face of Jackson's stand, and then soon unraveled altogether. After the trains had delivered Confederate reinforcements, the counterattack began, and the Federal lines soon broke into complete disarray. What had begun as a promising battle ended in a panicked retreat by the Army of the North. It was a stampede of, not only, soldiers but also of the civilians, and politicians who had come south from the capital to watch the spectacle. All of them rushing back to Washington in disorder hoping the Confederates would not follow. The defeat stunned both the citizens and politicians of the North; it was a complete embarrassment. There had previously been a sense that the war might be over in ninety days or less. That thought disappeared quickly.

After the battle McDowell said *"The people demanded the advance. I was ordered to advance. I did,"* in a statement that reflected both resignation and quiet indignation. Though not disgraced nor denigrated, McDowell was promptly relieved of command. He continued to serve in various administrative and subordinate roles, for which he was more qualified, throughout the war, but he would never again be entrusted with command of an independent field army.

General McDowell was not a man of towering ambition or battlefield brilliance. He was a bureaucrat thrust into a job that demanded decisiveness, instinct, and the ability to inspire, qualities he did not possess. He became the first in a long line of Union generals who would fall short in the hopes of the president, in their attempts to subdue the Confederacy. The Battle of Bull Run (Manassas Junction) was a lesson for the nation and a turning point for Lincoln, who now fully understood that the road ahead would not be a smooth one. That first battle was fought on July 21, 1861, it started in the morning, and the retreat began in late afternoon. During that short amount of time the Union losses (killed, wounded, and missing or captured) numbered some 2,900 while the South's numbers were 1,982. That trend of destruction was set to grow by unfathomable numbers.

McDowell was appointed to his command on May 27, 1861, and was relieved of his command on June 25.

George McClellan, Young Napoleon

After the disastrous result at the battle of Bull Run, President Lincoln urgently needed someone to transform a disorganized rabble of an army into an actual fighting force. The man chosen for that task was a 34-year-old rising star named George Brinton McClellan. This appointment was once again at the urging of the treasury secretary, Salmon Chase. A West Point graduate he finished second in the class of 1846. McClellan had distinguished himself in the Mexican-American War and later gained experience as a military observer during the Crimean War, which pitted Russia against the Ottoman Empire, Britain and France between 1853-1856. He observed the war and eventually wrote a book on European and Russian war technology. When civil war broke out in the United States, he was leading Union forces in western Virginia and had already achieved minor victories that gave him a reputation for competence and promise.

In July 1861, McClellan was brought east to command what would become the Army of the Potomac, and soon after, he was appointed General-in-

Chief of all Union armies. Press and public quickly dubbed him "The Young Napoleon." He was charismatic, dashing, and popular with his men, who admired his organizational brilliance and the discipline he instilled in the troops. Within months, he had turned a completely disorganized mass of army volunteers into a drilled, uniformed army that looked every bit the part of a professional fighting force.

But for all his skill in preparation, McClellan seemed unable, or unwilling to fight. Obsessed with the idea that the Confederate forces vastly outnumbered his own, McClellan repeatedly delayed offensive operations. He relied on faulty intelligence from the Pinkerton detective agency, which wildly exaggerated enemy troop strength. *"I am here in a terrible place,"* he wrote to his wife in 1862. *"The enemy have from 100 to 120,000 men… I have not 75,000 effective troops."* In reality, the Confederate force near Washington numbered closer to 50,000.

To say that McClellan was full of arrogance would be grossly understated. It was a trait that often exasperated the President and his Cabinet. McClellan's letters and telegrams to Lincoln often carried a tone of superiority, condescension, or petulance. In one of his most famous private letters to his wife, McClellan referred to Lincoln as a *"well-meaning baboon,"* ridiculing the president's understanding of military matters. On another occasion, McClellan wrote to Lincoln: *"If you do not want me to command the Army, withdraw the order; otherwise, allow me to do so without interference."*

McClellan's long-awaited Peninsula Campaign in spring 1862 was a logistical marvel, an amphibious landing on Virginia's southeastern peninsula aimed at seizing Richmond. But McClellan advanced at a glacial pace, constantly requesting reinforcements even when he had a manpower superiority and never capitalizing on enemy weaknesses. When Confederate forces under General Joseph E. Johnston finally attacked the Union Army at Seven Pines, McClellan failed to respond effectively. Even after Johnston was wounded and replaced by Robert E. Lee, McClellan hesitated. He was repeatedly outmaneuvered during the Seven Days Battles, retreating even after holding the field. At one time during the Peninsula Campaign, McClellan's forces were within five miles of Richmond with a superior force, and he failed to advance. Had he executed his plan, could it have shortened the war? Almost certainly!

Lincoln became increasingly frustrated with his new General in charge. He lamented once that McClellan had *"the slows."* And at one point, when the general refused to move his massive army, Lincoln famously quipped, *"If General McClellan does not want to use the army, I would like to borrow it for a while."*

McClellan's moment of redemption nearly came in September 1862. After Lee's first invasion of the North, McClellan's forces intercepted the Confederate plans, Special Order 191, dropped by chance and found wrapped around cigars. Armed with his enemy's secrets, McClellan had the opportunity to destroy Lee's army. But again, he moved too cautiously. The result was the Battle of Antietam, the bloodiest single day in American history. Though a tactical draw, it forced Lee to retreat and gave Lincoln the political cover he wanted to issue the Emancipation Proclamation. Still, McClellan refused to pursue Lee and argued that further action would have been too risky. Lincoln had seen enough. In November 1862, he removed McClellan from command for his lack of aggression in pursuing Lee.

In his short tenure (November 1861 – March 1862) as General in Chief of the United States Army, McClellan had at least three opportunities to cause significant harm to the Confederate army in Virginia and likely shorten the war. He had vastly superior manpower, but also had faulty intelligence, believing he was outnumbered. He refused to advance when the outcome seemed obvious to those around him. General Hooker said following the Peninsula Campaign *"He is not only not a soldier, but he does not know what soldiership is."*

McClellan returned home to a hero's welcome. His soldiers still adored him; many believed he had been unfairly treated. In 1864, he reemerged as the Democratic nominee for president, running against Lincoln on a platform that, while murky, leaned toward peace with the South.

In hindsight, George McClellan remains an enigmatic figure, a man of immense ability whose caution and extraordinary arrogance often paralyzed him. He could build an army, but he could not bring himself to unleash it. His story is one of brilliance undone by self-doubt, a general who might have ended the war early, but instead became a symbol of what could have been.

John Pope, Failed Arrogance

The summer of 1862 was a time of political anxiety and military embarrassment for the Union. George McClellan's Peninsula Campaign had failed to take Richmond and his victory at Antietam, where he failed to pursue Lee and put an end to the war was the last straw for the president. Lincoln, eager for a more aggressive approach, turned westward in search of a fighting general.

He settled on John Pope, a man whose recent captures of New Madrid and Island No. 10 on the Mississippi River had earned him fame and the label of *"successful."*

Pope was a West Point graduate of the Class of 1842 and had served with distinction in the Mexican-American War. His battlefield competence was genuine, but so too was his arrogance. When he was given command of the newly created Army of Virginia, formed by consolidating three disparate corps, Pope arrived in Washington full of bravado and contempt for McClellan and his cautious style. In a now-infamous order to his new army, Pope declared, *"Let us understand each other. I have come to you from the West, where we have always seen the backs of our enemies—from an army whose business it has been to seek the adversary, and to beat him when he was found... I presume that I have been called here to pursue the same system and to lead you against the enemy."* His proclamation was not only tone-deaf to the weary soldiers of the East who had a love for their previous commander but deeply resented by fellow officers. It was a boast he would come to regret.

Lincoln had hoped that Pope would take the fight to the Confederates while McClellan reorganized the Army of the Potomac, something he was good at. But Pope quickly found himself in over his head. He lacked familiarity with the Virginia terrain, and his force was smaller and more poorly supplied than he had anticipated. More importantly, he was facing Robert E. Lee, who now commanded a rejuvenated Confederate army and was determined to strike a decisive blow against the Union forces.

In late August 1862, Lee executed a brilliant maneuver. He split his army, sending "Stonewall" Jackson on a wide flanking march to seize the Union supply depot at Manassas Junction, drawing Pope away from his strong positions. Pope, believing he had Jackson isolated, rushed to attack. But Lee and Longstreet, moving with impressive speed, reunited with Jackson's forces in time for the Second Battle of Bull Run, fought on August 28 - 30. The battle was a disaster for the Union. Jackson held the line while Longstreet's massive wing launched a crushing counterattack into Pope's exposed flank. The Union army was routed. Once again, northern forces fled the Manassas battlefield the very same ground where McDowell had been humiliated a year earlier.

Pope blamed his subordinates for the defeat, particularly Fitz John Porter, who had hesitated to launch an attack that Pope had ordered. Porter was later court-martialed and dismissed from the army, a sentence that would be hotly debated and eventually reversed decades later. Lincoln, exasperated, dissolved the Army of Virginia. Pope was sent west to Minnesota to deal with the Sioux uprising; a quieter post far removed from the eastern headlines. He would never again hold major field command in the Civil War.

In the end, John Pope was a competent soldier undone by his own hubris and the misjudgment of those who elevated him. His career in the Eastern Theater lasted only weeks, but it left a deep mark. Lincoln's search for a general who could win, continued.

John Pope was appointed to his post in June 1862 and was relieved of the same on September 12. In less than six months the Union Command had seen three leaders, and each had been dispatched.

Ambrose Burnside, Knowingly Unfit

Ambrose Burnside was another man placed reluctantly in a position he never sought and ultimately could not command. Burnside was born in Indiana in 1824, the son of a frontier family, and graduated from West Point in 1847, near the middle of his class. He served capably in the Mexican-American War and then in various army and civilian roles, including as a railroad executive and arms manufacturer. When the Civil War broke out, he returned to uniform and performed well in early campaigns, particularly along the North Carolina coast, where his expeditions captured strategic Confederate ports. His success earned him promotion and growing attention in Washington.

Ambrose Burnside was a man who was well aware of his capabilities as well as his limits. He was a man of modest ambition and little interest in politics. When offered command of the Army of the Potomac after the second battle of Bull Run debacle, he turned the commission down, insisting he was not fit for such a role. *"I do not feel myself competent to command such a large army as this. I would prefer to remain in command of a corps."* Only after Lincoln and Secretary of War Edwin Stanton made it clear there were no other better options, did Burnside reluctantly accept his new role.

The first major encounter for the Union under command of Ambrose Burnside was the Battle of Fredericksburg. It ended as one of the of the most lopsided and tragic defeats that the Union Army would suffer. In December 1862, Burnside led over 100,000 Union soldiers across the Rappahannock River toward the Confederate stronghold of Fredericksburg, Virginia. The crossing itself was delayed by logistical blunders as the pontoon bridges arrived late, allowing Lee ample time to entrench his forces on the high ground behind the town. Burnside, under pressure from Washington to strike quickly, pressed on with the attack despite the terrible disadvantage.

What followed was a frontal assault of horrific proportions. Union soldiers charged up Marye's Heights, a ridge fortified with artillery and defended by Confederate infantry behind a stone wall. Wave after wave of blue-coated troops were mowed down in what one Confederate soldier described as *"butchery, pure and simple."* By the end of the day, over 12,000 Union soldiers had fallen, compared to fewer than 5,000 Confederates.

Burnside was shattered by the slaughter, reportedly considered leading a final charge himself at the head of his old IX Corps. His subordinates dissuaded him. Following the defeat, Burnside became withdrawn and dispirited. He had taken personal responsibility for the attack, and his confidence which was already fragile when he accepted command, collapsed entirely. Officers around him noted that he seemed uncertain, reactive, and emotionally overwhelmed.

The defeat at Fredericksburg devastated morale in the North and led to a public outcry against the war's conduct. Burnside accepted responsibility for the disaster. He did not blame his men or his generals, though some had privately questioned his plans. In January 1863, after a massive failure of a second offensive known as the "Mud March," Burnside offered his resignation which Lincoln, with regret, accepted.

In many ways, Burnside personified the tragedy of the Union command in the war's early years: a man of integrity and patriotism, elevated beyond his capacity by circumstances and political necessity. He did not seek greatness, and when it eluded him, he bore it with humility.

Ambrose Burnside was appointed to his command on November 9, 1862, and relieved of his command January 25, 1863.

Joseph Hooker, Unable to Decide

In the wake of the bloody catastrophe at Fredericksburg the Union Army was in disarray and its leadership shaken. Morale among the troops had plummeted, and the Lincoln administration once again faced the painful task of choosing a new commander for the Army of the Potomac. The man who stepped forward, confidently and boastfully was General Joseph Hooker, a general known equally for his battlefield aggression and political ambition. A native of Massachusetts, Hooker had graduated from West Point in 1837 and fought in the Mexican-American War, earning distinction and a reputation for boldness. By 1863, he had become a divisional commander and then a corps commander, admired by his men for his swagger and criticized by his peers for the same.

Nicknamed "Fighting Joe", a moniker created accidentally by a misprint in a newspaper. Hooker had been among the more vocal critics of Ambrose Burnside and the Fredericksburg campaign. His appointment was not without controversy. Lincoln, who was wary of the general's vast ego, accompanied the promotion with a now-famous letter warning him to remember that *"the Government is not in the field, but in the Cabinet."*

Hooker, to his credit, began his tenure of command with energy and reform. He improved camp sanitation and reorganized supply lines. He established a centralized cavalry corps and instituted furloughs to boost troop morale. Soldiers adored him, at least at first, and he restored a sense of confidence to a demoralized army. Hooker's greatest test came in the spring of 1863, in Chancellorsville, Virginia.

Armed with over 130,000 troops, Hooker devised a bold plan to flank and trap Robert E. Lee's army, which numbered barely half that size. His early movements were promising. He sent a large portion of his army west of Fredericksburg to come down on Lee's flank, while another force held the Confederates in place at the Rappahannock River. By late April, Hooker was poised to crush Lee between two wings of a superior force. Then, at the moment of advantage, he hesitated as had too many commanders before him. Whether due to Lee's aggressive countermoves or his own faltering confidence, Hooker suddenly pulled back his forces and assumed a defensive posture at Chancellorsville, ceding the initiative to Lee. In one of the most audacious maneuvers of the war, Lee divided his already outnumbered army in the face of the enemy and sent Stonewall Jackson on a daring flanking march. On the evening of May 2, Jackson's corps smashed into the exposed Union right flank, throwing Hooker's army into chaos.

The next day, Hooker was physically stunned when a Confederate shell struck a pillar he was leaning against, knocking him unconscious for half an hour. Though he resumed command, he was disoriented and hesitant, and not competent to command. The battle slipped from his grasp, and within days, the Union army was in full retreat across the Rappahannock. The defeat was staggering. Though Hooker's army had lost fewer men than Lee's, the psychological blow to his army was enormous. Hooker, who had entered the campaign with supreme confidence, left it a broken man. *"I just lost confidence in Joe Hooker,"* he would later admit, referring to himself in the third person.

Lincoln kept Hooker in command through the early summer, but with Lee again on the move into Pennsylvania, the president feared another disaster and replaced him on June 28, 1863, just days before the Battle of Gettysburg. His replacement was the quiet and unassuming George Meade.

Joseph Hooker remains one of the Civil War's most contradictory figures: a general of great charisma and initial promise, undermined by self-doubt at the critical moment. His name is forever linked to Chancellorsville, a battle where opportunity slipped through his fingers, and Lee's genius exposed yet another failing in the Union's long search for capable leadership.

Joseph Hooker was appointed to his command on January 26, 1863, and relieved of his command on June 28. With five months under his command, he was somewhat successful compared to his predecessors.

George Meade, Capable in Victory

At around 3 a.m. on June 28, a courier arrived at General Meade's headquarters near Frederick, Maryland, with a sealed packet from General-in-Chief Henry Halleck. Meade, then commanding the Union V Corps, opened the envelope to discover that he was now in command of the entire Army of the Potomac. The letter was brief, giving him little choice in the matter but to accept the position. According to Meade himself, in a letter he wrote to his wife the same *day: "I am in command of the Army of the Potomac... As a soldier, I had no option but to accept and exert my utmost abilities to command success."* Meade was shocked and reluctant. He felt unprepared for such a vast responsibility, especially in the midst of an active campaign against Robert E. Lee's advancing army. In that same letter to his wife, he expressed anxiety about being made a scapegoat if things went poorly: *"I had no knowledge till the arrival of the order that I was even thought of... I am moving at once against Lee..."* Still, Meade quickly took control.

Just three days later, his army would face down the great Robert E. Lee in the largest battle ever fought on American soil. It was a battle to define his legacy.

Meade's appointment came not from political ambition or behind-the-scenes lobbying, but from sheer necessity. His predecessor, Joseph Hooker, had lost Lincoln's confidence and resigned under pressure. Meade, though not well-known to the public, had earned a reputation as a disciplined and competent corps commander. He was respected by his men as a no-nonsense professional with a temper as sharp as his judgment.

Born in Spain in 1815 to American parents, Meade graduated from West Point in 1835. He was a career officer with engineering expertise and a strong record in both the Mexican-American War and the Civil War's early battles. Yet unlike many of his peers, Meade was not flashy. He disliked politics, distrusted the press, and had little appetite for self-promotion, qualities that earned him little favor in Washington.

But Meade had something more valuable: steadiness. When he took command on the eve of the battle of Gettysburg, the Army of the Potomac was in motion, shadowing Lee's forces as they moved north into Pennsylvania. Meade had no time to reorganize, no chance to lay out a long-term plan. He was forced to make decisions on the move and in the face of the most aggressive and skilled opponent the Union had encountered.

The battle that followed, from July 1–3, 1863, was a clash of epic scale and consequence. Meade had the advantage of terrain, positioning his army on the high ground south of the town of Gettysburg. His generals, including John Reynolds, Winfield Scott Hancock, and George Sykes, held key positions on Cemetery Hill, Culp's Hill, and Little Round Top. Meade directed operations calmly but assertively from his headquarters at the Leister House, gathering intelligence, shifting reinforcements, and keeping his lines coherent under enormous pressure.

On the third day, Lee launched Pickett's Charge, a massive frontal assault aimed at breaking the Union center. Meade had anticipated such a move and had reinforced his position. The charge was repulsed with staggering Confederate losses. By the evening of July 3, Lee's army was defeated. On July 4, the same day Vicksburg fell in the West, Lee began his retreat to Virginia.

Meade had won the greatest Union victory of the war, albeit with staggering losses. There was not much celebration among superiors. Lincoln was bitterly disappointed that Meade had not pursued Lee more aggressively during his retreat. Many in Washington believed he had missed an opportunity to destroy the Army of Northern Virginia once and for all. The press offered lukewarm praise, focusing more on the battle than the man who had won it.

Meade remained in command of the Army of the Potomac for the rest of the war but was placed under the overall authority of Ulysses S. Grant in 1864. Their relationship was professional, though occasionally strained. Meade continued to fight capably during the Overland Campaign, the Siege of Petersburg, and the final push to Appomattox, but the spotlight had shifted. Grant became the face of victory.

Meade died in 1872, relatively uncelebrated, and largely forgotten by the public. Yet George Meade deserves remembrance. At a time of crisis, when the Union desperately needed a calm, competent hand, he delivered under very difficult circumstance. He won Gettysburg not through bravado, but through judgment, preparation, and trust in his officers. He was a soldier's general; irritable, exacting, but loyal and fair. In a war too often defined by bold but flawed leadership, Meade's steady command stood apart.

George Meade was appointed to command the Army of the Potomac on June 28, 1863. He was not relieved of his command until the war had ended with the Lee surrender at Appomattox.

Ulysses S. Grant, Relentless Commander

In the early years of the Civil War, Ulysses S. Grant was an unlikely candidate, maybe one of the least likely officers of the Union, to end up in command of the Union's armies. He had resigned from the Army in 1854 over a choice to be court martialed or resign. He had failed in several civilian ventures and was working as a clerk in his father's leather goods store in Galena, Illinois, when war broke out. But like Lincoln himself, Grant would emerge from obscurity not by brilliance or pedigree, but by force of character, clarity of purpose, as well as sheer tenacity.

Grant's return to military service began modestly as a political appointee to be colonel of a group of untrained Illinois volunteers. However, train them he did, and battle successes came quickly. In February 1862, he captured Fort Henry and Fort Donelson in Tennessee, earning the nickname *"Unconditional Surrender"* Grant and delivering the first major Union victories of the western war. His boldness at Shiloh, while criticized for the battle's heavy losses, proved he would not shy away from brutal, sustained fighting.

Eventually, it was his brilliant Vicksburg Campaign in 1863 that secured his reputation as a master strategist. Rather than strike the city directly, Grant marched his army down the western bank of the Mississippi River, crossed the river below Vicksburg, and came up from behind, winning a series of battles, severing supply lines, and ultimately besieging the Confederate stronghold. On July 4, 1863, Vicksburg was surrendered, giving the Union control of the

Mississippi River and effectively splitting the Confederacy in two. That same day, far to the east, Lee was retreating from Gettysburg. The war had turned with those twin victories.

President Lincoln now saw the type of leadership and war acumen that had eluded him in so many others: a general who understood the nature of the war. Grant and Lincoln both knew that the war would only be won through destruction of the Confederate armies but the will that sustained them. Grant was not universally respected in Washington, but he was by the only man who counted. Lincoln said of Grant, *"I can't spare this man, He fights."*

In March 1864, Lincoln named Grant General-in-Chief of all Union armies at an elaborate ceremony on the grounds of the White House. Lincoln said, *"General Grant, the nation's appreciation of what you have done, and its reliance upon you for what remains to be done in the existing great struggle, are now presented with this commission, constituting you Lieutenant General in the Army of the United States."* Grant responded modestly, saying: *"Mr. President, I accept the commission with gratitude for the high honor conferred. With the aid of the noble armies that have fought on so many fields for our common country, it will be my earnest endeavor not to disappoint your expectations."*

Unlike his predecessors, Grant made no excuses and asked for no special conditions. He left Meade nominally in command of the Army of the Potomac but traveled with Meade's army, setting the tone for the final year of the war. His strategy was to apply constant, simultaneous pressure on Confederate forces: himself against Lee in Virginia, Sherman marching through Georgia, and others driving into the Deep South.

What followed was a campaign of unparalleled intensity, as well as relentlessness. In the Overland Campaign, Grant bled Lee's army in a series of brutal battles, the Wilderness, Spotsylvania, and Cold Harbor. His losses were many, but Grant kept moving forward. He laid siege to Petersburg, knowing that once it fell, Richmond would soon follow. *"I propose to fight it out on this line if it takes all summer,"* he declared, and he did just what he said he would do.

Through it all, Grant's relationship with Lincoln was one of mutual trust and respect. Grant avoided the political intrigues that had consumed so many of his predecessors. He did not write manifestos to newspapers or jockey for personal fame. He delivered results. Finally, in April 1865, with Petersburg evacuated and Richmond fallen, Grant pursued Lee's dwindling army to the McLean House in the village Appomattox Court House, where he offered generous terms of surrender: no humiliation, no vengeance, just peace.

Ulysses S. Grant was not a fabulous orator or a brilliant tactician in the classical sense. He was quiet, modest, and methodical. He understood that war was a contest of endurance as well as arms and that victory would require resolve as much as genius. His critics called him a butcher, but his soldiers called him a leader. Lincoln, after almost four years of searching, finally found a general who wouldn't accept loss.

The story of Union generalship is, in many ways, a mirror of the war itself, chaotic, painful, and marked by extraordinarily costly trial and error. From the first cannonades at Bull Run to the surrender at Appomattox, the path to victory was anything but straight and most often very uncertain. The Union did not begin the war with brilliant or even competent military leadership; it stumbled into it with caution, politics, as well as misplaced arrogance. Its earliest generals were often chosen for their political connections or reputations, not their capacity to wage war. From the hindsight of history, there were many occurrences where the war could have been put to an end much more quickly than it was, and with significantly fewer casualties.

Irvin McDowell never sought high command and proved unequal to the position to which he was commissioned. George McClellan dazzled in preparation but was paralyzed in execution, giving the South opportunities to survive and grow in confidence. John Pope charged in with swagger and left in disgrace due to poor decision making. Ambrose Burnside only reluctantly entered service to lead the Union Army, and he proved to be a very bad choice for the position. Joseph Hooker served the army well until it was time for battle and then he cracked under pressure. Even George Meade, who won Gettysburg, did so with grim competence rather than triumphal flair. He failed to pursue a broken enemy and was quickly overshadowed.

Within this parade of flawed leadership, a kind of hard wisdom emerged. Each failure taught something painful but essential. The war could not be won by half-measures, nor by men more concerned with reputation than results. It would take a new and different kind of general, one who could endure criticism, sustain massive losses, and press forward regardless of cost. That general was Ulysses S. Grant.

With Grant came a shift, not only in tactics but in vision. He understood that the Confederacy would not break until its armies were destroyed, its infrastructure shattered, and its political will exhausted. Crucially, Grant was not alone. In men that supported him, like William Tecumseh Sherman, who later cut a swath through Georgia and effectively ended the war with the surrender of Atlanta, and Philip Sheridan, who ravaged the Shenandoah Valley, Grant had found a new group of commanders who shared his unflinching resolve for victory, no matter the immediate cost.

For Lincoln, the journey leading to Grant was long and often lonely and way too often filled with failure. He watched one general after another promise victory and deliver retreat. He endured doubt from most around him as well as public outcry, political meddling, and crushing battlefield losses. Through it all, he never gave up, not on the Union, and not on the belief that the right men could be found that would finally put an end to the unfathomable bloodshed. It was not brilliance that won the war for the Union, but a dogged persistence and entrenched belief from Lincoln in the necessity to save the Union as a whole. It was not one single genius, but a team forged by adversity with a singular mindset. The Union had begun the war searching for a Napoleon. It ended it with men who, while far from perfect, understood how to win, and why the cost was worth the result.

CHAPTER 6
GRANT AND LEE

The American Civil War produced no two military leaders more deeply etched into the national memory than Ulysses S. Grant and Robert E. Lee. Their personalities, origins, and methods differed profoundly, so much so that they came to symbolize not only the two armies they led but the cultures of the regions they represented. Yet as the war reached its decisive years, these two men, initially distant in command and temperament, began to converge in purpose and clarity. Their eventual collision would decide not just the fate of the war, but the course of American history.

Where they Came From

Robert E. Lee was born into the Virginia aristocracy in 1807. The Lee family was of the elite plantar aristocracy with extensive holdings of land and enslaved persons. He was the son of a Revolutionary War hero Henry Lee III ("Light-Horse Harry"). Harry was a cunning officer who had a skill for conducting guerrilla-style raids and scouting missions and deceiving the enemy. After the war Harry married the heiress of another large plantation using enslaved labor. He soon represented Virginia in the Confederation Congress and following that became a member of the House of Representatives in the U.S. congress. Following his stint in Congress he was elected governor of Virginia. Harry inherited a lot of wealth and lost it all through ill-informed speculation. He was sent to debtors' prison in 1809, losing the inheritance from his wife's family. This was Robert's lineage.

Robert E. Lee was shaped by an upbringing steeped in honor, family tradition, and the values of the Old South. He graduated second in his class from the 1929 class of West Point without a single demerit, excelling in engineering. As an officer, he proved meticulous and disciplined, rising through the ranks with a quiet dignity. To many in the South, Lee embodied the virtues of the Southern gentleman modest, devout, commanding, and loyal. He was revered by the men he led, who saw in him both a moral and martial leader.

Ulysses S. Grant, by contrast, was born Hiram Ulysses Grant in 1822 in Point Pleasant, Ohio. His father was a tanner, and Grant's early life was practical and unadorned, but reportedly more comfortable than most in his town. From an early age Grant had obtained a reputation for skill in training and riding horses. He had no interest in pursuing his father's business or in pursuing a military life. But his father, Jesse, admired military prestige and saw that career as a way to secure a respectable future for his son. Grant was sent to West Point at the age of 17. His father had sent several letters to his congressman asking that his son receive a commission.

Grant graduated from West Point in the class of 1843, though with less distinction than Lee, ranking 21st in a class of 39. He did not rank in the top of his class in any academics but did in horsemanship. His military service in the Mexican-American War was more than competent but largely unnoticed. After resigning his commission from the army in 1854 under threat of court martial due to drunkenness, Grant struggled with poverty, business failures, and alcoholism. He was nearly forgotten by the time the Civil War broke out, working in his father's leather shop. But once given the opportunity, Grant demonstrated an unexpected capacity for command. He was calm under pressure, decisive in movement, and relentless in attack.

Lee's style of leadership was steeped in the chivalric code. He favored maneuver, boldness, and personal responsibility. He approved wide latitude to his lieutenants, sometimes to a fault. His campaigns in the east, particularly at Second Bull Run, Fredericksburg, and Chancellorsville, revealed a commander willing to take great risks to achieve decisive victory. But that same aggressiveness would cost him dearly at Gettysburg.

Grant, on the other hand, was methodical, patient, and increasingly focused on the use of overwhelming force. He emphasized logistics, coordination, and persistent pressure. At Vicksburg in 1863, he demonstrated a masterful campaign of maneuver and siege, cutting the Confederate stronghold off from supply and finally forcing its surrender. His ability to wage total war and press the advantage, regardless of criticism or casualties, became central to the Union strategy.

War Philosophy

Lee and Grant approached war through fundamentally different lenses, shaped by their upbringings, training, and worldviews. Their distinct philosophies not only guided their battlefield decisions but came to symbolize the broader differences between the Confederacy and the Union.

Robert E. Lee believed in the power of swift, decisive engagements. Steeped in the traditions of the Napoleonic art of war, he sought dramatic victories that would cripple the Union's will to fight. Lee aimed to win through bold maneuvering and brilliant battlefield execution, believing that a single overwhelming victory could secure Southern independence. His preference was for offense, even when defending; he often struck first, having significantly few numbers, to keep the enemy off balance.

Lee once said, *"It is well that war is so terrible, otherwise we should grow too fond of it."* The remark, made during the carnage at Fredericksburg, reveals his complicated relationship with war. He had a profound respect for its horror and an undeniable attraction to the art of command and combat. Even in defense of Richmond, Lee preferred to attack rather than retreat, risking high casualties in hopes of a decisive blow. This philosophy carried inherent risks. His strategy often assumed that Confederate soldiers' superior fighting spirit could overcome the North's numerical and industrial advantages. This belief sometimes led to high, unsustainable losses, as seen in the disastrous frontal assaults at Gettysburg.

In contrast, Ulysses S. Grant approached war with a colder, more calculated mindset. Grant was less concerned with winning spectacular victories and more concerned with destroying the enemy's ability to continue to fight. He grasped early what many Northern leaders did not and that was victory would come not simply by capturing territory but by annihilating Confederate armies and breaking the South's capacity to fight. Grant's war philosophy was summed up in his famous observation: *"The art of war is simple enough. Find out where your enemy is. Get at him as soon as you can. Strike him as hard as you can and keep moving on."*

Grant understood that the North's superior manpower, industry, and logistics were weapons just as potent as any rifle or cannon. He waged a relentless campaign of pressure forcing Lee's army to retreat again and again. Unlike many generals who had preceded him, Grant refused to be deterred by high casualties if the strategic objective demanded sacrifice. He saw war as a grim necessity, not a forum for displays of martial elegance. Another Grant quote captures his pragmatic view: *"I propose to fight it out on this line if it takes all summer."* He wrote this during the brutal Overland Campaign of 1864, signaling his determination to grind down Lee's forces no matter the cost.

While Lee prized honor, maneuver, and rapid decision, Grant embraced endurance, coordination, and overwhelming force. Grant's methods would come to define modern warfare with large-scale, sustained operations designed not merely to win battles, but to exhaust the enemy's entire system of resistance. In the end, both generals fought to exhaustion. But it was Grant's philosophy, that total commitment, total war, and the destruction of the enemy's armies were necessary that would prevail and bring the bloody conflict to its close.

Ulysses S. Grant was nicknamed *"The Butcher"* by some of his contemporaries and later critics because of the enormous number of casualties suffered by Union forces under his command. This label, however, reflects a deep misunderstanding of Grant's strategy, the context of the war at that point, and how it compared to Lee's own approach to battlefield command. The nickname *"The Butcher"* tells us more about the political pressures of the time and the war-weariness of the Union public than it does about Grant's generalship.

Ironically, Lee often viewed with reverence for his tactical brilliance and concern for his men, was responsible for similarly high casualty rates, especially in his offensive campaigns. At Antietam, Lee lost nearly a third of his army in one day. At Fredericksburg, he permitted the enemy to break itself against his defenses.

At Chancellorsville, Lee's bold maneuver worked, but he again took significant risks with his outnumbered army. And at Gettysburg, Lee ordered Pickett's Charge, a frontal assault against a fortified center, resulting in over 6,000 Confederate casualties in less than an hour. The entire Gettysburg Campaign cost Lee more than 28,000 casualties, again nearly a third of his army. These were losses from which the South would find it very difficult to recover. His aristocratic demeanor, courtly behavior, and battlefield presence fed into the myth of the noble warrior, in contrast to Grant's muddy boots and blunt manner.

While Lee remains remembered for his tactical brilliance and daring and Grant for his grim tenacity, both men commanded through the same crucible, facing choices where thousands of lives hung in the balance. The difference was that Grant's strategy, though costly, brought the war to a close. In the end, the question was not whether lives would be lost, but whether they would be lost in the service of victory, or in pursuit of a cause that could no longer be sustained.

The contrast between the two men extended beyond tactics. Lee was formal, polished, and reserved in manner. He rode a stately horse and was the picture of battlefield decorum. Grant was modest in dress, often dusty, riding a simple horse and wearing a private's uniform with his general's stars pinned to the shoulders. He disliked ceremony and rarely gave long speeches. Both men shared a trait critical to leadership, they inspired loyalty from the troops they led. Their troops followed them not because they demanded it, but because they had earned it.

In 1864, as General-in-Chief of all Union armies, Grant began to coordinate multiple battle fronts, including his direct confrontation with Lee in Virginia. The Overland Campaign, waged through the Wilderness, Spotsylvania, and Cold Harbor, demonstrated a convergence of strategy. Lee, now on the defensive, fought tenaciously to repel Grant's advances. Grant, for his part, refused to retreat. The war had entered a new phase: one of attrition and pressure rather than sweeping battles.

This strategic convergence was profound. Both men learned that the war could not be won through one extraordinary engagement. Lee sought to hold ground long enough to exhaust the North's will. Grant sought to apply constant pressure until the South's resources collapsed. They mirrored each other not in style, but in understanding that the war's end would not come through maneuver alone, it would come through endurance.

What separated Grant and Lee in life, background, demeanor, and culture was bridged in war by mutual respect and a shared capacity for excellent leadership under unbearable strain. Their convergence was not in creed, but in commitment: to their cause, to their men, and, in the end, to the peace that would follow.

Leadership Style

The leadership styles of Robert E. Lee and Ulysses S. Grant mirrored their philosophies of war and reflected the worlds from which they came. Each commanded not only armies but the loyalty, imagination, and endurance of tens of thousands of men. Robert E. Lee embodied the ideal of the aristocratic commander. He inspired by character rather than by command volume. Lee projected an almost serene authority; his soldiers revered him, often calling him *"Marse Robert"* in affectionate loyalty. His leadership relied heavily on personal dignity, mutual respect, and moral authority rather than detailed micromanagement.

Much of Lee's approach to leadership was built around delegation. He entrusted large operational decisions to his corps and division commanders, believing that giving them autonomy would encourage initiative on the battlefield. In some cases, this faith yielded remarkable results, such as the daring maneuvers at Chancellorsville. But at other times, especially later in the war as his officer corps weakened, Lee's deference contributed to breakdowns in coordination, most tragically visible during Pickett's Charge at Gettysburg. One of Lee's most quoted remarks about command reveals his reliance on personal honor and mutual trust: *"Duty is the sublimest word in our language."* He expected his officers and men to internalize a deep sense of obligation, to God, to country, and to one another, and to act without constant direction.

Ulysses S. Grant, by contrast, led with a quieter, more businesslike approach. Grant preferred to give clear, simple orders and then expected them to be carried out in earnest and without flourish. He built strong working relationships with subordinates like Generals Sherman and Sheridan, valuing competence and results over personal grandeur. Grant was noted for his calm under pressure, even in the face of near disaster. One officer remarked, *"In battle, Grant was always himself. No matter what happened, he could not be flurried."* This steadiness gave his armies confidence that their general would neither panic nor act rashly.

Unlike Lee, Grant was more inclined to maintain tight strategic control over campaigns, coordinating multiple armies across vast distances to apply simultaneous pressure on the Confederacy. His leadership in the Vicksburg and Overland Campaigns showed a masterful ability to orchestrate complex movements without losing the thread of overall purpose. Grant's humility also shaped his leadership style. Reflecting on his own rise, he once remarked, *"There are but few important events in the affairs of men brought about by their own choice."* He understood that circumstances, persistence, and quiet resolve often mattered more than bold declarations or aristocratic bearing.

In the end, Lee led from the heart and tradition, inspiring with ideals; Grant led from the mind and persistence, inspiring with determination. Both men forged powerful bonds with their armies, but in very different ways. Lee was the noble father figure, Grant, the steady and unyielding craftsman of victory.

Thoughts on Slavery

Though Robert E. Lee and Ulysses S. Grant shared many of the manners and experiences of antebellum officers, their views on slavery diverged sharply, a division that would grow even starker as the Civil War wore on.

Lee is often remembered in postwar mythology as a reluctant slaveholder, a man burdened by an institution he privately detested. The truth is more complex. While Lee did once call slavery a *"moral and political evil,"* he also believed that it was sanctioned by divine will and that human beings had no right to hurry its end. In a letter to his wife in 1856, Lee wrote: *"The blacks are immeasurably better off here than in Africa, morally, socially, and physically. The painful discipline they are undergoing is necessary for their instruction as a race."*

As executor of his father-in-law's estate, Lee actively enforced the system of slavery at the Arlington plantation, even going so far as to sanction harsh punishments for enslaved people who resisted. His actions during this period, especially the punishment of Wesley Norris and others who sought freedom, suggest that Lee was not merely a passive participant in the institution but a determined enforcer of its rules when he believed it necessary.

Lee's decision to side with Virginia and the Confederacy was deeply tied to his concept of duty, but it also aligned him with a society built upon slavery. While he did not frame his personal cause as a defense of slavery, his actions and his chosen allegiance helped prolong the system's life.

Ulysses S. Grant's relationship with slavery evolved over time but moved steadily toward strict opposition. As a young man living in Missouri with his wife's family, Grant briefly owned a single enslaved man named William Jones, who was a gift from his father-in-law. In a striking act of conscience, Grant freed Jones in 1859, even though he was struggling financially and could have sold him for a significant sum.

Grant's early views on slavery were shaped more by pragmatism than by ideology. But the war radicalized him. As he witnessed firsthand the loyalty, labor, and courage of African American soldiers, and as he recognized the Confederacy's reliance on enslaved labor, Grant came to see the destruction of slavery as inseparable from Union victory. Writing to Congressman Elihu Washburne in 1863, Grant declared: *"The negro is now a soldier. If he can fight, he can vote."*

By the end of the war, Grant had become not just an opponent of slavery but an advocate for advancing Black rights during Reconstruction. As president, he would push for the Fifteenth Amendment and use federal power to suppress the Ku Klux Klan. The 15ᵗʰ amendment states: *"The right of citizens of the United States to vote shall not be denied or abridged by the United States or by any State on account of race, color, or previous condition of servitude."*

The contrast between Lee and Grant on slavery was not merely academic. It represented two fundamentally different visions for the future of America. Lee's world sought to preserve a hierarchical society rooted in tradition and race. Grant's actions helped lay the groundwork for a Union that, at least in aspiration, was dedicated to equality and civil rights.

Appomattox

By the spring of 1865, Robert E. Lee's Army of Northern Virginia was broken, starving, and it was surrounded. The long siege of Petersburg had shattered Confederate defenses. Richmond, the Confederate capital, fell on April 3, 1865. Lee attempted a westward retreat, hoping to link up with other Southern forces in North Carolina, but relentless Union pursuit, led by Grant, left him no path forward. The Confederate troops were exhausted, many barefoot and despondent, with scarcely any supplies. Desertions swelled by the hour. In the final hours before the surrender Lee said to his staff officers: *"There is nothing left for me to do but to go and see General Grant, and I would rather die a thousand deaths."*

After the fighting on April 8, Lee sent word asking for a meeting with the Union Commander. That day General George Custer had intercepted and captured Confederate supply trains, which Lee's army desperately needed for survival.

The McLean house in the village of Appomattox Court House was chosen as the meeting place because of its convenient location. The parlor of the McLean House was small and sparsely furnished, with a low-burning fire casting soft shadows on the walls of the room. Robert E. Lee sat erect in a simple wooden chair, immaculate in his finest gray uniform, sword at his side, boots polished, his face a portrait of calm resignation.

Grant was finishing up some paperwork and when done, quickly road to the meeting along muddied roads. Grant and Lee had never met face-to-face until Grant entered the McClean home in Appomattox, Virginia on April 9, 1865. Grant entered dressed in a wrinkled private's blouse, and muddy from his ride. As always, their contrast in personal style was marked. As he entered the door, at a little after 1:00 p.m., Grant removed his hat and sat across from Lee with a small table between them. They stared at each other for a few moments.

Then as Grant later recalled "*When I went into the house, I found General Lee. We greeted each other, and after a little conversation about old army times, I stated the object of our meeting.*"

Despite their differences, the meeting was marked by thoughtful courtesy. Grant later recalled feeling sympathy for Lee, writing in his memoirs: "*I felt like anything rather than rejoicing at the downfall of a foe who had fought so long and valiantly.*"

Grant did not come to the meeting with written terms of surrender. When asked by Lee what were his terms, Grant himself wrote them down in long hand. The terms Grant offered were generous and well thought out. Confederate officers and men would be paroled and allowed to return to their homes without fear of arrest, provided they laid down their arms and pledged not to take up arms against the United States again. Officers could keep their sidearms, horses, and personal baggage, an act of mercy intended to ease their return to civilian life. No prisoners would be taken, no one would be prosecuted. Grant called in an aide to write a formal copy. Lee made sure that his enlisted men could keep their horses to help work their farms back home.

Lee, relieved by the leniency, accepted the terms without protest.

When Lee left the McLean house and faced his men, he simply said, "*Go to your homes and resume your occupations. Obey the laws and become as good citizens as you were soldiers.*" He also reportedly also said: "*General Grant has behaved with magnanimity at our interview and on every occasion since.*"

As Lee had mounted his horse only about an hour and a half after arriving at the house, and was riding back to address his men, some reported that he was sobbing "*unmanly*" tears.

One poignant moment came after the signing, as Lee rode away from the McLean House, Union soldiers began to cheer in celebration. Grant, sensitive to the gravity of the moment, quickly ordered them to stop. Victory was not to be marked triumphally over defeated countrymen. Grant understood that if the nation was to heal, it must begin with dignity and restraint. Thus, the Civil War effectively ended not with vengeance, but with solemn respect between two soldiers, one offering mercy in victory, the other accepting defeat with grace.

The surrender at Appomattox symbolized far more than military capitulation. It marked the collapse of the Confederacy, the preservation of the Union, and the beginning of the long, painful struggle to build a new nation, one no longer chained to slavery. In the quiet room at Appomattox, Lee and Grant, for all their differences, shared a final, unspoken understanding: that the time for fighting had ended, and the time for rebuilding, in all its complexity. had begun.

Conclusion

In the end, the contest between Robert E. Lee and Ulysses S. Grant was not just how they commanded battles on muddy fields and in blood-soaked trenches. They commanded armies that were battling for the moral soul of the nation. Lee fought to preserve a world where human beings could still be bought, sold, and whipped into submission, even as he cloaked that cause in the language of honor and duty. Grant fought with a brutal clarity, understanding that victory would demand not just broken armies but the breaking of an entire way of life. When the guns finally fell silent, it was Grant's grim vision, of a Union preserved, and of slavery destroyed, that carried the day. In their clashes, America bled, but it also began, however slowly and painfully, to redeem itself.

PART 3: BEYOND THE BATTLEFIELDS OF THE CIVIL WAR

CHAPTER 7
DAILY LIFE IN A WAR-TORN NATION

While elected officials and military brass were making life and death decisions on a daily basis in the military and in government, there was very little normalcy to the life of the common person. The war interrupted and reshaped the daily lives of millions of citizens, almost every person in the Union and in the Confederacy. Life in the North and the South diverged dramatically, but both were marked by anxiety, scarcity, and dramatic social shifts.

In 1863 there were about 31.4 million people living in the total country, 18.5 million living in the north while the Confederacy had 5.5 million free people and 3.5 million enslaved people. There were another 2.5 million free people in the border states with 500,000 enslaved people. By the end of 1863, it is estimated that a minimum of 625,000 people had died or been wounded in the war. Numerous persons had gone missing and are not counted in those numbers. That number of killed and wounded represented roughly 2 percent of the entire population of the country. The war touched every corner of geography, and every living soul in the Union and in the Confederacy.

Long before the end of 1863, Americans in both the Union and the Confederacy had learned that the war was not just being fought with rifles by regiments. It was being fought and absorbed with excessive grief in kitchens that had only empty shelves, in chapels filled with prayer, hope and doubt, and on printing presses inked with outrage, sarcasm, and sometimes faith. It was fought in the weary arms of women sewing bandages, in the brave feet of enslaved people escaping toward freeing cannon fire, and in the soft voices of children singing songs about a home that was no longer the same and never would be. Grief was everywhere, open and hidden and it could not be escaped. The toll on the psyche of all was intense and unforgiving.

The lines between the war front and the home front were blurred. Victory at Chancellorsville did not fill bellies in Richmond or comfort the mothers and fathers of the fallen in Fredericksburg. The Emancipation Proclamation did not stop mobs in New York from burning Black orphanages but rather incited them. And in cities far from any battlefield, a mother reading her dead son's letters became nearly as much a casualty of the war as the soldier who had written them.

In this war, everyone had been impacted in a uniquely negative manner, humor became defiance, music at times became a comfort and at times incited more pain. Faith became the thread that held fragile communities together. Some believed the war would purify the nation. Others feared it would destroy it. Most simply hoped to survive it.

The North's Wartime Mobilization

In 1863 northern cities bustled with economic activity. Much of it due to the needs of the war. Industry boomed amongst several sectors: iron and steel, textiles, and manufacturing. Agricultural needs skyrocketed and their exports to European countries increased, as mechanized tools for their production became commonplace. Ship building was multiplied many times at the demand of the Navy. Railroads were almost choked with the movement of war supplies.

However, the prosperity realized from the grand production of war necessities was very uneven. The poor, especially immigrants in the major cities like New York, felt crushed by rising prices and forced conscription and the limited compensation for their efforts. The rich became richer by supplying the Union forces in the war effort as well as those that commanded the war effort, and there was very little trickle down. The New York Draft Riots in July 1863 exposed some of the tension between rich and poor, black and white, immigrant and slave as well as exposing a great amount of bigotry in the North.

Women were not permitted to carry arms into the battlefront; they were not allowed to participate in the killing. But they were forced by circumstance to step out of their tradition home making roles. They stepped into factories as workers as well as managers, and they occupied post offices, and hospitals. They took over the management of farms and managed other businesses left by their husband solders fighting and dying in the war between the states.

"Government Girls" took over clerical roles in Washington, once solely the domain of men, working for the Federal government in numerous important office positions. War widows opened boarding houses, mostly as a means of survival. Some of the North's most valuable spies were women, many acting with uncommon valor. Many women took to organizing volunteers and to raising money however possible to supply troops with badly needed food, clothing and medical supplies.

The war greatly intruded on everyday life, in every aspect even though the war was mostly being fought far from where they lived. Letters from soldiers were read aloud at the dinner table, often with tears flowing from all those listening. Newspapers printed casualty lists daily, with families anxiously and painfully reviewing the lists looking for the names of their loved ones. Families stared at portraits of sons who might never return. Some citizens sought comfort in church, others in theater, music halls or prize-fighting. Children played "Blue and Gray" with toy rifles, unaware they were mimicking their fathers and brothers. One Boston housewife wrote in her diary: *"We scrub the floor in the morning and bury the dead in the evening. This war creeps into everything."*

The South Under Siege

The Confederate home front was different than that of the North. The war was sometimes being fought in their own back yards. Often, especially in Virginia, citizens heard gunshots and cannon fire much of the time. As the war dragged on, food supplies increasingly dwindled, staples such as coffee became luxuries. Much of the reason the South was so strained was because of a port blockade by the Union Navy, exhaustive inflation, a worthless currency, and extraordinary fear. Cities like Richmond and Atlanta swelled with refugees from the rural poor. Prices soared, paper was a rarity, salt nearly priceless. Southern women, especially from planter families, found themselves managing farms and plantations, bartering for necessities, and fending off deserters. In some towns, "bread riots" erupted as women stormed markets and government stores, demanding food.

Before the war the chief export, and the chief agricultural product was cotton. Because of the Union naval blockade of Southern ports, the need for cotton abroad from southern growers had nearly vanished. Many farmers switched from growing cotton to producing food crops. Before the war most industrial activity was located in the north. The South had very little industry and by 1863 what little industry they had was focused on providing those items necessary to sustain the war effort. Texas remained mostly isolated from the war and was able to produce beef, hides, and salt as well as other goods that could be shipped east along overland routes.

The women in Virginia witnessed more battles than those in any other state, not to diminish fears elsewhere, just in Virginia it was more intense. As husbands and fathers departed for the battlefield and politicians and journalists urged civilians to do their patriotic duty, white women were confronted with the strange new expectation of demonstrating authority and civic involvement. The days of the antebellum had definitely expired.

The demands of war encouraged white women to develop a political outlook and prove their patriotism, in contrast to the antebellum period when they were considered too delicate and pure to become entangled in the public world of politics. Many Confederate women sewed presentation flags for local regiments or became involved in organizations that sponsored every war-influenced cause from directly aiding soldiers with food and clothing, to supplying hospitals with nursing services, to arming gunboats. And like in the north many had to fill the rolls previously occupied by their husbands.

In rural areas, people adapted as best they could, most always in fear that soldiers, Union or Confederate, would soon be marching by and would confiscate their crops and their animals, leaving then with little or nothing on which to survive. Confiscation was allowed by law for the Southern Army to do so to southern farms, and the Union would do so as a cost of war. Clothes were patched endlessly. Ink was made from pokeberries, and paper was very hard to come by. Evening meals shrank to cornmeal and molasses, when meals were possible at all.

For enslaved people, daily life was filled with anxiety and, at times, a ray hope. News of the Emancipation Proclamation filtered slowly southward and sparked secret prayers and cautious celebration. In Union-occupied areas, many enslaved persons walked off plantations and flocked to *"contraband camps,"* seeking freedom for whatever hardship it might cost. One ex-slave later recalled: *"We heard Mr. Lincoln had set us free, and we started walking. We didn't know where to go, but we knew we couldn't stay."* But hope was not always present. During 1863, especially after the Emancipation Proclamation, discipline became harsher on the plantations. When slave owners feared that their slaves may soon be freed, they tried to extract as much labor as possible from them.

All of that said, children still played, weddings still happened, there was still some laughter, and meals were shared when possible. The war shattered the rhythm of life but did not erase it. The lives lived in 1863, famous or anonymous, were not always frozen in response to the war, there were normal daily pursuits. People loved, mourned, joked, and hoped. They made do, made art, made music, made mistakes. While history remembers battles and speeches, it is the daily choices of people, from the woods of Maine to Georgia cottonfields, that remind us of the true cost and complexity of that year.

Long before he became the towering literary voice of postwar America, Samuel Clemens, later known as Mark Twain, briefly joined the Confederate cause in 1861. He enlisted with a local Missouri militia group known as the Marion Rangers. But Twain's military career lasted all of two weeks. He later wrote: *"I was not anxious to see the war end. I was anxious to see it begin. I wanted to see it begin right away and come off with a rush. But it didn't. It dragged its slow length along... and so did I."* Disillusioned by the idea of war and disinterested in violence, Twain abandoned the war and headed west, launching his path to fame as a journalist with an obscure newspaper in Virginia City, Nevada a boomtown in the middle of nowhere.

Though not a central figure in 1863, Twain later reflected on the era with his trademark humor: *"When I was a boy everybody was poor, but didn't know it; and everybody was comfortable, and did know it."*

Music, Humor, and the Lighter Side

Music echoed across battlefields as well as at kitchen tables and in the saloons in 1863, shaping identity and sustaining morale. In the North, the song *"The Battle Cry of Freedom"* by George F. Root became a rallying anthem. *"Yes, we'll rally 'round the flag, boys, we'll rally once again, Shouting the battle cry of freedom!"*

Confederate troops, not to be outdone, appropriated the tune of the song and rewrote the lyrics to suit their cause *"The Southrons Cry for Freedom"* a reminder that both sides tried to cloak their war aims in liberty's language.

If war was the drumbeat of 1863, music was the melody that gave people reason to keep marching. Songs, fiddles, foot-tapping jigs, and parlor ballads filled the spaces between battles and heartbreak. When there was a lull in the fighting, camp life revolved around music. Soldiers brought banjos and harmonicas, and many companies had regimental bands. A Southern diarist noted: *"Our camp was soaked in rain, the coffee was burnt, and our socks full of mud, but when Corporal Hodge played his fiddle, it all seemed far away."*

Sometimes impromptu dances broke out. Soldiers removed cartridge boxes and danced with one another for a brief moment of joy. Union drummer boys sometimes beat out rhythms, and when women were scarce, soldiers improvised: *"Private Thompson makes a fair lady if you don't look at his boots."*

On plantations, enslaved people preserved and transformed African musical traditions. Work songs like *"Follow the Drinking Gourd"* carried secret instructions for possible escape, while spirituals like *"Go Down Moses"* merged Biblical yearning with the hope of deliverance. *"Let my people go,"* they sang, deep and rising, their voices carrying beyond the fields, *"When Israel was in Egypt's land…"* These songs often doubled as encoded maps or rallying cries, unintelligible to white overseers but powerful to the community.

In towns and cities, minstrel shows were the most popular public entertainment. While deeply racist in content, they dominated American stages, with performers like Dan Emmett, composer of *"Dixie"* garnering national fame. Even Abraham Lincoln reportedly said of the song: *"I have always thought 'Dixie' one of the best tunes I ever heard."*

For those not in uniform, domestic parlor music was a daily ritual. Middle- and upper-class homes featured pianos, and songbooks circulated widely. One of the most beloved composers was Stephen Foster, whose songs like *"Hard Times Come Again No More"* felt almost prophetic in 1863: *"Tis the song, the sigh of the weary, Hard times, hard times, come again no more…"*

Meanwhile, dance remained one of their favorite escapes. Square dances, reels (Irish / Scottish form of dance), and cotillions were held during wartime, though often shortened when news from the front arrived. A Northern teenager wrote: *"We waltzed while the telegraph ticked out names of the fallen."* It celebrated Union resolve and the new moral direction of the war. The Confederacy had its own version with altered lyrics, preserving its claim to states' rights and Southern honor. *"Our Dixie forever! She's never at a loss: Down with the eagle and up with the cross!"*

Even amid the misery of war, soldiers found ways to laugh. Perhaps there was a necessity to find a small amount of joy and laughter to soften the near constant pain and desperation. Their humor was often dry, self-deprecating, and aimed at the exposed conditions of the war such as poor food, incompetent officers, or the absurdity of army life.

One Union soldier, writing from Tennessee, observed: "*We march by day and joke by night. If ever we lose our sense of humor, we'll lose this war before a single bullet finds us.*"

Q: What's the difference between a soldier and a baked potato? A: One's boiled alive and the other's still edible.

"*Hardtack is so hard, I'm thinking of using it as a breastplate.*"

Private's letter home: "*Tell mother not to send any more soap. It only reminds me how dirty I am.*"

Soldiers quipped that their hardtack (a nearly indestructible biscuit) was *"half flour, half fossil."*

The Southern heat, Union soldiers said, was *"hotter than abolitionist sermons in Charleston."*

One popular gag among privates: *"What's the difference between our general and a mule? One's stubborn, slow, and hard to steer, the other is a mule."*

Confederate troops weren't far behind in their gallows wit: *"We may be short on boots and bullets, but the Yankees can't match our sarcasm,"* wrote a soldier at Vicksburg.

The 1860s was also the golden age of satirical papers. Publications like The Southern Punch and the Northern Vanity Fair ridiculed politicians and military blunders alike. Cartoons mocked both Jefferson Davis and Lincoln, often in the same issue.

Mark Twain, not yet famous but already cutting in sarcasm, later recalled his experience as a failed Confederate volunteer in 1861: *"I was not eager to die. I had seen dead people and was not anxious to join their company."*

Humor also made its way into makeshift plays and performances. One Union encampment in Maryland staged a comedic farce where a soldier played a cross-dressing Southern belle who repeatedly fainted at the sight of Yankees, only to revive miraculously at the mention of whiskey. And in the North, with men at war, humor became a political weapon. One broadside read: "*Vote Democratic, because losing the war faster sounds like a plan!*"

Famous People Beyond the Battlefield

Frederick Douglass stood at the moral center of the Union cause. He was a former slave turned devout abolitionist. Douglass spent 1863 urging President Lincoln to not just declare freedom but ensure equality for enslaved persons. His powerful speeches and editorials pushed for Black enlistment into the army and for their fair treatment. He often shouted, *"He who would be free must himself strike the blow."* Douglass published articles demanding pay equality for Black soldiers and directly lobbied the White House for Black rights. He had already met Lincoln once and would again. Of that first meeting, he wrote: *"I was not the President's favorite man, but he treated me as a man."*

Walt Whitman brought tenderness to a brutal war. Though never a soldier, he spent 1863 in Washington helping ease the pain of wounded Union troops in hospitals. He wrote poetry, held hands, brought small comforts, and memorized the faces of dying boys. His notebook entry from February 1863 reads: *"I do not ask the wounded person how he feels, I myself become the wounded person."* His hospital experience later bled into the pages of *Drum-Taps* and *Leaves of Grass*, capturing the sacred and profane beauty of suffering.

Clara Barton, already known as *"The Angel of the Battlefield,"* nursed the wounded (though she had no formal nursing training) on front lines from Antietam to Fredericksburg. In 1863, she began organizing medical supplies to assist relief operations. She did so with unmatched intensity and endurance. Her reputation for fearlessness grew. She once said: *"I may be compelled to face danger, but never fear it, and while our soldiers can stand and fight, I can stand and feed and nurse them."* After the war she dedicated herself to identifying missing soldiers and marking graves, answering thousands of questions from grieving families. In 1881 Clara Barton founded the American Red Cross.

Mark Twain was still known by his birth name Samuel Clemens. In early 1863, when he ventured to Nevada and started working as a journalist for the Territorial Enterprise in Virginia City. That year, he first adopted the pen name "Mark Twain." Twain first used his pen name on February 3, 1863, when he wrote a humorous travel account titled "*Letter From Carson, re: Joe Goodman; party at Gov. Johnson's; music"* and signed it "Mark Twain." This was the point at which he began honing his uniquely American wit. In one editorial, he described a local political debate as *"A contest between a drunk and a liar. It was difficult to tell which one was more sincere."* His rare gifts were already capturing the satirical spirit that would later define the postwar generation.

Harriet Beecher Stowe, whose book, Uncle Tom's Cabin had helped awaken Northern conscience a decade earlier to the immorality of slavery continued to write in defense of emancipation and Christian morality. She had a significant impact on the moral climate surrounding the Civil War, and in 1863, she was personally involved in events celebrating the emancipation of enslaved people. In 1863, she toured Union camps and corresponded with the Lincoln administration. The President allegedly greeted her by saying: *"So you're the little woman who wrote the book that made this great war."* Though apocryphal, the quote illustrates her perceived impact.

Louisa May Alcott, served for six weeks as a nurse in Washington caring for soldiers before she became ill with typhoid. She was treated for her fever with mercury, which permanently damaged her health. She wrote many letters home to her family which served as the foundation for her book, *Hospital Sketches*, in 1863 revealing the raw humanity of the wounded. This work, inspired by her experiences as a civil war nurse, but was a fictionalized account of her time in a military hospital. She also published short stories and other works during this period.

Horace Greeley was one of the most influential American journalists of the 19th century, best known as the founder and longtime editor of the New-York Tribune. A staunch advocate for reform, Greeley supported abolition, labor rights, temperance, and women's suffrage, and used his editorial power to shape public discourse on these and other major issues of the day. In 1863, Greeley stood at the center of the national conversation, not as a politician or soldier, but as a moral and political voice in print. Greeley editorialized in favor of the Emancipation Proclamation and championed the recruitment of Black soldiers, seeing them as both a moral and military asset to the Union cause.

A Prizefight to Remember

Prizefighting at the time was not fought with gloves but with bare fists. It persisted through 1863, though it occupied a strange space in American culture during the Civil War. It was technically illegal in most states but for the most part it was ignored by law enforcement. Prizefighting was often conducted in secret and in rural locations, and it remained popular among working-class men, particularly in urban centers and among soldiers looking for diversion. While the Civil War was in full force, prizefighting didn't stop, it actually thrived especially among soldiers in both Union and Confederate camps. Matches were sometimes held informally between regiments or among troops at rest. Soldiers gambled on their favorites and gathered in large numbers to watch the bare-knuckle contests.

Religious groups and newspapers, particularly in the North, frequently condemned prizefighting as brutish and immoral. Their points were all very valid, it was often very brutal. The fights were normally characterized by a lot of wrestling holds and body punches. Throwing the other fighter was allowed. Headbutting, eye-gouging, biting, and kicking were prohibited. A foul was called if a man was struck while he was down. There was an umpire from each side, as well as a referee overseeing the match. A line was drawn in the center of the ring before each round. If a fighter could not make it to the line, he would forfeit the match. Fighters were often romanticized as symbols of toughness and masculinity.

Newspapers would often run detailed accounts of matches, indicating a popular fascination. In a time of mass violence and uncertainty, the brutal clarity of a one-on-one fight, two men in a ring, no weapons, clear but brutal rules, held a strange appeal. Some saw it as a test of masculinity, national strength, or ethnic pride, especially among Irish and English immigrants.

While armies clashed across fields and rivers, and emancipation reshaped the meaning of liberty, Americans still found time for this brutal spectacle, and few displays rivaled the brutal endurance contests of bare-knuckle prizefighting. The usual fighting area was a 24 x 24-foot square ring, although it could be almost any size. The ring was cordoned off by ropes, the floor of the ring was the field in which it was placed.

In 1863, a match between Joe Coburn and Mike McCoole, two Irish-American champions, came to symbolize the nation's appetite for grit and survival. It had a $2,000 purse that was to go to the winner. This was about 13 years' worth of pay for the typical Union soldier. But before the bout the combatants made a $700 bet on themselves. This fight was for purse, for sure, but also the victor was to be called Champion of America. Coburn was 5'10"and weighed about 180 pounds, while McCoole was 6'2"and was about 200 pounds. The smaller Coburn was agile and quick, while McCoole was a brute.

An estimated 2,000 spectators assembled to witness the fight at Charlestown, Maryland, near the North East River. It was a remote location selected to evade law enforcement. Most of the spectators likely paid about $3 to watch the fight, which is equivalent to about $75 in 2025. Those closest to the ring paid more. There were many gamblers in attendance, with most of the fight revenue coming from side bets, not attendance. The fight started at about 12:30, with McCoole having to wait 20 minutes in the ring for his opponent to arrive. A mostly round by round description of the fight was relayed in the New York Herald.

The fight lasted 67 rounds; each round terminated when a fighter is knocked to the ground. Although many rounds ended when a fighter voluntarily fell to the ground (that was illegal), but more often than not accepted by the referee. There was a 30-second rest between rounds.

Mike McCoole was bleeding from his engorged eye from the very first round. Joe Corbon had strongly initiated the fight, looking like a polished prize fighter.

From the New York Herald, "*Round First — McCoole, after some little sparring, rushed in, and Coburn retreated ; Mac followed him up. let fly, but being out of distance missed, and Joe assaulted him on the neck with the left and planted his right on the cheek, under the left eye, raising a mouse immediately and drawing blood. Mac at once clinched; some slight mutual fibbing occurred, and Coburn was thrown. First blood for Coburn claimed and allowed.*"

For 67 rounds, according to the Herald, McCoole sustained blow after blow, some of which were claimed to be illegal, as the crowd cheered, jeered and sometimes laughed. Each of the fighters was accused of cheating at various times during the fight. On the end of the fight the Herald reported: *Joe forced the fighting in Mac's own corner, turning his blows with beautiful precision and as straight as a dart. He was now so much the stronger man that he could throw Mac easily. The latter was feeling the effects of the tremendous hitting he had received, was bleeding hat and his eyes closing ; but his courage was as undaunted as ever. It was clear he could not win, barring accident, and Coburn was fighting coolly and carefully, without a scratch on him. So, it continued until the Sixty - seventh and Last Round — When Mack came up weak, led off and missed, Joe nailing him heavily and knocking him down totally exhausted. On being taken to his corner his seconds, seeing his chances gone, and unwilling to subject the brave fellow to more unnecessary punishment, threw up the sponge in acknowledgment of his defeat.*"

Making prizefighting illegal did little to stop its popularity, especially among working-class immigrants who saw in the fighters a mirror of their own struggle for respect and survival. Newspapers covered the matches with the same drama as battlefield dispatches, and fighters were treated as folk heroes. In a year marked by historic transformation, the bloody persistence of a 67-round fight was, in its own way, a reflection of the American character, unyielding, bruised, but determined to stand back up.

CHAPTER 8
LEGISLATION AND DESERTION - STRUGGLES IN CONGRESS AND CAMP

While cannons roared on distant fields, and bodies of soldiers were seemingly strewn everywhere, newspapers continued to chronicle the daily rise and fall of armies, counting and naming the dead wherever they were reported. In both Washington and Richmond, the congresses of both sides of the war pressed forward with the quieter but consequential work of legislation. The year 1863 saw both the Union and the Confederacy pass pivotal laws that not only supported their respective war efforts but also reshaped national identity, civil liberties, economic policy, and military structure. Below is a synopsis of some of those legislations.

Union and Confederate Legislation

During the Civil War, the U.S. Congress was scheduled to have one Official Session during the year. The session typically started at the beginning of December and lasted several months. The specific duration was not defined. The final session of the 37th Congress started on December 1, 1862, and concluded on March 3, 1863. Special sessions could be called by the president as he deemed necessary. Committee work and emergency measures were continuous throughout the year.

Enrollment Act (March 3, 1863) – The Federal Conscription Law often called the Conscription Act, was the first in U.S. history to mandate military service for all male citizens and immigrants who had filed for citizenship. All men ages 20 to 45 were required to enroll and be subject to military duty. The act allowed for substitutions or payment of a $300 commutation fee to avoid service, a provision that sparked accusations of class bias and led directly to the July Draft Riots in New York.

National Banking Act of 1863 (February 25, 1863) This legislation was one of the most significant pieces of economic legislation in U.S. history. It established a system of national banks and a uniform national currency, helping to stabilize Northern finances and reduce reliance on disparate state-issued currencies. It laid the groundwork for a modern financial infrastructure and was part of Salmon Chase's effort to fund the Union war through controlled banking and the sale of war bonds. Prior to the act money was a mess, state-chartered banks operated independently, issuing their own currency. In the north there were over 7,000 kinds of bank notes with varying reliability. Confidence in paper money was not high.

Habeas Corpus Suspension Act (March 3, 1863) President Abraham Lincoln had acted unilaterally early in the war, suspending habeas corpus in certain regions just days after the fall of Fort Sumter. His action aimed to quell rebellion, suppress secessionist sympathizers in border states like Maryland, and give military authorities the power to detain those considered threats to the Union. Critics decried these actions as a grave violation of civil liberties, accusing Lincoln of overstepping his constitutional authority. Congress passed the Habeas Corpus Suspension Act, formally granting the president the power to suspend the writ of habeas corpus "*whenever, in his judgment, the public safety may require it*" during the ongoing rebellion. The act effectively ratified what Lincoln had already been doing and gave retroactive protection to officials who had detained civilians without trial.

Internal Revenue Acts (amendments in 1863) To fund the escalating cost of war, Congress revised and expanded the federal income tax introduced in 1861. It increased the rates and broadened enforcement under the Internal Revenue Bureau. It also taxed luxury goods, licenses, and inheritances. All incomes above $600 would be taxed. Incomes between $600 and $10,000 were taxed at 3 percent, while those above $10,000 faced a 5 percent rate. The 1863 update improved administrative mechanisms for determining income, defining allowable deductions, and punishing evasion. Dozens of common consumer goods received excise taxes. Licenses were required for various occupations, and tax assessors and collectors were hired, some 3,000 in all.

The West Virginia Statehood Act West Virginia was admitted as the 35th state on June 20, 1863. The act was a response to the secession crisis and the Civil War, with the residents of the northwestern counties of Virginia desiring to establish a separate state, separate from the Confederacy. The act was controversial, as it challenged constitutional interpretations about state formation, but it was a political and symbolic victory for the Union. It was a direct challenge to Confederate legitimacy, a strategic boon to the Union, and a precedent-setting use of wartime federal power. The process of West Virginia statehood faced several challenges, including concerns about the legality of forming a new state from part of an existing state, as well as questions about the validity of the process used to establish the new state. As a condition of statehood, Lincoln required the new constitution to include a gradual emancipation clause, a sign of how closely slavery and war aims were now entwined.

Pacific Railroad Amendments Although the original Pacific Railway Act passed in 1862, it was amended in 1863 to address technical issues, land grants, and financial arrangements. The railroad's promise to bind the coasts played heavily in Lincoln's vision of a united, industrial future. The 1863 Pacific Railroad Act amendment primarily focused on standardizing the track gauge for the transcontinental railroad. It established a standard gauge of four feet eight and one-half inches (1.435 meters), which became the standard gauge for US railroads and is still widely used today.

The Confederate Congress typically met for one or two sessions per year, with each session normally lasting about three months, or however long it took to legislate the business of the Confederacy. In 1863 they convened twice once from January 12 to May 1, and then again at the end of the year from December 7 to February 17, 1864.

Impressment Act (March 26, 1863) This law gave the Confederate government sweeping authority to seize food, fuel, slaves, and other goods for military use, at government-determined prices. The act codified an existing Confederate army practice of seizing resources to support military operations. It was deeply unpopular with Southern farmers and small landowners and symbolized the growing power of the central Confederate state over individual rights and state sovereignty.

Tax-in-Kind Act (April 24, 1863) The Confederate Congress passed the Tax-in-Kind Act requiring farmers to deliver one-tenth of their agricultural produce directly to the Confederate government. This included staples like corn, wheat, oats, sweet potatoes, cotton, sugar, tobacco, and even livestock. The collected goods were to be used to feed the Confederate Army, support government operations, and sustain the war effort in the face of monetary collapse.

The act applied to all agricultural producers, although there were some exemptions for poor farmers and regions devastated by fighting. In practice, enforcement was inconsistent and often heavy-handed. Confederate tax agents, called tax-in-kind collectors, traveled from farm to farm, often accompanied by wagons and troops, to gather goods. Many rural Southerners resented the intrusion, seeing little difference between federal tax collectors and Confederate tax collectors. The act deepened tensions between the central Confederate government and its citizenry.

Confederate Conscription Act Amendments (February 17, 1863)
The original 1862 conscription act had already sparked controversy. The original Conscription Act required all white males between the ages of 18 and 35 to serve in the Confederate military for three years, whether they volunteered or not. This measure expanded the existing army by forcibly drafting men who had not yet enlisted, and, just as controversially, it extended the service of men already under arms, whose original terms were set to expire.

Though militarily necessary, the act struck a blow to the core of Southern ideals. The Confederacy, founded on a fierce commitment to states' rights and individual liberty, now wielded federal authority in the most personal way possible, forcing men into military service. Many Southerners, especially in the more independent-minded mountain regions, saw the act as a betrayal of the very principles for which they had seceded.

The 1863 Conscription Act extended the draft age to those men between the ages of 17 and 50, and established the Twenty Negro Law, which exempted one white male per 20 owned slaves. Resistance was strong and immediate in certain areas. Draft evasion, desertion, and even armed opposition to conscription agents became common, especially in Appalachia and other Unionist-leaning parts of the Confederacy. In some cases, entire communities offered sanctuary to draft dodgers or refused to cooperate with Confederate authorities.

Suspension of Habeas Corpus (various instances) Though Jefferson Davis and the Confederate Congress were reluctant, several temporary suspensions of habeas corpus were enacted in regions deemed dangerous or rebellious, particularly in eastern Tennessee and parts of Georgia. The action was controversial in a Confederacy that had styled itself as a guardian of liberty against Federal tyranny.

Currency and Finance Laws Facing runaway inflation, the Confederate Congress passed multiple acts in 1863 to issue more currency, regulate gold and silver trade, and impose penalties for hoarding. These laws were primarily focused on funding the war effort. However, without sufficient backing or taxation, Confederate currency continued to spiral downward. These laws helped establish a Confederate banking system and issued treasury notes, which were backed by bonds, which had been intended to be a long-term investment and not immediately payable.

Legislation to Regulate Deserters and Guerrillas The Confederate Congress passed laws aimed at cracking down on widespread desertions and rogue militias. These included harsh penalties, and in some areas, martial law. It became illegal for civilians to transport, feed or shelter deserters. But enforcement was inconsistent, and local resentment sometimes turned armed citizens against Richmond. In early 1863 General Lee issued an order offering amnesty to any deserter who returned to service. This offer was codified after the battle of Gettysburg by legislation in congress.

A Georgia legislator wrote in a private letter: "*We have become the very tyranny we seceded to avoid.*"

Desertion From Both Sides

While tales of heroism and sacrifice filled the headlines of newspapers, a quiet crisis brewed beneath the banners, drums and bugles: desertion. By 1863, as the war dragged into its third agonizing year, thousands of soldiers, both Union and Confederate, began slipping away from their posts, many never to return. The Union Army had about 1 million soldiers in service at various times during 1863.That year, official reports suggest that approximately 85,000–100,000 men deserted the Union ranks during the calendar year. Desertion rates fluctuated by region and unit, rural regiments, immigrant-heavy units, and draftees often saw higher rates.

The Confederate Army was significantly smaller than that of the Union, with perhaps 400,000–500,000 men during 1863. Desertion rates in the South were even higher than in the North, especially as major battles seemed to turn the direction of victory toward the North. With supplies dwindling, and morale faltering soldiers left their posts in droves. Estimated Confederate desertions for 1863 range from 60,000 to 100,000 men.

Both sides struggled to maintain troop numbers and deal with desertion, with Confederate authorities eventually passing legislation against sheltering or encouraging deserters. The prevalence of desertion reflected the complex factors influencing soldiers' decisions, including their perception of government and military obligations, and the conditions they faced on the battlefield. Historians estimate that over 200,000 Union soldiers and more than 100,000 Confederate soldiers deserted during the Civil War. Some fled after a single battle. Others left after months in the mud; malnourished, homesick, and doubting the cause for which they fought.

For the Union Army, desertion rates spiked after major defeats or long winter encampments. Soldiers from immigrant communities especially Irish and German regiments sometimes felt little allegiance to a government they believed treated them unfairly.

In the South, desertion became rampant by late 1863 as food supplies were sometimes non-existent and Confederate promises of food and clothing often did not materialize. The reasons for desertion were as varied as the men themselves: fear, hunger, homesickness, political opposition, or simply exhaustion. Some left to care for family members. Others despaired that they may never see home again.

Punishments ranged from branding (like cattle) and hard labor to execution by firing squad, particularly in the Confederate ranks where morale often hinged on visible discipline. Posters and newspaper ads offered cash rewards for returning deserters. In both North and South, patrols were dispatched to capture them, sometimes referred to grimly as *"bounty hunters in blue or gray."* Most deserters were never caught. Some changed their names and settled in new states. Others were quietly accepted back into their regiments as they either returned freely or were forcibly returned, especially as both sides grew desperate for manpower.

Stories beneath the shadows

Beyond official records and statistics, personal stories from deserters and their families provide a haunting window into the human cost of war. One Union soldier, Private Samuel Delaney of the 126th New York, deserted in early 1863 after writing to his sister: *"I cannot hear from home, I have no boots, and I have not seen bread in three days. I fear I will die for nothing."* He was later captured in upstate New York and sentenced to hard labor, though his sentence was quietly reduced due to illness.

In North Carolina, a Confederate wife named Rachel Whitaker wrote to her husband's commanding officer, begging for leniency: *"John is not a coward, but our son is sick and our fields are dying. I cannot hold the farm alone. He will come back when he can."* John was never apprehended, and years later, their grandson would recall how the family survived on blackberries and cornmeal until the war's end.

Another poignant account came from Union soldier Henry White, who deserted after witnessing the deaths of his two closest friends at Chancellorsville. He later surrendered to a provost marshal in Pennsylvania and pleaded for forgiveness. Lincoln personally reviewed his case and granted him clemency. White returned to service and survived the war. His descendants would later share the pardon, signed by Lincoln, as a family heirloom.

Many, perhaps most, of the men had good cause for leaving their posts, at least in their minds: *"I know I did wrong to leave, but my children had no bread, and my wife was too sick to stand. God will forgive me though the army will not."* Anonymous Confederate deserter, letter to his brother, 1863. *"I could not hear another letter say the children cried themselves to sleep hungry. Let them hang me if they must. My duty is at home."* Union private from Ohio, deserting after the Battle of Chickamauga.

Private John F. Appleton of the Union Army recounted how a fellow soldier deserted during a night march, only to be captured two days later by his own unit. He was publicly flogged and forced to march for a week in shackles. *"I do not know if he was brave or broken,"* Appleton wrote, *"but he cried like a child."*

"Vicksburg broke something in me. We buried men with our bare hands and ate mule meat. I don't care who wins anymore." Confederate soldier from Mississippi, recorded postwar in a local oral history *"We have marched three hundred miles in thirty days, eaten what a pig would shun, and slept in swamps. If this is glory, they can keep it."* Union deserter, letter intercepted in Kentucky, 1863

In Georgia, Confederate soldier Thomas Brooks deserted after learning that his wife had died, and his children were starving. He walked nearly 300 miles home. *"I had given them to the Cause,"* he later wrote, *"but the Cause had taken all."*

Lincoln's Dilemma

Lincoln, ever sensitive to the burden of ordinary men, personally reviewed many desertion cases brought to his attention. He pardoned some, especially young or first-time offenders. *"I do not believe the boy meant to betray his country,"* he once said. *"I believe he simply missed his mother."* But he also knew the importance of discipline. His challenge was to balance justice with mercy, knowing that every decision set a precedent and revealed the character of the man making it. Desertion rarely made the headlines. But it told its own story one of fatigue, sorrow, and the private battles fought behind the front lines.

In March 1863, Lincoln offered amnesty to many Union soldiers who were absent from their regiments, provided they returned to their units. This policy was part of a broader strategy to end the war and restore the Union. It reflected Lincoln's understanding of the contractual nature of military service during the Civil War, where many soldiers felt they had obligations to the state and the government. Lincoln also believed that a sincere repentance for desertion warranted pardon, according to the New York Times.

The War Within the War

Beyond the battlefields and legislative chambers, 1863 was a year of reckoning. It was the year the war became truly total, touching every class, every race, and every corner of the divided nation. Black Americans, long excluded from national identity, began claiming their place with their blood and bravery. Legislators in both North and South grappled with wartime contradictions, liberty versus control, equality versus privilege. And as soldiers deserted, they exposed a truth the cannons couldn't drown out. The will to fight had its limits. This war was not just about victory. It was about defining the essence of the country. And in 1863, that essence was being tested in the courts, in the administration, in the camps, as well as in the conscience of every American.

The Rise and Role of Independent Militias

As desertion increased and central armies thinned, a different breed of soldier began to take shape across both the North and South. Where discipline faltered or manpower ran short, independent militias, state-organized, community-based, or entirely irregular, partially filled the void. Their emergence in 1863 was not the product of grand strategy, but of necessity, fear, and local resolve. Private Herman Sidney Cook of Company A, 26th Pennsylvania Emergency Militia, documented in his diary on June 23, 1863, *"Received Springfield Rifle Muskets, accoutrements, and forty rounds of cartridges."*

In the Union, these forces often materialized as emergency militias, called up to respond to crisis. Pennsylvania's rolling countryside, peaceful one day, sprang to arms the next as Lee's Army of Northern Virginia moved north. Thousands of citizens, many with little or no training, enlisted in hastily-formed defense regiments to protect Harrisburg and Philadelphia. Governor Andrew Curtin, determined to raise a line of defense with or without federal reinforcement, relied heavily on these ad hoc formations. Many of these men would never see combat, but their presence projected resolve, and in several instances, they performed valuable service securing supply lines and calming public fear.

Elsewhere in the North, militias found themselves in a more combustible role. When the Enrollment Act was passed in March of 1863, it ignited widespread resistance. In cities like Boston, Chicago, and especially New York, opposition exploded. When mobs took control of large sections of Manhattan during the Draft Riots in July, the New York State Militia ironically deployed in Pennsylvania during the Gettysburg campaign, had to be rushed back to restore order. Their return marked the beginning of the end of the riots, but not without deep scars. The experience revealed how thinly stretched federal authority was and how vital state militias remained to the domestic security of the Union.

In border states like Missouri and Kentucky, militias operated in a world of constant uncertainty. Skirmishes, raids, and sabotage were common, and Union-loyal militias often took on a quasi-military, quasi-policing role. Some acted as defenders against Confederate raiders. Others, in truth, were barely distinguishable from vigilante bands, fighting not just rebels, but neighbors with opposing loyalties. The chaos of guerrilla warfare blurred the line between patriotism and revenge.

Across the lines, in the embattled Confederacy, independent militias played an even more complex and contradictory role. Built upon the ideological foundation of states' rights, the Southern war effort was often hindered by governors who refused to subordinate their state forces to Confederate command. Nowhere was this more pronounced than in Georgia, where Governor Joseph Brown repeatedly defied Richmond's demands, insisting that his state militia remain within Georgia's borders. To Brown, these troops were defenders of Georgia first, and the Confederacy second. In a letter dated May 11, 1863, Confederate soldier Derastus E.W. Myers wrote from *"Camp Near Hamilton's Crossing"* to his brother and sister: *"We have been on the move constantly, and the men are weary, but their spirits remain high. The militia units have been essential in supporting our efforts, especially in guarding supply lines and maintaining order in the rear."*

Local defense units, known as Home Guards, took up the work of enforcing conscription, capturing deserters, and, in many areas, maintaining slave discipline. With many white men off at the front, the fear of slave insurrections gripped plantation districts. These militias, often older men or boys patrolled back roads and plantations, a presence that was as much psychological as military. They also became a bitter reminder to poor whites that the war, increasingly, was being fought to protect the institution of slavery and the wealth of the planter class.

Some militias evolved into more mobile, semi-official fighting forces. Confederate legislation had authorized Partisan Ranger units; irregular cavalry granted broad latitude to strike Northern supply lines and create havoc behind enemy lines. In Virginia, John S. Mosby's Rangers became the most famous of these, operating with uncanny efficiency in disrupting Union communications. Though technically under Confederate control, Mosby's operations were deeply autonomous, earning him both admiration and suspicion.

Not all militias remained loyal to the cause. In the mountain regions of North Carolina, Tennessee, and Alabama, resentment toward the Confederacy ran deep. Unionist militias formed in secret, aided escaped slaves, and even attacked Confederate supply trains. To Confederate commanders, they were traitors. To many civilians, they were defenders of neglected communities.

In Missouri and Arkansas, where guerrilla warfare was normal, bushwhackers, and jayhawkers, irregular fighters aligned with neither formal army, committed acts of violence that bordered on anarchy. These men, sometimes driven by political loyalty and other times by simple vengeance, raided towns, looted farms, and left a trail of misery behind them. In such areas, militias were often indistinguishable from gangs.

By late 1863, it was clear that the war was no longer confined to clean lines of battle or grand maneuvers by great armies. Increasingly, it was fought on back roads, in farm fields, and among the tangled loyalties of local communities. The rise of independent militias reflected both the weakening grip of central authority and the growing desperation of a war that touched every corner of the nation. While some of these forces provided vital protection or assistance, others deepened the chaos and bitterness that would outlast the conflict itself.

CHAPTER 9
THE INDIAN WARS

For the Native American peoples of the United States, the Civil War was not simply a distant contest between white factions. The force of the Union army reshaped the political geography of the West, disrupted fragile tribal alliances, and opened the door to an even more aggressive era of U.S. expansion. The year 1863 marked an inflection point. Under cover of national crisis, the federal government carried out some of its most devastating campaigns against indigenous resistance. Native lands were seized, tribes forcibly relocated, and traditional economies disrupted by war, displacement, and disease.

Though they fought bravely the Native nations found themselves increasingly isolated. Neither North nor South would ultimately honor its promises to its Indian allies. The postwar period would bring even greater betrayals. For the Dakota fleeing Sibley's troops, for the Navajo watching their crops burn in Canyon de Chelly, for the Cherokee torn by civil strife, 1863 was not a year of emancipation or preservation. It was a year of significant disruption and betrayal. In the shadows of Gettysburg and Vicksburg, this was another war that raged. It was less visible, but no less tragic for those who were losing their war.

While the eastern battlefields absorbed the attention of the Union and Confederate high commands, the wars against Native Americans continued in the shadows of everything else going on in 1863. The Indian Wars were bloody, consequential, and largely ignored by national leadership. Neither side dispatched its best men to the frontier. The Union's top generals, like Grant and Meade, were consumed with breaking the Confederate lines in the East and Mississippi Valley. As a result, the campaigns against tribes such as the Dakota in the northern plains and the Navajo in the Southwest were led by lesser-known officers, frontiersmen, local politicians, or former generals who had failed in the main war effort.

Men like Henry Sibley, Kit Carson, and James Carleton lacked the stature or strategic acumen of their Eastern counterparts, yet they wielded enormous power on the frontier. Their orders were often reduced to scorched-earth destruction and forced removals. Their reputations not built on military brilliance but on ruthless efficiency. Indian Territory itself was left to tribal militias and divided loyalties, with Confederate support under men like Stand Watie being symbolic more than substantial. In truth, the Indian Wars of 1863 were managed not by the nation's finest, but by those who were available and often by those no longer welcome elsewhere.

In 1863 the American Civil War was seemingly out of control. Either side occasionally relinquished control. The Indian Wars were another kind of war, less remembered but deeply consequential. For the Native American tribes whose lands stretched across the Great Plains, the Southwest, and the upper Missouri basin, the year 1863 brought devastation, betrayal, and a growing sense that their world was vanishing. The war between North and South offered no clear allies for many tribes; instead, it accelerated their dispossession and exposed them to brutal military campaigns and political manipulations.

Even as President Lincoln drafted words for the Gettysburg cemetery and Robert E. Lee maneuvered at Chancellorsville, Union columns were marching through Dakota Territory, Navajo homes were being burned in the canyons of New Mexico, and tribal warriors allied with the Confederacy were skirmishing with Unionist tribal neighbors in Indian Territory. The Civil War had expanded the frontier not only of battle, but of conquest.

Aligned with the North or South

Long before the Civil War, the Cherokee and Choctaw Nations, along with several other southeastern tribes, stood at a complicated intersection of cultural adoption and resistance. As part of their strategic efforts to maintain sovereignty and avoid removal, these tribes adopted certain European-American customs such as written constitutions, centralized governments, Western-style dress, Christianity, and, in some cases, the ownership of African American slaves.

By the mid-19th century, slavery had become embedded in segments of both Cherokee and Choctaw societies. The Cherokee Nation passed laws in the 1820s and 1830s codifying slavery, modeled on southern U.S. statutes. Enslaved people were often laboring on farms or working as skilled craftsmen. They were considered personal property, and their status was inherited through the maternal line. A census taken in 1860 found that approximately 4,000 Black people were enslaved by Cherokee citizens, and about 2,000 were enslaved in the Choctaw Nation.

This was not mere imitation. It was part of a painful calculus that by aligning themselves with the economic and cultural norms of the southern states, Native leaders hoped to prove that they were *"civilized"* in the eyes of the U.S. government, and thus worthy of retaining their ancestral lands. That hope, as history showed, was in vain. Despite their efforts, most of these tribes were forcibly removed west of the Mississippi during the 1830s and 1840s during the infamous Trail of Tears.

Once relocated to Indian Territory (present-day Oklahoma), the system of slavery continued. And when the Civil War began, these dynamics fractured the tribal nations internally. In both the Cherokee and Choctaw Nations, debates raged over whether to support the Union or the Confederacy. Ultimately, many leaders, especially those who were slaveholders, sided with the Confederacy, believing it would offer greater respect for tribal sovereignty and the protection of slaveholding rights. Confederate agents also actively courted tribal support with promises of autonomy.

Prominent Cherokee leader Stand Watie, himself a slaveholder, became a brigadier general in the Confederate Army, the only Native American to achieve that rank. He led mixed forces of Cherokee, Creek, and white Confederate troops in battles across the Indian Territory and Arkansas. The Choctaw also fielded troops aligned with the South, and Choctaw leaders signed formal treaties with the Confederacy in 1861.

Many Cherokee, particularly in the full-blooded, non-assimilated communities of the Keetoowah Society, fought on behalf of the Union, forming what were called the Loyal Cherokee. Within the Cherokee Nation, the American Civil War was also an internal civil war.

After the Union victory, the U.S. government imposed new treaties on the tribes that had sided with the Confederacy. Among their terms was the abolition of slavery and a controversial requirement that the freed men, the formerly enslaved Black residents of Indian Territory, be granted full tribal citizenship. This provision led to a long and bitter legacy of legal battles, discrimination and exclusion that, in some cases, persists even into the 21st century.

The fact that some Native Americans held Black people in bondage complicates the popular narrative of oppressed versus oppressor. It reminds us that history resists simplification. It also underscores a tragic irony that peoples who had been displaced and subjugated by white Americans found themselves, at times, participating in the very systems of domination that had been used against them.

By 1863, the Union had recruited several regiments of Indian Home Guards, composed of pro-Union tribal members, especially from the Creek, Seminole, and some segments of the Cherokee Nation. These men fought not only Confederate soldiers but also their tribal rivals, seeking to reclaim homes and communities lost to Confederate-aligned tribal leaders.

Elsewhere in the West, some tribes tried to maintain neutrality. The Pawnee, for instance, offered intermittent support to Union forces on the plains, viewing them as a counterbalance to their traditional Sioux enemies. In California and Oregon, smaller-scale conflicts between settlers and tribes continued in relative obscurity, often framed as *"pacification"* rather than war.

Wapshasha was a Dakota Leader and was in support of the Union forces. Wabasha opposed the 1862 uprising led by Little Crow. He sided with the Union, trying to maintain peace and protect his people through cooperation. He later helped lead the forced relocation of Dakota survivors to Crow Creek, South Dakota, a grim resettlement effort plagued by disease and starvation. His story reveals the agonizing choices faced by Native leaders: resist and face annihilation or cooperate and endure displacement.

Meanwhile, Indian Territory was torn by a civil war of its own. The Five Civilized Tribes: the Cherokee, Choctaw, Chickasaw, Creek, and Seminole, had been forcibly relocated there in the 1830s. By 1861, they faced yet another fateful decision, whom to support in the Civil War. Southern diplomats promised sovereignty, respect, and political representation. Many tribal leaders, especially among the slaveholding elite of the Cherokee and Choctaw nations, aligned themselves with the South. In July 1861, the Confederacy signed treaties recognizing tribal governments as sovereign nations.

Support for the Confederacy was far from unanimous. Other factions within the tribes, particularly among the Creek and Cherokee, viewed the Union as a better guarantor of Native rights, or at least the lesser of two evils. These divisions led to brutal internal strife, with entire tribal communities split into pro-Union and pro-Confederate camps. The result was a savage and often personal war, marked by ambushes, arson, and revenge killings. In Indian Territory, the

Civil War was not just between blue and gray. It was a war of brothers, cousins, and clans.

Kit Carson and the Navajo Campaigns

Kit Carson was perhaps the most famous Indian Fighter of them all in 1863. By that time, the name Christopher "Kit" Carson was already etched into the American imagination as the quintessential frontiersman. He was a renown scout, trapper, guide, and soldier. Born in Kentucky in 1809 and raised on the Missouri frontier, Carson had spent decades navigating the untamed landscapes of the West. He guided expeditions for General Fremont in the 1840s, fought in the Mexican-American War, and served as an Indian agent in New Mexico Territory. His reputation, burnished by popular dime novels and embellished newspaper accounts, was that of a quiet but fearless man who knew every canyon and trail west of the Rockies.

But in 1863, Carson's role changed from guide and observer to that of a military commander. Appointed colonel of the 1st New Mexico Volunteer Infantry in the Union Army, Carson was ordered by General James Carleton to carry out a brutal campaign against the Navajo Nation. The Navajo had long resisted encroachment by settlers and had engaged in raiding to defend their territory and retaliate against rival tribes. Carleton viewed the Navajo not as a nation but as a persistent obstacle to U.S. control of the Southwest and he ordered Carson to break their resistance by any means necessary.

What followed was one of the most devastating episodes of the Indian Wars. In the summer and fall of 1863, Carson led a scorched-earth campaign through Navajo lands by burning crops, destroying food stores, slaughtering livestock, and razing villages. The campaign was methodical with a clear intent to starve the Navajo into submission. Carson, who reportedly had complex personal views on Native Americans and had previously served as an Indian agent, later expressed discomfort with the cruelty of the operation. Still, he carried it out with grim efficiency. His forces were accompanied by Ute scouts and other auxiliaries familiar with the terrain.

By the winter of 1863–64, the Navajo, facing starvation and destitution, began to surrender. The campaign reached its tragic climax with the Long Walk, a forced march of over 300 miles that began in early 1864, as thousands of Navajo men, women, and children were herded from their ancestral homeland to the bleak Bosque Redondo reservation near Fort Sumner, New Mexico.

Hundreds died on the journey or shortly after arrival from hunger, cold, and disease.

Carson's role in this episode remains one of the most controversial aspects of his legacy. Though some have tried to portray him as merely following orders or as a reluctant participant in a cruel system, others argue that his command and his silence, make him complicit in what many now view as an early form of ethnic cleansing.

After the Civil War, Carson was promoted to brigadier general and served briefly in various posts, including as an Indian agent once again. He died in 1868 at the age of 58, just as the mythology around his name was reaching its full height. In the end, Kit Carson was a man of contradictions: a trailblazer who opened the West and a soldier who helped close it to the peoples who had lived there for centuries. Carson's campaign in the Southwest served as a grim reminder that not all freedom marches moved forward, and not all Union victories were just.

Dakota Punitive Campaigns

The leader of the Dakota Sioux was a man known as Little Crow (Taoyateduta). He was a complex and intelligent leader who tried to balance diplomacy with the U.S. government and the mounting desperation of his starving people. In 1862, he reluctantly led the Dakota Uprising in Minnesota, which spilled over into 1863 with lingering skirmishes and punitive expeditions by Union troops. He spoke English, wore European-style clothing, and had even visited Washington, D.C., years earlier. But broken treaty promises and withheld annuity payments left his people destitute. The war ended with a brutal response with mass trials and the largest mass execution in U.S. history (38 Dakota men hanged in Mankato). Little Crow was hunted down and killed in 1863 while foraging near Hutchinson, Minnesota. His scalp and remains were displayed for years, a tragic symbol of how Native leaders were dehumanized even in death.

It could have been even worse. Abraham Lincoln commuted the sentences of 265 other Sioux who had also been sentenced to hang. But these men were only guilty of fighting and were not engaged in the murder and rape of innocents. It was one of the few times that Lincoln was directly involved in the Indian Wars.

In the summer of 1863, Brigadier General Henry H. Sibley led a large Union force westward from Minnesota into the Dakota plains in pursuit of fleeing Dakota bands. This expedition was not just retaliatory but intended to exert lasting military control over vast territories. At battles such as Big Mound, Dead Buffalo Lake, and Stony Lake, Sibley's troops engaged Native warriors in fierce skirmishes. Though these were often more running fights than pitched battles, the effect was devastating. Villages were burned, food supplies destroyed, and tribal communities driven further into hardship.

To the southwest, a parallel campaign was underway against the Navajo people. In New Mexico Territory, Colonel Kit Carson, already a legend on the frontier, carried out a scorched-earth policy against the Navajo under orders from General James Carleton. Carson's campaign destroyed crops, stole livestock, and turned vast tracts of homeland into lifeless ruin. The strategy was not simply to defeat the Navajo in battle but to force their complete submission through starvation and terror.

The Apache Wars

In the arid mountains and deserts of the Southwest there was another war of survival, betrayal, and retribution. For the Apache, a proud and decentralized people made up of several bands, Chiricahua, Mescalero, Jicarilla, and others, the Civil War created both opportunity and peril. With U.S. Army forces redeployed to the eastern front, Apache leaders saw a chance to reclaim ancestral lands long encroached upon by miners, settlers, and military forts. Yet this brief vacuum of power only invited more chaos.

Among the most formidable of these leaders was Cochise, chief of the Chiricahua Apache, a man whose very name would come to symbolize both resistance and honor in the Southwest. In 1863, Cochise was not yet the widely feared and mythical figure he would become in later years, but he was already deeply respected among his people and feared by his enemies. His territory spanned the rugged mountains and hidden canyons of what is now southeastern Arizona and northern Mexico, land so forbidding that it served as a natural fortress for the Apache.

The roots of the Apache conflict with the U.S. Army went back decades, but recent years had brought a fragile peace. Cochise himself had signed on to that uneasy calm, preferring to trade with settlers rather than raid them. He had even allowed passage through his land for wagon trains and stagecoaches, believing coexistence might be possible. But that hope had been shattered in 1861 with the so-called Bascom Affair, in which Cochise was falsely accused of kidnapping a white boy and a small group of Apache women. He was lured to a meeting under a white flag, only to be seized by Lieutenant George Bascom. Cochise escaped, but members of his family, who had also come under the flag of peace, were hanged. It was a wound that would never heal.

By 1863, the war between Cochise and the United States had become a long, grinding affair marked by ambushes, reprisals, and disappearances into the vast wilderness. Union troops, stretched thin by the demands of the national conflict, could do little to contain him. That year, General James H. Carleton, commander of the Department of New Mexico, launched a campaign to *"pacify"* the Apache and Mescalero, particularly those in the mountains of New Mexico and Arizona. His methods were brutal. Apache men were hunted, their camps destroyed, and survivors, including women and children, were herded into what he called the Bosque Redondo, an experimental reservation hundreds of miles from their homeland. Conditions were horrific: scarce food, disease, no clean water, and bitter cold. Many died trying to escape.

Cochise, however, evaded capture. He refused to be drawn into open battle, relying instead on classic Apache guerrilla tactics: hit-and-run raids, vanishing into mountain passes, and striking only when the enemy was weakest. To the settlers and soldiers who feared him, he was a ghost. To his people, he was a shield.

In one telling episode from 1863, an Apache war party, likely led by Cochise or one of his lieutenants, ambushed a wagon train guarded by Union soldiers along the Apache Pass Trail. The narrow canyon, hemmed in by high rock walls, was perfect terrain for an ambush. Arrows, musket fire, and rolling boulders turned the path into a killing ground. Survivors who fled were often picked off or lost to the heat and thirst of the desert.

Cochise kept a sense of limits in his war. He reportedly spared civilians when he could and released captives after negotiations. Unlike other commanders in that era, he did not kill for pleasure or conquest but fought to protect a way of life under siege. And he knew that his war was not just against the blue coats, but also against time.

By the end of 1863, the tide had begun to shift again. The Union was slowly reasserting control in the West, and Apache leaders saw more soldiers, more forts, and more settlers arrive. Cochise, though still free and defiant, understood that the struggle would only grow harder.

The Press and the Indian Campaigns

If the fighting on the Great Plains, in the canyons of New Mexico, or in the tribal lands of Indian Territory was largely overlooked by the nation's highest military planners, the press followed suit but not entirely. Throughout 1863, newspapers in both the North and South did offer coverage of the so-called Indian troubles, though the column space was limited, and the tone often more inflammatory than informative. These reports served to stoke settler anxieties, justify the federal government's campaigns of removal, and reinforce the prevailing belief that westward expansion was both inevitable and righteous.

In the northern states, especially Minnesota and the surrounding territories still raw from the bloodletting of the Dakota War of 1862, the press took a keener interest. Papers like the St. Paul Pioneer, The Minnesota State News, and The Dubuque Herald printed serialized accounts of General Henry Sibley's pursuit of the Dakota across the plains. Dispatches breathlessly detailed encounters near Big Mound, Dead Buffalo Lake, and Stony Lake, often written with a lurid flair that emphasized the danger posed by *"marauding bands"* and *"hostile Indians."* These stories painted the Dakota people in the language of fear and menace, describing them not as sovereign peoples defending their homes, but as dangerous remnants of a crushed rebellion that had not yet learned their lesson.

The national papers such as the New York Times, Harper's Weekly, and The Philadelphia Inquirer, occasionally picked up wire reports or reprinted stories from the frontier, but they rarely led with them. Their editors were far more concerned with the battles of Chancellorsville and Gettysburg, the draft riots in New York, or the movements of General Grant along the Mississippi. When they did reference the Indian campaigns, it was often with a paragraph or two noting a successful skirmish, the destruction of a village, or the capture of a group of refugees, always framed as signs of progress and civilization pushing westward.

In the Southwest, the local press more regularly chronicled the campaign against the Navajo. The Santa Fe New Mexican, under the guidance of territorial loyalists, reported enthusiastically on Kit Carson's scorched-earth campaign in the canyons and mesas of northern New Mexico. Stories lauded Carson's destruction of crops and confiscation of livestock, presenting the suffering of the Navajo as an unfortunate but necessary step toward peace and development. The military's plan to forcibly remove the entire Navajo population to Bosque Redondo was described as a rational solution to an *"Indian problem."* The human cost of this policy, the starvation, exposure, and death that would soon follow went largely unmentioned.

Meanwhile, in Indian Territory, the press coverage was sparser and more deeply colored by politics. Southern newspapers such as the Richmond Examiner and the Charleston Mercury occasionally praised the efforts of General Stand Watie and his Cherokee troops, portraying them as symbols of Southern strength and Native loyalty to the Confederate cause. Yet the coverage was often cursory, written from afar, and laden with romanticized notions of *"noble savages"* fighting for the Southern homeland. Little space was given to the internal civil war among the Five Civilized Tribes especially the blood feuds and retributive killings between pro-Union and pro-Confederate Native factions. In truth, most Southern editors were more interested in Watie's occasional raids on Union supply lines than in the broader suffering of the Cherokee Nation, which had already endured a forced removal within living memory.

Northern coverage of Indian Territory was equally limited, and what little there was focused on tribal loyalty as a political issue. Editorials in papers like The Chicago Tribune or The Cincinnati Gazette questioned whether Native allies could be trusted, particularly as Union recruiters struggled to raise troops in border states. Some coverage hinted at betrayal or barbarism among Confederate-aligned tribes, while pro-Union tribal militias, such as the Indian Home Guard were praised but rarely featured in any depth.

What united nearly all this press coverage, North and South, was a fundamental dehumanization of Native people. Descriptions of massacres, village burnings, and mass displacements were stripped of moral ambiguity. The narratives rarely questioned the legitimacy of U.S. expansion, or the brutal tactics used against Indigenous communities. To the average reader in New York, St. Paul, or Charleston, the stories from the West were confirmation that the frontier was dangerous, that the military was bringing order, and that Indian resistance was a stubborn relic of a bygone age. There were few dissenting voices. A scattering of abolitionist and Quaker publications raised concerns about the treatment of Native Americans, citing broken treaties and wanton cruelty but they were peripheral, their warnings drowned in the roar of Civil War headlines.

In essence, the Indian campaigns of 1863 were a war within a war, and the press treated them as such. They were important only insofar as they touched on the safety of white settlers or the strategic movement of troops. For Native Americans, the stories told in the press were often the first and last, public recognition of tragedies that would unfold in silence.

The Indian Wars of 1863 unfolded in scattered battles, desperate ambushes, retaliatory raids, and government campaigns marked by destruction and forced removal. And though the attention of the nation was fixed on the Civil War, thousands of miles from the eastern battlefields, Native peoples were engaged in a war to survive.

In the northern plains, the aftermath of the Dakota Uprising bled into the new year. General Henry Sibley's pursuit of fleeing Dakota warriors led to a string of violent engagements in the Dakota Territory, at Big Mound, Dead Buffalo Lake, and Stony Lake. resulting in the deaths of as many as two hundred Dakota, with dozens more captured or driven westward. Thirty to forty Union soldiers also fell during these actions, far from the accolades of the Civil War theaters.

In the high deserts of the Southwest, General Carleton's campaign against the Mescalero Apache intensified. Villages were burned, food stores destroyed, and entire bands were marched to Bosque Redondo. Disease, exposure, and despair killed hundreds more. At the same time, Cochise and his Chiricahua warriors continued their elusive war from the mountains, frustrating military campaigns but also suffering from increasing scarcity and encroachment.

Farther west, in one of the most tragic and overlooked events of the year, over three hundred Shoshone men, women, and children were killed in a dawn assault along the Bear River in what is now Idaho. Carried out by Union troops under Colonel Patrick Connor, the attack was less a battle than a massacre, marked by indiscriminate killing and the destruction of a village. It remains one of the deadliest single acts of violence against Native Americans in U.S. history.

In total, the Indian Wars of 1863 may have claimed the lives of 1,100 Native people, many of them noncombatants. Roughly 150 to 250 soldiers and settlers died in related skirmishes and reprisals. The numbers are necessarily imprecise, scattered across journals, military dispatches, oral histories, and conflicting reports, but the pattern is unmistakable.

Each number masks a name, a family, a story. A son who would not return from a hunting trip. A village elder who died singing a prayer. A child whose grave was never marked. The year 1863 is rightly remembered for the turning points of the Civil War. But as the Union fought to define freedom and the Confederacy to preserve its vision of sovereignty, another America was being shaped in silence, one marked by conquest, resistance, and the erasure of nations that had been here long before the Republic.

The Indian Wars were not mere sideshows.

CHAPTER 10
BLOOD, BANDAGES, MEDICINE & MORTALITY

The Civil War was fought not only on fields of honor and carnage, but also in makeshift hospitals, tented encampments, and the dim interiors of commandeered churches and barns. For every shot fired on the front lines in 1863, there was a corresponding agony off the field: a soldier writhing in pain, a nurse wiping a brow, a surgeon reaching for the saw.

More soldiers in the Civil War died of disease than from combat. It is estimated that total deaths from the civil war were near 750,000 with an estimated 500,000 of those deaths caused by disease. Unsound hygiene, dietary deficiencies, and battle wounds set the stage for epidemic infection, while inadequate information about disease causation greatly hampered disease prevention, diagnosis, and treatment. Pneumonia, typhoid, diarrhea/dysentery, and malaria were the predominant illnesses. Infectious diseases, and epidemics played a major role in halting several major campaigns. These delays, coming at a crucial point early in the war might have prolonged the fighting by as much as two years.

In 1863, armies remained ignorant of the impact of germs, and sanitation was haphazard at best. Camp latrines, called *"sinks,"* were often dug too close to cooking or sleeping areas. Flies swarmed, carrying typhoid, dysentery, and cholera from feces to food. Drinking water came from contaminated streams or shared barrels. The very ground upon which these men camped and fought became a vector for infection.

Sanitation and Disease

The hospitals of the war in 1863 were not buildings designed for healing. Instead, they were converted churches, barns, schoolhouses, private homes, hotels, and, most often, canvas tents pitched hurriedly behind the front lines. The architecture of mercy was improvised, shaped by urgency and necessity, not design. There were two types of hospitals: field hospitals and general hospitals. Often homes, churches, barns and other local buildings were converted to rudimentary hospitals. Surgeries took place on dining tables or doors removed for that purpose. Doctors performed as quickly as possible because the hospitals were typically understaffed, and the number of wounded was often overwhelming.

During the First Battle of Manassas, Sudley Church was converted by Union forces into a field hospital. The pulpit was turned into an operating table and pews removed to make room for the wounded. Blankets and straw were laid down on the church floor for bedding. William Croffut, a local reporter who was present at the battle recorded *"it was a sickening spectacle... pulpit had the appearance of a drug store...the church floors were so overcrowded with wounded that it was difficult to get across by stepping carefully"*.

Homes close to the battlefield were also converted into hospitals, often without permission of the owner. One house called Portici was on the battlefield and converted into a hospital early on the afternoon of the 21st. Fannie Ricketts described the scene of a hospital she visited which apparently typifies the field hospital experience: *"Two men dead and covered with blood are carried down the stairs as I waited to let them pass. On a table in the open hall a man was undergoing amputation of the leg. At the foot of the stairs two bloody legs lay and through all I went to I went to my husband...In the opposite room are ten dying or wounded men. Next to us are three, one with a gangrenous thigh where it is amputated. The smell is horrible. In another room are five Carolinians, one dying, son of Henry S. Middleton. His father is with him... Downstairs there are some forty men in various stages of death or possible recovery. Blood runs on the floor, the smell is dreadful, but no language can describe it..."*

Approaching a field hospital in the aftermath of a battle like Antietam, Gettysburg or Chancellorsville, one would first notice the chaos outside. Ambulances, wagons pulled by two or four horses, stood in line, waiting to unload their human cargo. Wounded men groaned, some clinging to consciousness, others slumped motionless as blood soaked the boards beneath them. Tents, if available, were arranged haphazardly in rows. In some cases, no tents existed at all, and the wounded lay on the ground under makeshift shelters of canvas and poles. Bloody bandages were piled nearby, sometimes burned, often left to fester. The smell was unmistakable: a mix of smoke, blood, urine, and the ever-present stench of decay. Flies swarmed around wounds and discarded food. Buckets of water, often murky, sat outside for cleaning hands or instruments, though they were rarely changed. Occasionally, a flag bearing a red cross or other insignia fluttered in the breeze to mark the hospital zone, a courtesy often ignored by artillerymen on both sides.

If the hospital was in a building, pews would have been shoved aside, desks stacked in corners, beds crammed in rows, or men laid directly on the floor. Windows were opened for ventilation, when possible, but flies and foul air still hovered. If the hospital was under canvas, straw or old blankets covered the cold earth, and men lay side by side, limbs bound with cloth, eyes wide with pain or dulled by morphine. Light filtered in from oil lamps or sunlight through canvas, casting long shadows. The din was constant with moans, ragged coughing, orders shouted between attendants, and the clatter of surgical tools. Buckets of bloodied rags and amputated limbs were pushed to the side of the room. Surgeons operated on tables blackened with dried blood, surrounded by piles of instruments, bone saws, knives, scalpels, wiped on aprons or dipped in tepid water.

There was no separation by ailment or injury. Typhoid patients lay nearby to men with open gunshot wounds. Nurses did their best to tend to all, changing dressings, spooning broth or hardtack to feverish mouths, reading letters from home. In the rare moments of silence, the human spirit flickered. A wounded man murmuring a hymn. A chaplain offering last rites. A nurse adjusting a blanket. A handwritten letter clutched in a bandaged hand.

These makeshift hospitals, though primitive, were vessels of courage and compassion. Their walls, whether of brick or canvas, echoed with more suffering and salvation than any battlefield.

Disease tore through encampments with terrifying regularity. Measles, mumps, smallpox, and pneumonia were constant threats. Soldiers arriving from rural areas had little immunity to such contagions, and no vaccination campaigns existed to prepare them. Sanitation officers were appointed in some regiments, but their advice was frequently ignored. One Union officer remarked that men *"took more kindly to lice than to lectures."* General George McClellan tried to enforce strict sanitary codes early in the war, but by 1863 those codes were often neglected under the press of movement and battle.

In the general hospitals, it was easier to follow the Medical Department's rules and regulations set forth to maintain the cleanliness of a hospital and the well-being of the patients. Many general hospitals were fully equipped with their own kitchens, laundries, mess-rooms, baggage-room, linen-room, storeroom, and guardhouse. Some hospitals even had a bakery, chapel, bathhouse, dead-house, as well as offices, houses, stables and privies in which nurses, surgeons, ward-masters and matrons worked. Within these buildings, hundreds of medical staff worked to treat patients.

Daily life in a general hospital could be monotonous for both patients and staff. These hospitals were cleaned daily, and patients bathed. Clothing was washed, meals cooked, dishes cleaned, and medical supplies were inventoried. The staff made rounds to check on their patients, feeding them, changing bandages, and administering medicines. Some nurses stopped to talk with patients, write their letters, and provide comfort. Amanda Akin Stearns who worked at the Armory Hospital in Washington D.C, regularly worked an eighteen-hour day. She was *"up at six, dispensed medicines, served breakfast, dispensed medicines, served dinner, wrote letters, dispensed medicine, served supper, and wrote letters."*

For soldiers being treated in these hospitals, life could be monotonous for those bedridden, with little to do except chat with their neighbors, sleep, read, until the nurses made their rounds, or they had a visitor. One soldier, Albion F. Hubbard of the 1st Massachusetts Calvary was unable to write with his ulcers and so Walt Whitman took up the pen for him, writing for Hubbard on June 12, 1863:

Dear friend,

As I have a favorable opportunity, by means of a visitor to the hospital, who is now sitting by the side of my bed, I write you again, making the second time this week, to let you know that I am tolerably comfortable, have good care & medical attendance, & hope to be up before long—have been up & moving around the ward both this forenoon & afternoon though I move around pretty slow as I am weak yet—A member of the Massachusetts Relief society has called upon me & given me a few trifles - My diarrhea is still somewhat troublesome yet I feel in pretty good spirits—I send you an envelope with my address on— Keep a copy of it & this one you please put a stamp on & write to me—Please give my love to the friends in the village & tell them I should like to hear from them, & give them my direction here in hospital—Good bye for the present

Unfortunately, Private Hubbard died on June 20th, 1863

Medical Treatment and Amputations

The most notorious symbol of Civil War medicine was the amputation table. Bullets and shrapnel shattered bone and tore through muscle. With no reliable way to clean deep wounds, doctors favored amputation as the most effective way to save a life. Some surgeries were performed within minutes of injury, others hours later, under skies still smoky with cannon fire. Ether and a chloroform inhaler were most often used with increasing frequency by 1863, but not always. Many soldiers underwent surgery fully conscious, biting leather straps or screaming into rags. A skilled surgeon could remove a limb in under ten minutes. The blades were rarely sterilized. Tools were wiped on bloodstained aprons or rinsed in dirty water before reuse.

The typical field hospital was chaotic and grim. Wounded soldiers lay on straw-strewn floors, moaning in pain, often coated in dirt and blood. Supplies were scarce. Bandages were re-used. Instruments were limited. Maggots, ironically, sometimes saved lives by eating away infected flesh. Yet, the survival rate for amputees was higher than expected, nearly 75 percent if performed early enough and outside the chest cavity. But many survivors endured lifelong pain and disability. Prosthetics, crudely made from wood and leather, became a common sight among veterans.

Physicians, Nurses, and Competency

The army medical corps was overwhelmed. Most doctors had little to no surgical experience before enlisting. The war forced a brutal crash course in battlefield medicine. Some rose to the occasion. Others faltered. By 1863, the U.S. Sanitary Commission had begun to organize medical care more efficiently, creating an ambulance corps and establishing triage procedures. But there were still too few trained physicians and too many casualties.

Competence varied widely. The North generally had better resources and training. Confederate doctors often operated under appalling conditions with minimal supplies. Confederate Surgeon General Samuel Preston Moore worked tirelessly to improve standards, creating examination boards for new surgeons, but the South's isolation and lack of industrial base limited what could be done. One Union doctor, Jonathan Letterman, revolutionized battlefield medicine by introducing the first true ambulance system and reorganizing field hospitals into structured units of care. His innovations at Antietam and Fredericksburg were refined by 1863 and saved countless lives at Gettysburg and beyond.

Before the war, nursing was not considered a profession. By 1863, thousands of women had upended Victorian norms by tending to the wounded. Clara Barton, who would later find the American Red Cross, worked tirelessly at the front lines, delivering supplies and comfort. Dorothea Dix, appointed Superintendent of Army Nurses, demanded strict qualifications and discipline among her volunteers, though many male surgeons resented their presence.

African American women and formerly enslaved people also worked as nurses and aides, often with little recognition. Some were pressed into service by

Union or Confederate forces. Others volunteered. Harriet Tubman herself led missions behind enemy lines and later worked in Union hospitals. The devotion of these caregivers added a human touch to the war's otherwise industrial slaughter. Letters from soldiers often mentioned *"angel nurses"* whose kindness seemed to transcend the hellscape around them.

Medical personnel worked with limited resources. Southern doctors especially faced severe shortages due to the Union blockade. They reused bandages, made medicines from local herbs, and salvaged tools from dead soldiers. A Confederate doctor near Jackson, Mississippi, wrote: *"We perform miracles with whiskey, willow bark, and thread. The men deserve more. We do what we can."*

Officers and Enlisted Men: Unequal Wounds

Medical care was not democratic. Officers were treated more swiftly and with better resources. They were more likely to receive private tents or access to rear-area hospitals. While battlefield triage was evolving, especially under competent surgeons in the Union army, treatment often reflected rank. Officers were more likely to be treated earlier, especially when resources were limited. They were also more likely to be removed from the front more quickly for care. In cases where amputation or experimental procedures were on the table, officers might receive more conservative treatment, aiming to preserve limbs or quality of life. A Union soldier from the Army of the Potomac wrote bitterly in 1863. *"The captain was removed to a house nearby and given the attention of two surgeons. We lay on the grass all night with only our comrades to bind our wounds."*

Officers, if their injuries allowed, were more likely to be evacuated to private homes, hotels, or dedicated officers' wards in military general hospitals. Some wealthier officers could pay for private doctors or nurses, which was not an option for enlisted men. And the more skilled surgeons took care of wounded officers. A Confederate surgeon from North Carolina admitted in his diary. *"It is hard to admit, but we are told to focus our efforts on those whose recovery may bear fruit for the cause. This generally means the officers, while the privates... must be left to Providence."*

Enlisted men, on the other hand, lay in open fields or packed ward tents, awaiting help that sometimes never came. Officers were also more likely to survive amputations, not only due to priority treatment but because they generally had better overall health and diet. Enlisted men, often immigrants, farmhands, or the urban poor, were already malnourished and susceptible to disease.

Yet in many hospitals, nurses and volunteer workers blurred the line of class. They tended to all who suffered. Many wrote memoirs detailing both gallantry and misery without regard to rank. The war had a way of stripping away societal layers, if only briefly, in the face of shared suffering.

Officers who died were more likely to have their bodies returned home, sometimes in the accompaniment of honor guards. Common soldiers were most often buried in mass graves or hastily dug trenches, often without being identified.

Medical Technology and Innovation

Eventually design was implemented in providing ambulances, both two and for wheel varieties, allowing injured soldiers to get to where they could be treated more quickly. In the same vein, stretchers were improved to allow easier transport over rough ground.

While germs were not often considered during treatment, the war accelerated innovation in medical technology. Surgical kits were mass-produced. Standard-issue medical manuals, like The Handbook for the Military Surgeon, were distributed to field doctors. Quinine became a staple for treating malaria. Bromine was discovered to prevent gangrene. And though primitive by modern standards, the war laid the foundation for post-war advancements.

The U.S. Sanitary Commission and Christian Commission helped standardize nursing care and improve hospital conditions. Innovations included the use of chloroform and ether for anesthesia, the adoption of triage systems to prioritize care , an ambulance corps to transport the wounded more efficiently. Still, infection was rampant. Sterilization was poorly understood. Many soldiers who survived gunshots later died of gangrene or sepsis.

The sheer number of casualties, more than 50,000 at Gettysburg alone, created an urgency that spurred organization. Battlefield triage, mobile field hospitals, and medical supply chains emerged from chaos. These became the precursors to modern emergency medicine.

Despite the horror, medical personnel developed critical innovations. Field hospitals became more organized. Survival rates for amputations improved. And the war created a generation of doctors and nurses who would bring their experience into postwar medical reform. One Union nurse, Louisa May Alcott, later wrote: *"I had no dream of heroism — only duty, sorrow, and an endless ache in the hands. But I would do it all again."*

It had been invented earlier, but the stethoscope was used extensively during the Civil War for diagnosing chest injuries and respiratory conditions like pneumonia and tuberculosis.

Prison Camps: Hell Beyond the Battlefield

Although medical care improved over the course of the Civil War, prisoners often received inadequate and sometimes negligent medical care in prison camps. When prisoner exchange ended in the summer of 1863. both the Union and Confederate armies began placing large numbers of captured men into prison camps. Both sides were unprepared for this turn of events, and what followed proved disastrous. Soon the prison camps were populated with two or three times more soldiers than for which they were designed

Nowhere was the medical crisis more horrifying than in the prison camps. By 1863, thousands of captured soldiers languished in Confederate and Union prisons. Andersonville in Georgia would become infamous later in the war, but even in 1863, places like Libby Prison in Richmond and Camp Douglas in Illinois were overcrowded, unsanitary, and lethal.

Diseases ran rampant. Medical staff were scarce. Rations were poor or rotting. The overall mortality rates in prisons on both sides were similar, and quite high. Many Southern prisons were in regions with high disease rates, and were routinely short of medicine, doctors, food and ice. Northerners often believed their men were being deliberately weakened and killed in Confederate prisons and demanded that conditions in Northern prisons be equally harsh, even though shortages were not a problem in the North. About 56,000 soldiers died in prisons during the war, accounting for almost 10% of all Civil War fatalities.

Letters from prisoners describe the stench, the rats, the silence of death and sometimes, the kindness of a chaplain or fellow prisoner who shared their last crust of bread.

Perhaps the most notorious prison camp of the war was that of Andersonville, Georgia where nearly 13,000 Union prisoners died. Guards and prisoners often suffered alike, but Confederate camps lacked food and medicine far more acutely. Latrines overflowed. Fresh water was rare. Medical care was nearly nonexistent. Prisoners were treated as combatants who had forfeited certain rights, but the line between criminal neglect and systemic collapse was thin.

CHAPTER 11
CONFEDERACY ABROAD

Even as the Confederate States of America fought to forge a nation on the battlefield, it struggled to sustain itself economically. International trade of cotton, their only real export was of paramount importance to the ability of the Confederacy to sustain a war. The South also exported to a lesser extent, tobacco, and goods for navies (tar, pitch, turpentine, and resin), that were necessary for wood ship building. Industry in the south was sparse, agricultural was king. Prior to the war exporting agricultural goods was the lifeline of the South.

Foreign sales could provide solid currency, supply weapons and equipment, and Southern leaders hoped to compel Britain and France to support the Confederate cause. From the earliest days of the war, that hope collided with the harsh reality of the Union's naval blockades of key southern ports, shifting markets, and the relentless reach of Union sea power, which grew significantly as the war wore on.

At the center of the South's export ambitions stood cotton, the crop that had made the region wealthy in the antebellum years. Known in political and diplomatic rhetoric as *"King Cotton,"* it was believed to be a commodity so essential to British and French textile industries that those powers would have no choice but to intervene in the conflict or at least formally recognize Confederate independence. Confederate President Jefferson Davis and his advisors embraced that belief, and in 1861 they made a fateful decision to withhold cotton exports voluntarily, aiming to create a *"cotton famine"* in Europe that would pressure governments to act.

The strategy backfired. In Britain, where industrialists had stockpiled Southern cotton in anticipation of war, the initial disruption was manageable. When shortages did hit in earnest by 1862, alternative sources from India, Egypt, and Brazil helped to fill the gap. With those new trade partners Britain was no longer reliant on the Confederacy to supply their textile economy. Moreover, public opinion in Britain, particularly among the working class, leaned against the

South due to its defense of slavery. Instead of forcing intervention, the embargo not only expanded the trading partners of Britain but also deepened the South's economic adversity.

By mid-1861, the United States Navy had begun implementing a blockade of Southern ports. This action was part of the so-called Anaconda Plan, devised by General Winfield Scott. The plan was basically to surround the South by land and sea and slowly tighten the noose until it could survive no more.

The blockade in 1861 included a total of 42 warships, but by the end of the war there were 600 ships. Though initially porous, the blockade quickly became more effective as the Navy built and sailed more ships. By 1863, most major ports including New Orleans, Charleston, Savannah, and Mobile were either captured or tightly sealed from exporting. The South was effectively choked off from legal, large-scale trade.

Of course, trade did not cease entirely. The Confederacy turned to blockade running, using fast, low-profile steamships to evade Union patrols. These ships, often built in British shipyards and operated by British crews under British flags, ran routes from Southern ports to neutral havens like Nassau, Bahamas, Havana, Cuba and Bermuda. These activities were not officially sanctioned by the British government. From these waystations, Southern cotton could reach Liverpool, and in return, the Confederacy could receive arms, ammunition, boots, cloth, and even luxuries like coffee and wine.

When a Union warship intercepted a blockade runner, usually after a tense chase often conducted at night or in fog, the vessel was boarded, and both ship and cargo were seized. The captains and crews were taken prisoner, though they were often treated civilly, especially if they were British or other foreign nationals. The Union Navy then placed a prize crew aboard the captured ship and escorted it to the nearest Union prize court, usually located in Northern port cities like New York, Philadelphia, or Boston.

The seizure was subject to legal review under the rules of naval warfare and maritime law. These "prize courts" examined the circumstances of the capture, the ship's registry, manifest, and ownership documents to determine whether the vessel had indeed violated the blockade.

If the court ruled that the capture of the vessel was legal, which it almost always did, then the ship and cargo were auctioned, which often brought substantial sums of cash to the captors. Proceeds from the auction were distributed as prize money to the capturing vessel's officers and crew, providing a strong financial incentive to enforce the blockade. Some captured ships were refitted and repurposed by the Union Navy to serve as gunboats, patrol vessels, now on the side of the Union.

Confederate sailors from the captured vessels were treated as prisoners of war and were most often sent to prison camps. British or neutral crews were more complicated. If they were found to have been knowingly attempting to break the blockade, they would likely be detained temporarily or fined, but they were often released, particularly early in the war when the Lincoln administration was careful not to provoke Britain or France, because their neutrality was very important in the North's war effort. In some high-profile cases, such as the Trent Affair, diplomatic tensions flared, especially when neutral rights seemed to be at stake.

The profits could be enormous for those who succeeded in running the blockades and were able to take their goods to British colonies. If they were able to successfully outmaneuver the blockade, they could be expected to profit $10,000 per trip or more, depending on what they were carrying. In the early years of the war, as many as eight out of every ten blockade runners made it through. But as the Union Navy grew and the blockade tightened, the risks rose. By 1864, only about half of the attempts succeeded, and each run became more dangerous. The Union Navy captured or destroyed nearly 1,500 vessels during its blockade, and the Confederacy struggled to replace its losses.

In an attempt to circumvent the Gulf blockade, the South also turned westward. The Texas-Mexico border, especially the twin towns of Brownsville and Matamoros on opposite sides of the Rio Grande, became a critical trade route. Cotton was carted overland to the river, ferried across to Mexico where the Union blockade held no jurisdiction and sold to European merchants. From there, it could be shipped legally to Europe. In return, Confederate agents brought back munitions, medicines, and textiles. The Matamoros trade remained active until mid-1864, when Union forces occupied the region.

Despite the enormous obstacles, the South's cotton did make its way to Europe though in quantities far smaller than prewar levels. British and French merchants were eager to buy, and Confederate agents such as James Bulloch in Liverpool coordinated clandestine shipments and purchases of war matériel. Cotton was even used as collateral in European financial markets. The most famous example was the Erlanger Loan, a series of bonds sold in Europe in 1863, backed by Southern cotton. While the bonds were initially popular, investor confidence waned as Union victories mounted, and the likelihood of Confederate success diminished.

Other exports continued to be shipped, but on a smaller scale. Tobacco, once a major Virginia export, found its way to France, where demand remained strong. Naval goods such as turpentine, tar, and rosin, essential for shipbuilding and industrial processes, were also traded, though the volume paled in comparison to cotton. Livestock, foodstuffs, and raw minerals were sometimes exported through Texas or with the aid of smugglers operating in the Caribbean.

By 1865, with Union armies advancing from all directions and the Southern economy in shambles, Confederate trade was reduced to a trickle. The dream of funding the war with cotton wealth had evaporated. The South's ports were sealed, its foreign partners reluctant, and its treasury nearly empty. In the final analysis, the Confederacy's limited export capacity hampered by geography, diplomacy, and Northern steadfastness contributed greatly to its inability to sustain a protracted war.

The failure of King Cotton diplomacy was not merely a blow to Confederate pride; it was a fatal miscalculation. Cotton was indeed powerful, but not powerful enough to turn war in the favor of the South.

The Confederacy had not sought the help of Russia in its diplomatic efforts, and in 1863 Russia sent naval fleets to New York and San Franciso. Officially the ships were stationed there to protect Russian interests, but their presence also served as a show of goodwill to the Union and a warning to Britain and France to stay out.

For the Confederate States of America, diplomatic recognition by a European power was most sought and coveted from Great Britain and France. Such recognition was seen not merely as a badge of legitimacy, but as a potential lifeline to establishing their sovereignty. From the earliest days of secession, Southern leaders believed that the economic lure of the expansive cotton industry in the south would prove irresistible to much of Europe but especially to the two great powers it needed on its side.

President Jefferson Davis, himself a former U.S. Secretary of War, understood the power of perception in international affairs. He appointed respected envoys such as James Mason to Britain and John Slidell to France with the aim of winning over European opinion. At the end of October 1861, these two slipped through the Union blockade to Havana, Cuba, and boarded the British mail steamer *Trent* enroute to Europe. Their mission was simple: to persuade Britain and France to recognize the Confederacy as a sovereign nation and to encourage formal alliances. On November 8, 1861, the *USS San Jacinto*, under the command of Captain Charles Wilkes, intercepted the *Trent* in the neutral waters of the Old Bahama Channel. Wilkes ordered the seizure of Mason and Slidell and brought them aboard his ship, escorting them as prisoners to Fort Warren in Boston Harbor.

The mission of these diplomats was to present the South as a peace-seeking nation under siege, one defending its liberty against a tyrannical and centralized Northern government. They were to play upon Europe's lingering fears of American democratic radicalism and sought to frame the Confederacy as a bulwark of order and conservative values. The Trent issue was of great concern to Britain, feeling their sovereignty had been attacked, and soon British sentiment against the North grew. Lincoln ordered the release of the southern diplomats early in 1862 to avoid conflict with Britain. Eventually Mason and Sidell returned to Europe, but the momentum of their intended efforts had subsided, they were unable to obtain formal recognition of any European nation.

The South's case was hampered from the outset by the moral stain of slavery. Though slavery still existed in some European countries, abolitionist sentiment was growing steadily in Britain, particularly among the working classes and liberal intellectuals. The spectacle of a new nation built explicitly to preserve human bondage did not sit easily with much of British or French public opinion. Lord Palmerston, Britain's Prime Minister, and his Foreign Secretary, Lord John Russell, were intrigued by the prospect of a divided America but wary of acting without clear justification. Recognition, they feared, might mean war with the Union and damage to British commercial interests in the North.

The Union, for its part, made it a central priority to make sure it prevented any such recognition. Secretary of State Seward was an experienced and canny diplomat. He coordinated a far-reaching campaign to neutralize Confederate influence abroad. His efforts were supported by an increasingly effective network of U.S. diplomats, commercial agents, and journalists stationed throughout Europe. Seward warned foreign governments that recognition of the Confederacy would be viewed as a hostile act by the United States and might provoke war.

At the same time, Union diplomacy cleverly turned the South's King Cotton narrative on its head. While Britain did indeed suffer a brief *"cotton famine"* that put thousands out of work in Lancashire, England and elsewhere, the North supplied Europe with grain during a time of poor harvests, a commodity far more essential than cotton to their actual survival. Northern wheat and corn shipments helped offset food shortages in Europe and gave the Union considerable leverage.

Throughout 1862, Confederate hopes for recognition remained high, particularly as General Robert E. Lee won a string of victories in Virginia. Confederate agents met regularly with European leaders, and the French Emperor, Napoleon III, seemed more amenable than the British to recognizing the South, especially if Britain took the first step. Yet the crucial link never came. A joint Franco-British intervention was discussed privately but never materialized.

Any potential for European recognition of the Confederacy began to weaken definitively in late 1862 and early 1863. Lincoln's preliminary Emancipation Proclamation, announced in September 1862 and enacted on January 1, 1863, reframed the conflict in terms of slavery and human freedom. Lincoln was acutely aware of the foreign policy implications of the Emancipation Proclamation, especially its impact on preventing Great Britain from recognizing the Confederacy. In fact, it was one of the central motivations for issuing the proclamation when he did. Though it applied only to areas still in rebellion, the Proclamation made it politically untenable for any European government, particularly one like Britain where abolition was a powerful movement, to support the Confederacy.

Britain had already abolished slavery throughout its empire in 1833, and public opinion, particularly among the working class, was firmly anti-slavery. This tension placed the British government in a precarious position: while economic interests leaned toward recognition of the South, moral and political considerations cautioned against it. Lincoln understood this and in his cabinet meetings he expressed both the military and diplomatic urgency of issuing the Proclamation.

In 1863, the British House of Commons voted against recognizing the Confederacy. This was followed by a de facto diplomatic crisis that soured Southern relations with Britain, France, and Spain. In a dramatic and telling move, Confederate Secretary of State Judah Benjamin took steps in October 1863 that reflected the deepening isolation of the Confederacy on the world stage.

As hopes for European recognition faded, Benjamin issued an order banning all foreign residents in the Confederacy from communicating with their diplomats in Washington. This extraordinary restriction effectively severed private diplomatic correspondence and underscored the Confederate leadership's growing distrust of foreign nationals, especially those from neutral nations suspected of harboring Union sympathies or of reporting Confederate conditions back to their home governments.

At the same time, Benjamin ordered the expulsion of all foreign diplomats and consular officials from Confederate-held territory. It was a striking break with conventional international norms. By doing so, the Confederacy not only cut itself off from any remaining diplomatic presence within its borders but also signaled to the world that it would tolerate no backchannel ties to the U.S. government, even at the risk of appearing belligerent or diplomatically irrational. Some saw the move as defensive posturing; others saw it as desperation.

Several British financiers built and operated most of the blockade runners, spending hundreds of millions of pounds on them. They were staffed by sailors and officers on leave from the Royal Navy and regularly used the British territories of Bahamas, Bermuda, and Nova Scotia as strategic stopovers. During the war, British blockade runners delivered the Confederacy 60 percent of its weapons, 35% of the lead for its bullets, 75% of ingredients for its powder, and most of the cloth used to make its uniforms; this assistance may have lengthened the Civil War by two years and cost 400,000 lives of soldiers and civilians on both sides

By transforming the Union war aim into a moral crusade, Lincoln closed the door on Southern hopes of international legitimacy. The war was no longer a mere civil conflict over sovereignty or federalism it was a battle over the future of slavery. Confederate diplomats, once treated with cautious interest, found doors closing around them. Public opinion in Europe shifted decisively in favor of the Union.

Military events reinforced this trend. The Union victory at Antietam gave the North the strategic boost it needed, while Confederate defeats at Vicksburg and Gettysburg in 1863 further weakened Southern credibility abroad. European leaders, always skeptical of the South's long-term prospects, saw little gain in backing a cause that increasingly looked doomed.

In 1863 Confederate diplomatic efforts moved their focus from Britain to France, with the Union's counter-diplomacy following. Weapon purchases also moved almost exclusively to France after the Union successfully argued in court that Confederate weapons purchases were a breach of British neutrality. Napoleon III's offers to mediate peace between the Union and the Confederacy were angrily rejected by Seward, and by 1864 he lost interest due to the lack of Confederate victories and the outbreaks of the January Uprising and the Second Schleswig War in Europe.

In the end, neither Great Britain nor France ever recognized the Confederacy. Both governments maintained a policy of official neutrality, while continuing limited trade and diplomatic contact with both sides. Had recognition come early, perhaps following a major Confederate victory, it might have changed the course of the war. But it did not, and the Confederate dream of international legitimacy died a quiet death, never having risen beyond the hopeful dispatches of its agents abroad.

The Union's triumph in the diplomatic war was no less significant than its victories on the battlefield. By holding Europe at bay, it denied the Confederacy the chance to shift the balance. The war remained a domestic conflict, and its resolution, for better or worse, would come from within.

In correspondence to a friend Lincoln said *"The emancipation policy, and the use of colored troops, constitute the heaviest blow yet dealt to the rebellion. Keep it and you keep the Union. Destroy it, and you will not only lose the Union, but destroy the democracy itself."*

Feeding the World with Northern Exports

Even as Union troops marched through Mississippi and the clash of troops engaged in confrontation from Tennessee to Virginia, the North had flourishing exports. Most important of which was grain. In 1863, there were food shortages in Europe, India and China. Grain was plentiful in the American North, and the Union became a lifeline to a hungry world.

While the South had banked its fortunes on cotton, the North quietly capitalized on breadstuffs, the essential grains that fed Europe's growing urban populations. Across the Atlantic, nations like Britain and France faced poor harvests and there was political unrest in Poland. In an effort to survive their crisis, they looked once more to American granaries. From the vast wheat fields of Ohio, Illinois, and Wisconsin, grain was shipped into the Great Lakes, through the Erie Canal, and eastward from the ports of New York and Boston.

Merchant vessels loaded with flour, corn, and salted meats sailed for Liverpool, Le Havre, and Hamburg. In return came gold, weapons, and finished goods, as well as something less tangible but no less important: a reinforcement of international neutrality from its trade partners. As long as the Union was feeding the world, it remained an economic partner too valuable to oppose.

Beyond agriculture, Northern manufacturers continued to produce and export machinery, tools, and rails, particularly to Latin America. The war had spurred innovation, and surplus output from armories and factories found markets abroad. Steam-powered sawmills, reapers, and mechanical looms became symbols of the Union's industrial might and became export staples.

Despite the constraints of war, Union shipping flourished. Merchant marine losses from Confederate raiders like the CSS Alabama (a ship manufactured in Britain) were real but did not cripple trade. In fact, some ships temporarily registered under foreign flags to protect themselves from *"piracy."* American-built clipper ships still sailed with unmatched speed and elegance across the globe.

And so, even in the midst of civil war, the North did not simply survive, it thrived as a commercial exporting power. It wielded economic leverage alongside military force, and in so doing, helped assure that no foreign nation would dare tilt the scale in favor of the Confederacy.

CHAPTER 12
NEW YORK DRAFT RIOTS

By 1863 voluntary enlistment in the Union Arny had slowed significantly. The military needed to be sustained, and the administration found it necessary to expand the ranks of the Army. The Enrollment Act of 1863 was introduced to the senate by Henry Wilson of Massachusetts, Chairman of the Senate Committee on Military Affairs. The act passed the Republican controlled Senate with a vote of 24-13 and with very little debate. It passed the Republican controlled House of Representatives, after an important structural amendment, with a vote of 115-49. The Senate then agreed with the House by a 35-11 vote.

On March 3, 1863, Abraham Lincoln signed the first conscription act in United States history into law. The act required all able-bodied male citizens, as well as immigrants who intended to become citizens between the ages of 25 and 45 to be *"liable to perform military duty in the service of the United States when called out by the President for that purpose."* African Americans were exempt from the draft since they were not yet considered citizens. All eligible men between the ages of 35 and 45 were to be enrolled into class one and drafted first. Class two consisted of married men between the ages of 35 and 45 and they were to be drafted only if class one had been used.

Any person enrolled and drafted could present a suitable substitute to go in his place. If someone could not find another person to go in for him, he could pay $300 to the Secretary of War for a substitute to be found and paid.

The following men were exempt from military duty due to this law:
o   Certain government officials including the Vice President, judges, heads of executive departments, as well as governors.
o   The only son of a widow who was dependent upon her support.
o   The only son of elderly or weak parents that were dependent on him
o   If there were two or more sons eligible for military duty that were taking care of their parents, the father would pick which son would be exempt. The responsibility would be given to the mother if the father was already deceased

o   The only brother of a child not yet 12 years old who had no mother or father.

o   The only father of a child not yet twelve years old.

o   If two members of a household were already in the military, the family could exempt up to two others.

The law was heavily skewed toward the war being fought by the children and husbands of the poor and middle class

In addition to the recently announced draft law, the Emancipation Proclamation had intensified fears among white working-class New Yorkers, particularly Irish immigrants, about job competition from freed African Americans. These anxieties were exacerbated by existing racial prejudices and economic insecurities, leading to increased hostility toward Black residents. The situation was further inflamed by sensationalist media and political rhetoric that stoked fears of African Americans undercutting wages and taking jobs .

At the time of the passage of the new conscription law, New York City was a Democratic stronghold, dominated by Tammany Hall, the powerful and corrupt Democratic political machine. The city's leadership, including influential former Mayor Fernando Wood, had at various times expressed sympathy for the South and hostility toward Lincoln. Wood even proposed that NYC secede from the Union and become a *"free city"* to continue its trade ties with the Confederacy. Many Irish and German immigrants in the city, fearful of job competition from freed slaves and angry over the forced draft, supported the Copperhead Democrats, a faction that opposed the war and emancipation.

Tensions Erupt

The first draft lottery in New York City occurred on Saturday, July 11, 1863, without incident. It was conducted at the Ninth District Provost Marshal's office, located at 77 Third Avenue, near 46th Street in Manhattan. A large crowd gathered to watch the drawing. The names of eligible men had been placed on slips of paper and drawn from a large, circular drum, not unlike a modern-day lottery machine. The process was intended to be orderly and impartial. Local newspapers were invited to observe. The first name drawn was Gilbert Mulqueen, an Irish-American laborer. There were an additional 1,200 names drawn from the Ninth Congressional District's enrollment list.

The draft was suspended on Sunday July 12, because the office was closed on Sunday. On Saturday there had been a large crowd to watch the drawing, and there had been some heckling and general discontent shown by the crowd. The Sunday pause gave local agitators and Democrats time to spread rumors that on poor Irish laborers were going to be forced into service. Church sermons, political and tavern meetings featuring anti-war oratory worked the people into a frenzy.

On July 13 when the picking of names continued, tensions had reached a boiling point. The crowd was littered with agitators, mobs, and gangs, as well as political ward bosses. A crowd led by volunteer firemen from Engine Company 33 attacked the draft office at Third Avenue and 47th Street, marking the beginning of the riots. The violence quickly escalated, targeting African Americans, abolitionists, and symbols of Republican authority.

The following day's edition of the New York Times reported: *"The excitement which had existed since the drawing of the draft on Saturday found vent yesterday in open and lawless violence. Crowds gathered at an early hour around the Ninth District draft office… A rough, turbulent mob surrounded the building, hooting and yelling, but few anticipated the rapidity and fury with which the first stone was thrown, the first torch applied… In less than an hour, the provost marshal's office was a heap of smoldering ruins."*

New York City erupted in fire and fury. Two leaders of the American Republic found themselves hurtling toward a quiet collision; one the governor of New York and one the President of the United States. The President had been worn thin by war. He clung to the fragile center of a fractured nation. The governor with national political ambitions and a support base of immigrant laborers, stood at the eye of the political storm. Horatio Seymour and Abraham Lincoln would never meet face-to-face, but their clash would reverberate through the Union for the next year.

Governor Seymour had returned to Albany from New York City just days before the first draft lottery names were drawn. A polished speaker and ardent Copperhead Democrat, Seymour was a fierce political opponent to the president. He had opposed the Emancipation Proclamation, questioned the constitutionality of conscription, and accused Lincoln of trampling civil liberties.

When the riots first erupted, Seymour rushed back to the city, but instead of condemning the violence, he addressed an angry crowd gathered at City Hall as *"My friends, I have come here because I am your friend."* With these words he urged the crowd to disperse peacefully and promised to advocate for a legal challenge to the draft. In the midst of arson, lynchings, and the beating of Black citizens, Seymour appealed, not necessarily for calm but for legal process. He promised to work to have the draft declared unconstitutional. He intended his tone to pacify the crowd, but it did nothing of the sort. The rioters had become even more emboldened. To Lincoln's circle of advisers, Seymore was on the edges of sedition. Later, Seymore tried to clarify his speech as trying to preserve peace and not to endorse violence.

Meanwhile, Lincoln remained largely silent in public. Privately, he was furious. In a letter to Secretary of State William Seward, he confided his alarm that the governor of the Union's largest state might be encouraging rebellion. Yet he resisted calls from radical Republicans to remove Seymour or declare martial law. Lincoln knew the danger of overreach. The war already walked a knife's edge in the border states; alienating New York's Democratic machine could tear the North in two.

But Seymour decided to take the promises of his speech to the president. In a letter to Lincoln dated July 18, 1863, he demanded that the draft be suspended in New York until its legality could be resolved in the courts. Lincoln's reply, dry and clipped, made clear his position: *"The draft will proceed. The rebellion must be put down."*

By year's end, the rift between the two men had become a canyon. Seymour was largely thought to be the likely Democratic nominee for the 1864 presidential race, though he would ultimately decline, paving the way for George McClellan. Still, the Draft Riots became a rallying cry for Lincoln's opponents. They portrayed Lincoln as a tyrant and Seymour as the champion of civil rights, quite ironical considering the race-based brutality of the riots themselves.

The Enrollment Act marked the first time the federal government enacted a compulsory draft of its citizens into the military. Its implementation was controversial from the beginning, especially in large urban centers. While the war had been raging for two years, many in the North, particularly among the working classes, had grown weary and resentful of the war. For months after the draft law was passed, registration efforts lagged as resistance quietly festered. Enrollment officers were met with suspicion, ridicule, and, in some neighborhoods, open hostility. Newspapers debated the legality and morality of the draft, and opposition simmered in saloons, churches, and labor halls.

What especially inflamed tensions was the inequity of the system. The law appeared to formalize class divisions, confirming fears that the war was being fought on the backs of the poor while the wealthy bought their way out.

By early July, with the first drawing of names scheduled for July 11, anxiety began to give way to fury. Editorials across the city warned of unrest. The New York Herald cautioned, *"There is a storm brewing... the draft will strike like lightning through the poorer wards."* Meanwhile, The New York Tribune defended the policy but acknowledged, *"The unequal burden of sacrifice has become a source of deep bitterness among the laboring classes."*

An anonymous letter published in The Irish-American read: *"If the government can afford to let the rich man buy his safety, it must also afford to listen when the poor man objects to being used as cannon fodder."*

New York's newspapers had become a battleground of their own, with some dedicated to fanning the flames of dissent, others trying in vain to extinguish them. Southern newspapers seized upon the chaos as evidence of Union hypocrisy and instability. The Richmond Examiner declared, *"The Yankee experiment is unraveling, not in the fields of Virginia, but in the streets of its own cities."*

Abolitionist voices, meanwhile, responded with horror and determination. The Liberator wrote, *"This is not a rebellion against conscription, it is a rebellion against justice, against freedom, and against the very soul of this republic."*

Frederick Douglass published an editorial in Douglass' Monthly stating, *"These riots reveal what we have long known: that slavery's shadow darkens every corner of this nation, not just the South, but the North as well. Yet we will not be turned back. This is the moment to press forward with greater resolve."* On the second day of the lottery, as the names were posted and the conscription offices began their work, the city exploded.

While Union victories were being celebrated at Gettysburg and Vicksburg, another front had opened, this one not on a battlefield, but in the heart of New York City. From July 13 to 16, 1863, the city descended into chaos as thousands of angry citizens, many of them Irish immigrants and working-class laborers, violently protested the implementation of the first federal military draft.

The City Burns

On the morning of Monday July 13, rioters unleashed their fury on the Ninth District Draft Office. They stormed the office and set it aflame. The fire ultimately destroyed an entire city block. The mob also directed its anger at New York's wealthy population, ransacking and burning mansions along Fifth

Avenue. However, the rioters' primary target was the city's African American community. What began as a protest against conscription quickly turned into the most destructive civil disturbance in American history, second only to the Civil War itself. Over four days, New York City was gripped by terror, as mobs vented their rage on government offices, political opponents, symbols of wealth, and above all, African Americans. The mobs prevented the firefighters of Engine Co. No. 18 from extinguishing the fire that they had set at the Colored Orphan Asylum.

There were an estimated 120 African Americans killed during the riots, many of which were thrown into the east river. Lynchings and beatings occurred in several neighborhoods many of which were not recorded. Blacks were hunted down by the mobs, dragged out of their homes and from their workplaces. They were attacked with bricks, clubs, and guns and some lynched. Men, women and children were treated the same. The Colored Orphan Asylum on Fifth Avenue, home to over 200 Black children, was looted and set ablaze. Miraculously, the children escaped before the flames consumed the building.

The mob didn't simply lash out at symbols of federal power; they destroyed homes of abolitionists, businesses that employed Black workers, and even hospitals that treated Black patients. One eyewitness noted that the rioters *"seemed not merely to kill, but to unmake, tearing the skin, the bones, the voice from the person."*

After the rioters burned the draft office to the ground they moved through the streets with loosely coordinated fury. Telegraph lines were cut. Bridges were blocked. Police were overwhelmed, beaten, and scattered. Mayor George Opdyke and Governor Horatio Seymour were both criticized for their hesitant responses. Harper's Weekly reported: *"Hell has broken loose in the city. Law is suspended. The mob is master."*

The violence grew in intensity with each passing hour. Armed with clubs, axes, and stolen firearms, the rioters moved in coordinated bands, using lookouts and messengers to direct the next target. By the second night of rioting, the Governor ordered whatever military was available into the city to help the police. The Invalid Corps were volunteer soldiers who had been found unfit for field service. They were called in to defend public buildings.

Militia units arrived by boat and train to aid police, and together they fought running street battles through lower Manhattan. Artillery was brought in and aimed down Broadway. At one point, gunshots were fired into a crowd near First Avenue, scattering the rioters with deadly effect.

When the riots were finally crushed by July 16, more than 120 blacks had died, many more wounded or unaccounted for. It is reported that dozens of the white rioters were killed and about 15 Union soldiers and police were murdered. Also, several bystanders and other innocents were killed. Over $5 million in property had been destroyed. Black families fled the city, some never to return. The demographic landscape of New York was permanently altered.

The draft was resumed weeks later, protected by troops. But the memory of the riots lingered, a grim reminder of the explosive tensions in the Union itself, and of the dangerous undercurrents of racism, class conflict, and fear that surged beneath the war's patriotic surface.

One rioter was quoted as shouting, *"We won't fight to free the niggers, but we'll die before they take us!"* Harper's Weekly reported: *"The city was at the mercy of the mob. Blood ran in the gutters, and smoke blotted out the summer sun."*

While flames lit the Manhattan skyline and mobs dragged Black citizens from their homes, Washington was reeling from the news: the largest civil disturbance in American history was underway, and it was in the North's crown jewel city. Lincoln needed to act, not just politically, but militarily. At that very moment, the Army of the Potomac was licking its wounds after the bloodbath at Gettysburg. Just days earlier, General George Meade had defeated Robert E. Lee in the most significant Union victory to date. The 11th and 7th New York regiments, among others, had fought bravely in Pennsylvania. Now, without even a week to rest, they were being ordered home, not to parade, but to police.

On July 15th, under Lincoln's orders and Secretary of War Edwin Stanton's swift logistics, several units, including the battle-hardened 152nd New York Infantry and the 20th U.S. Infantry were diverted from Pennsylvania and Maryland toward New York City.

The first reinforcements arrived from nearby forts and armories in New York and New Jersey, but they were few and mostly ill-prepared for urban combat. It was not until July 15 and 16, as the violence reached a peak of brutality, particularly in its targeting of Black homes, that battle-hardened troops from the Army of the Potomac began arriving in force. Units such as the 152nd New York Infantry, the 11th New York Volunteers (formerly the Fire Zouaves), and elements of the 7th New York National Guard were rushed into the city by rail and steamer.

Command of military operations was placed under Major General John Wool, the elderly but experienced commander of the Department of the East. However, the day-to-day suppression of the riots fell to General Harvey Brown, a West Point graduate and veteran of the Mexican-American War, who had served with distinction in the defense of Fort Pickens. Brown coordinated with city police and militia units, but it was the arrival of thousands of Union soldiers that truly turned the tide.

The troops were ordered to use force if necessary, and they did. Soldiers patrolled the city in tight formations, armed with loaded rifles and fixed bayonets. When confronted by mobs, they responded decisively. At First Avenue and 19th Street, rioters refused to disperse and hurled bricks and paving stones at the soldiers. The troops fired volleys directly into the crowd, killing an estimated 12 to 15 people and wounding dozens more. While critics later decried the use of deadly force, it proved effective. In the face of military discipline and superior firepower, the mobs began to retreat.

Skirmishes occurred throughout the city, especially in working-class neighborhoods like Harlem, Yorkville, and Hell's Kitchen, where anti-draft sentiment was most virulent. Troops cleared streets, guarded critical infrastructure like telegraph lines and arsenals, and stood watch over homes and businesses owned by Black residents or Republican politicians. The Colored Orphan Asylum, which had been burned to the ground on the second day of the riots, was now surrounded by soldiers to prevent looters from returning to the ruins.

By July 17 there were roughly 5,000 Federal troops in New York City. With their presence the riots had subsided. Federal troops remained on alert, but the mass gatherings had ceased. The city was under de facto martial law, though it was never formally declared. It was a remarkable use of military force on the domestic front. Their presence likely prevented further bloodshed and halted the spread of violence into neighboring boroughs and towns.

The cost of the riot was staggering in terms of lives lost and those with significant injuries. In the four days of rioting the killing of US citizens by other citizens and then by federal troops was the fodder for newspapers all over the country. Millions of dollars in property damage had been inflicted on a wide swath of the city. Racial animosities would remain raw for generations. Yet from the perspective of federal authority, the use of troops had succeeded in reestablishing control.

Lincoln never publicly condemned Seymour or the city's Democratic leadership, choosing instead to let the facts speak for themselves. But privately, many within the administration believed that only the presence of Union soldiers saved New York from deeper rebellion was a sobering reminder that the Civil War's battle lines did not always lie between North and South but sometimes ran through the very heart of Union territory.

Political and Social Fallout

The Draft Riots left not only physical ruin but political turmoil in their wake. New York's elite were shaken by the intense violence of the rioters, and the federal government began to fully recognize the fragility of public support for the war effort in the North, but especially in New York, the largest city in the Nation. President Lincoln, already mentally stretched by the demands of the major battles of Gettysburg and Vicksburg, now faced internal rebellion in the very heart of Union territory. But Lincoln never did deliver a public address concerning the riots.

The speech by Governor Seymour was seized upon by Republicans and the Lincoln administration as evidence of sympathy with the rioters and betrayal of the Union cause. Lincoln never forgave Seymour's perceived softness, and it intensified partisan divisions that would continue into the 1864 election, when Seymour's political allies would rally behind George McClellan.

Socially, the riots had a lasting effect. New York's Black population, already small, dwindled by over 20 percent in the months that followed. Many survivors of the violence fled to Brooklyn or left the city and the state entirely. Black churches, schools, and communities were left in ruins. Trust between Black and Irish working-class communities, already strained by job competition and racial animosity, collapsed completely. The Colored Orphan Asylum was never rebuilt. Though the children were rescued, their trauma became symbolic of how deeply racism was woven into the very fabric of Northern society.

Newspapers and political cartoonists across the North debated the meaning of the riots. Some warned that the administration's push for emancipation and equality had provoked a backlash among white workers who feared being replaced. Others argued the violence proved the moral necessity of Lincoln's cause.

Frederick Douglass declared that the riots revealed *"the work yet to be done, a war not only for Union, but for justice. Until the Black man is safe in the North,"* he said, *"no flag can claim purity."*

The New York Draft Riots of 1863 exposed America's inner contradictions, its simultaneous fight for liberty and Union while engaging in the practice of exclusion. The riots revealed that the war's battlefields stretched beyond Virginia and Mississippi and into the streets of New York itself.

PART FOUR: KEY BATTLES

CHAPTER 13
FREEDOM AND THE 54TH MASSACHUSETTS

When President Lincoln signed the Emancipation Proclamation on January 1, 1863, it not only altered the war's moral course, but it also opened the door for Black men to officially join the Union Army or Navy. Though many had already served unofficially as laborers and scouts, they had not yet been granted formal recognition as soldiers and had not served in actual combat.

Among the first and most famous regiments was the 54th Massachusetts Infantry Regiment. This unit was raised in the spring of 1863 under the authorization of Massachusetts Governor John Andrew, who was acting on orders from Secretary of War Stanton. The governor immediately set about organizing and promoting the new regiment. Governor Andrews knew the Shaw family and thought that their young son Robert might be a good candidate to lead the regiment.

Robert Shaw was born into affluence in Boston and was raised by a prominent abolitionist family. He was initially educated in Europe and finished his education at Harvard. When the Civil War broke out in April 1861, like many young men of his class, he was swept up in patriotic fervor. He briefly joined the 7th New York Militia for a short 30-day enlistment, serving in the early defense of Washington. In May 1861, Shaw accepted a commission as a second lieutenant in the 2nd Massachusetts Infantry, a unit composed largely of young men from similar social backgrounds. The regiment was sent to northern Virginia as part of the Army of the Potomac.

Shaw saw his first real combat in the Shenandoah Valley of Virginia serving under Major General Nathaniel Banks in battle against Stonewall

Jackson. He experienced close combat at the Battle of Cedar Mountain in August 1862, after which he was promoted to captain. He subsequently fought at the Battle of Antietam in September 1862, where he experienced the trauma and horror of war with friends dying at his side. He had that aloof air of a societal elite but was recognized as being reliable and reserved.

His letters from the field to his family reflected a maturing view of the war. While still personally reserved and sometimes cynical, he began to show signs of disillusionment with the Union Army's leadership and the general conduct of the war. He also grew more reflective about the causes of the war, including slavery, though he was not initially as much a radical abolitionist as his parents.

Shaw was offered the command of the 54th Regiment by the Governor of Massachusetts. He was initially hesitant to accept the assignment because he had a strong belief that he would not be permitted to take his fighting force to the front lines. But Shaw became convinced by his mother of the moral and symbolic importance of the role. Shaw soon came to accept the command to lead these men as a moral calling and an honorable duty. He understood that leading the 54th was not just about military service, it was a political and social statement. He realized the success or failure with this unit could influence the future of Black men in the army and their broader place in American society.

In a letter to his fiancée, Shaw admitted his initial reservations but said he had come to see the appointment as *"an honor,"* and that he would *"take it with all my heart. I feel convinced I shall never regret having taken this step, as far as I myself am concerned; for while I was undecided, I felt ashamed of myself. Now, I feel as if I had something to work for. And I shall try to do my duty to the utmost."*

The command came with a promotion to the rank of Colonel, which was equal to the position of regimental commander.

The regiment was composed entirely of African American enlisted men, many of whom had never held a weapon, but had long carried the weight of freedom's promise. Recruits came from across the North, not just Massachusetts. Some of the men had been born free, and a few had escaped southern slavery. There were many more free black men than former slaves volunteering for the regiment. Their volunteering was for a cause. Frederick Douglass, played a key role in recruiting soldiers, including his own two sons.

Shaw finally accepted the commission in February 1863. He was a strong disciplinarian who was determined to train his men to the highest standard. He wrote his father in March: : *"Everything goes on prosperously. The intelligence of the men is a great surprise to me. They learn all the details of guard duty and camp service infinitely more readily than most of the Irish that I have had under my command. There is not the least doubt that we will leave the State with as good a regiment as any that has marched."*

The 54th Massachusetts trained at Camp Meigs in Readville, Massachusetts, just outside Boston. Shaw had sought experienced drill instructors to instill readiness and discipline. The men endured the same punishing drills, discipline, and expectations as any white regiment, perhaps more so based on the demands of their commanding officer. They marched through snow. They drilled from dawn until dusk. They faced ridicule from nearby civilians and often skepticism from white Union officers. Moreover they were underfunded. Clothes, food, weapons, barracks were all substandard to what the average white recruit would be afforded.

As he got to know their strengths, Colonel Shaw grew into being a fierce advocate for his men, mostly because they surprised him with their intelligence and great dedication to the cause for which they had volunteered. From his superiors, Shaw demanded equal provisions and supplies. His demands were met with stringent resistance, but he always persisted until his demands were at least minimally met. When the War Department offered to pay Black soldiers less than white soldiers ($10 per month instead of $13), with clothing costs deducted from that salary, the men of the 54th refused their pay entirely. Shaw stood with them. *"If they cannot receive the full recognition of soldiers,"* he wrote to his parents, *"then they will at least have the full dignity of men."* The men of the 54th held their ground for 18 months without pay until Congress finally acted to right the wrong in June 1864, which allowed for retroactive pay to the date of enlistment.

Shaw knew the nation had many skeptics that would be watching, and he wanted the 54th to prove the capability and professionalism of Black soldiers beyond question. To do so without the same benefits as the white trainees would be a difficult task. *"We are striving to make ours the model regiment in the service,"* Shaw wrote in a letter, reflecting his commitment to excellence.

Captain Luis F. Emilio, who was just 19 when he joined the 54th Massachusetts, later wrote *A Brave Black Regiment* (1891), the most comprehensive firsthand account of the regiment's formation, training, and combat experience. Emilio, at age 19, already had more than two years of combat experience. He had garnered a reputation of being disciplined, intelligent and brave in battle. He entered the 54th as a second lieutenant, then was quickly promoted to a first lieutenant, then captain all before his 20th birthday. He became one of the most respected white officers in the unit and offered detailed, respectful descriptions of the men's discipline and spirit. *"The men of the Fifty-fourth were most eager to learn their duties. Their intelligent faces and willing obedience made it a pleasure to instruct them."*

"Colonel Shaw was earnest and devoted. He was determined that the Fifty-fourth should be second to none in discipline and efficiency. He demanded strict attention to duty and held his officers to the highest standards."

"Spectators came in crowds to witness the drills. At first, curious and skeptical, they soon were enthusiastic over the soldierly bearing of the men."

The 54th was finally dispatched from their training facility and marched through Boston on May 28, 1863, in an emotional and patriotic send-off. The men of the 54th, dressed in full Union blue, marched proudly through the streets of Boston, cheered by thousands of onlookers. Governor Andrew and prominent abolitionists, including Frederick Douglass were present and involved in the formation. The proud march of these men was not only military but political. It was a public statement of the state's support for the use of Black soldiers in the Union cause.

The regiment boarded a steamship at the docks in Boston Harbor later that day. The steamship was used to carry troops and supplies along the Atlantic coast. Though not a warship, it was sufficient for moving an entire regiment with its officers, equipment, and supplies. The voyage lasted several days and followed the Atlantic seaboard down to Hilton Head, South Carolina, where Union forces maintained a major base of operations. Hilton Head, along with nearby Port Royal and Beaufort, had been under Union control since 1861 and served as the Union's headquarters for operations in the Department of the South.

The 54th was eventually stationed at Beaufort. Their first assignments involved raiding Confederate supply lines and fortifications in the surrounding area. But mostly they were sent to Beaufort to provide physical labor at the loading docks. Colonel Shaw was anxious to show that these men could be a formative fighting force and applied for action various times meeting resistance time and time again.

In early June 1863, the town of Darien, Georgia, sat quietly along the banks of the Altamaha River. Once a thriving coastal settlement built on the wealth of rice and cotton, Darien had been largely abandoned by its white residents. The war had pushed many of the population inland. Still, the town stood with wooden homes, churches, and stores, shaded by moss-draped oak trees, its silence broken only by the occasional breeze off the marsh.

On June 11 Union boats arrived and Federal soldiers disembarked. Among them were men of the 54th Massachusetts. Their mission was to support a *"scouting expedition"* led by Colonel James Montgomery, a white abolitionist from Kansas known for his fiery anti-slavery rhetoric and ruthless guerrilla tactics. Montgomery commanded a group of Black soldiers from the 2nd South Carolina Volunteers, many of whom had been formerly enslaved. In his view, the South had to be punished militarily, economically and psychologically. *"We are outlawed, and therefore not bound by the rules of regular warfare,"* he reportedly said.

The town was defenseless and nearly empty. Shaw believed their orders were to confiscate supplies and disrupt Confederate logistics not to destroy civilian property. But to his dismay, Montgomery ordered the looting and burning of the town. Shaw protested arguing that burning Darien was both unnecessary and dishonorable. Montgomery was unmoved by the destruction he claimed would send a message. When Shaw hesitated to carry out the order, Montgomery snapped: *"You have only learned half your lesson. The other half is to make the Southerners feel the war. We are outlawed, and we must act accordingly."*

Under protest, Shaw reluctantly ordered his men to assist. Fires were set, and soon Darien was engulfed in smoke and everything was consumed. That night, Shaw was sick with guilt. He wrote to his mother: *"We went down and destroyed the little town of Darien, on the Altamaha. That is the only expedition I have been on, and I shudder to think of it. It was a vile affair, and I am ashamed of having been connected with it."*

The burning of Darien left a scar on Shaw's conscience. It deepened his resolve to ensure that his men would not be seen as raiders or tools of vengeance, but as professional soldiers fighting for the cause of freedom and the dignity of all men. Shaw wrote to his father: *"I told him I did not want to take the responsibility of it, and he was only too happy to take it on his own shoulders."* And to his mother Shaw wrote: *"I did all I could to prevent it, but Montgomery is the ranking officer, and he would not listen."*

The regiment was then reassigned to Morris Island, not far from Charleston, where they mostly dug trenches while under fire from the enemy. The trenches would be eventually used as an aid to the charge on Fort Wagner. Their first real combat happened on July 16 in a skirmish at Grimball's Landing on James Island, where they held the line against a Confederate attack and performed well under fire. In the skirmish, the 54th had one killed and 42 wounded or missing.

But it was in July 1863, just days after Gettysburg, that the 54th would write their names into the annals of American memory. Colonel Shaw and his regiment were placed under the command of General Quincy Gilmore and sent to Charleston, South Carolina. On July 11, General Gilmore had ordered an assault on Fort Wagner that had failed, so he decided to order a second, direct frontal assault. It was commonly known that there would be waves of soldiers in the assault and the first wave would experience the most casualties.

Brigadier General George Strong under the command of General Gillmore directly ordered Shaw to have his regiment ready to be the first wave in the next day's assault. General Strong reportedly said to Shaw before the attack: *"You and your men, I know, will do well; tomorrow night the nation will ring with the story of the Fifty-fourth."*

Charge on Fort Wagner

Before their march toward Fort Wagner, the 54th Massachusetts was engaged in a skirmish at James Island, near a place called Secessionville. On July 16, Confederate forces launched a surprise attack on Union positions. The 54th helped repel the attack, fighting with distinction and demonstrating their discipline under fire, an important moment that helped prove the capability of Black soldiers in combat. Though casualties were limited, it was a sobering introduction to battle. The 54th held its ground, protecting the Union rear and allowing for an orderly withdrawal.

Immediately after the fighting on James Island, Union commanders pulled the 54th back to Folly Island, which had been used as a staging area for troops and artillery. There, the men had only a brief rest

On the afternoon of July 18, the 54th Massachusetts formed up and began their final march up Morris Island, a narrow spit of sand leading toward the Confederate defenses. It was hot, and the men had marched several miles in full gear, passing other Union units who had already seen the heavy fire from Wagner's artillery. As they neared the front, soldiers and officers along the way saluted them and called encouragement. The moment was not lost on either the Black soldiers or their white comrades.

That evening, as the sun began to set, Colonel Shaw assembled his officers and gave the order that would lead the frontal assault on the fort. They reached the edge of the beach, just south of Fort Wagner, just after dark within sight of its massive sand walls and bristling guns. The ensuing battle would be the fourth time that Black troops were to play a critical combat role during the war. This would become the most impactful of them all.

The 54th Massachusetts Infantry stood in formation. As is often the case in mid-summer in South Carolina, the weather was hot and humid. The men of the 54th were exhausted from a grueling approach march through marshes and beaches, they were soaked in sweat and spattered with the mud of the South Carolina coast. But they stood ready and according to Captain Emilio in *"excellent temper and spirits."* These men were very aware that what they were about to attempt was not only dangerous, but it was also monumental for the acceptance of their race into the military. The perceptions of Blacks in the military needed to substantially change if they were to bolster the possibility of an overall Union victory.

Their destination that day was Fort Wagner, it rested on a narrow spit of sand guarding the seaward approach to Charleston Harbor. It was one of the most formidable Confederate fortifications of the war. Perched on the northern end of Morris Island, its guns scanned the surf, and its sand-constructed walls defied the Atlantic winds, as well as incoming cannon fire. It was not a permanent fortress of stone or brick, but a hastily yet ingeniously constructed stronghold of sand, palmetto logs, and gabions, designed to deny the Union any foothold in Charleston's outer defenses.

Roughly 250 yards long and 100 yards wide, Fort Wagner stretched across the full width of the island, from marsh to sea. Its interior was filled with artillery, heavy smooth bores, shell guns, and mortars, mounted both on parapets and hidden behind earthworks. A water-filled ditch, deep and treacherous, protected the approach. Flank howitzers were concealed on the parapets to shoot any soldiers daring enough to reach the moat. Behind these defenses, a well-prepared garrison of seventeen hundred Confederate troops, under the command of Brigadier General William Taliaferro, waited with determination.

Life in the garrison was far from easy. Sand and salt clogged the air, the summer heat was relentless, and the threat of bombardment was ever-present. Shelters known as bombproofs, constructed with thick timber beams and buried beneath the sand, provided safety from the Union shelling. These spaces doubled as supply depots, sleeping quarters, and makeshift hospitals. Even in moments of quiet, the fort was a place of tension. For those stationed within, there was little glamour and no illusions, only duty and endurance.

On July 17 Colonel Shaw had received orders from his regiment commander that required him to lead his men in a frontal assault of Fort Wagner. It was both an honor and a brutal test, a suicide mission. Shaw wrote a brief note to his wife Annie that night, handed it to a fellow officer, and quietly made peace with what he envisioned lay ahead. Many soldiers in the 54th knew that if captured, they faced not just the probability enslavement but also that of execution under Confederate policy. Some, like William Carney, reportedly prayed and sang spirituals. Others wrote farewell letters. As the sun set, the men readied their gear. They fixed bayonets on their rifles and filled cartridge boxes.

The first charge on the fort had occurred on the morning of July 11, Union commanders, eager to capitalize on the momentum gained after seizing the southern end of the island just days before, decided to strike quickly. Major General Quincy Gillmore ordered a direct frontal assault on Fort Wagner's seaward face. He hoped that speed and surprise might overcome the defenses before the Confederates could reinforce. But the assault was plagued from the start.

At around dawn, under cover of darkness and fog, an attacking force of about 6,000 Union soldiers advanced quietly across the narrow beach. The lead regiments, including the 7th Connecticut and 76th Pennsylvania, trudged through the soft sand in columns, the crashing surf on their right and a swampy creek to their left. The beach offered no cover. Their only path was straight ahead into the teeth of the enemy.

As they came within range, the fog lifted just enough for Confederate lookouts to spot the movement of the Union troops. Suddenly, Fort Wagner came alive. From its sand walls and gun ports, Confederate cannon and musket fire exploded into the advancing blue line. Grape shot and cannon balls tore through the front ranks. Rifle fire poured down from the ramparts. The narrow beach became a killing zone. Still, the Union troops pressed forward, some reaching the moat before being cut down. The storming force was thrown into confusion, no scaling ladders had been brought, and the fort's earthen walls were too steep and high to climb under fire. Lacking artillery preparation or coordinated support, the assault collapsed within minutes.

The survivors fell back dragging wounded comrades with them. Bodies lay strewn across the sand. The attack had lasted less than an hour and had achieved absolutely nothing. By the time the firing ceased, the Union had suffered around 339 casualties. Confederate losses were minimal. Inside the fort, Colonel Robert Graham, the Confederate commander, later wrote that his men were surprised the Union had attempted such a rash charge. For the Union, the failed assault was a grim lesson as to the strength of Fort Wagner's defenses. General Gillmore, humbled by the defeat, recognized the need for a more thorough approach including sustained bombardment, and better coordination.

Despite the undeniable defeat suffered on July 11, Union command remained undaunted in their determination to take Fort Wagner. They considered the first disastrous effort as an intelligence reconnaissance. They would start the new engagement with a stronger bombardment of the fort from the sea as well as land and would engage in a nighttime assault instead of at dawn. They thought this approach would reduce troop exposure. On the evening of July 18, under darkening skies and amid the roar of cannon fire from the Union Navy, the Union command readied to launch a second and more daring assault using the 54th Massachusetts Regiment as the lead.

In the early morning of July 18 Union land-based artillery were supported by Navy ironclad gunships, and both opened fire on the fort. After about eight hours of shelling and exhausting 9,000 rounds of ammunition, the assault was finally called off in favor of the forthcoming infantry attack. The Union would later find that their artillery had basically no effect on the fort. The sand used to construct the fort absorbed the contact of the incoming shells, as its men were hiding in subsurface bunkers that were also covered in sand.

As the sun was sinking behind the marshes, and the Union bombardment fell silent. At about 7:45 p.m., a calm and focused Colonel Robert Shaw addressed his men briefly, then drew his sword. *"Now, men, I want you to prove yourselves. The eyes of thousands will look on what you do tonight."* The 54th surged forward in darkness, with Shaw leading the charge. They advanced in silence, but in a double-time march for about 500 hundred yards. When they came within range of the guns of the fort, the quiet of the evening was shattered. First came the Confederate artillery fire and as the men of the 54th drew closer, musket fire also erupted from the fort. Cannon swept the front ranks with grape and canister shot. Men fell in clusters. What followed was chaos and courage in equal measure. The dedicated, gallant men of the 54th continued forward sprinting in an attempt to gain some cover.

The 54th reached the outer moat of the fort but found it added little protection from the muskets of the Confederates defending Fort Wagner. It was a trench filled with water and debris, just beneath the parapet of the fort. Captain Emilio writes in his book *"When the head of the column had nearly reached the ditch,*

Colonel Shaw, springing upon a little knoll, shouted, 'Forward, Fifty-fourth!' and led the way through the ditch, over the slope, and on to the parapet of Wagner. With waving sword he shouted, 'Come on, boys!' and, with a gallant few around him, he stood a moment on the crest. Then he fell, pierced by three bullets, one through the heart."

The men of the 54th continued to pour forward, fighting hand to hand for hours, clubbing and stabbing in the darkness. Sergeant William Carney, later awarded the Medal of Honor, seized the regimental colors after the standard bearer was shot down. Carney advanced up the slope, waving the flag and urging his comrades forward, despite suffering multiple gunshot wounds himself. *"Boys, I only did my duty; the old flag never touched the ground,"* he would later say.

Captain Emilio wrote in his book, *"I found myself, as ranking officer, in command of the regiment. The enemy's fire was still murderous. Of sixteen officers who went into action, only me and three others remained unhurt. Two were wounded, and the rest were dead or missing."*

"We had charged with nearly six hundred men. When I mustered the survivors the next day, I could count barely over one hundred."

Emilio counted his survivors before all had made it back to safety but the devastation to his regiment was obvious. Behind the 54th came additional regiments of white soldiers from New York and Connecticut, but the narrowness of the beach made coordination nearly impossible. The assault bogged down under relentless Confederate fire. The 54th held a portion of the parapet for about an hour, but they were outnumbered and unsupported. When the Union's second and third waves failed to break through, the survivors were forced to withdraw.

Of the 600 men of the 54th who made the charge, nearly 280 were killed, wounded, or captured. It was a devastating loss. Colonel Shaw was among the dead. He was buried by the Confederates the next day with the fallen Black soldiers in a mass grave. It was a gesture meant to insult Shaw, his family and his regiment. Shaw's parents acknowledged that the Confederate officers had given Shaw exactly what he would have wanted, if given the choice: to be buried with the men he led and admired.

The following waves of troops backing of the initial charge were white troops who had to jump over the dead and wounded of the 54th. They fought through the night and retreated in the early morning. In all there were over 1,500 men dead and wounded on the beach in front of the fort. General Strong who had ordered the attack was mortally wounded while moving his staff and forcing his troops forward. He was shot in the thigh and died several days later.

Legacy and Meaning

Tactically, the assault on Fort Wagner was almost a complete failure. The fort withheld the attack, and without much Confederate sacrifice. The ultimate goal of attacking Fort Wagner was to proceed on and capture Charleston. That city would not fall into Union hands until the final months of the war in 1865. But symbolically, the attack was a resounding triumph. The courage of the 54th Massachusetts Regiment shattered the widespread doubts about the fighting capabilities of African American soldiers.

Fort Wagner was eventually abandoned rather than taken, but its legacy resounded throughout the Union. The 54th Massachusetts, baptized in blood, had proven the strength and valor of African American soldiers. Their charge had galvanized public support and furthered the cause of Black enlistment. For the Confederacy, the defense of Fort Wagner was a testament to their tactical ingenuity and willingness to fight tooth and nail defending every inch of ground.

News of the valor of the Union soldiers spread quickly. Frederick Douglass, whose sons served in the 54th, praised their bravery. Newspapers across the North ran headlines about the heroism of Shaw and his men, some of it glorified beyond reality. Union recruitment of Black soldiers surged in the months that followed. Eventually, nearly 180,000 African Americans would serve in Union uniform.

In death, the men of the 54th Massachusetts did what no argument or policy paper could. They proved, under fire, that Black Americans would fight for freedom, not only their own, but that of the nation. Their sacrifice at Fort Wagner became yet another turning point in the moral character of the war.

After the 54th and nine other regiments from two brigades were driven back from the Fort with very heavy casualties, the Union finally concluded that frontal assaults would not be successful. They initiated siege operations to reduce Fort Wagner over the next two months. After 60 days of siege operations, the Confederates decided to abandon the fort on September 7, 1863.

The 54th Massachusetts Regiment continued to fight with distinction in the Civil War in battles in South Carolina and Florida. What they proved to the nation and specifically to the Union Army was that they were disciplined, dedicated, and gallant fighters who were willing to die to further the Union cause and to retain their freedom.

Decades later, a bronze memorial would be erected on Boston Common, depicting Shaw and his men marching forward. The faces in the sculpture are not idealized, they are individuals, as the soldiers were.

CHAPTER 14
THE BATTLE OF STONES RIVER

As the calendar was about to turn from 1862 to 1863, the Union desperately needed a victory. The war had brought more frustration than progress for the North in the previous year. Despite some successes in the West, morale was sagging after the catastrophic Union defeat at Fredericksburg in December. Yet even almost before the smoke had cleared from that battle in Virginia, a massive and brutal battle was unfolding in central Tennessee near the town of Murfreesboro, along the Stones River.

In command of the Union Army of the Cumberland was Major General William Rosecrans who had recently been appointed to replace Major General Don Carlos Buell, who had a long-standing reputation for being cautious to a fault. After the Union victories at Shiloh and Corinth in the spring of 1862, Buell's Army of the Ohio was expected to advance rapidly into East Tennessee, a strategically important region with a populace that had strong Unionist sentiment. But Buell, as had other generals before him, moved slowly, painfully so, citing logistical issues, poor railroads, and Confederate cavalry raids.

His hesitancy frustrated President Lincoln, Secretary of War Stanton, and General-in-Chief Henry Halleck, all of whom were desperate for more aggressive action in the West. They began to lose patience as Buell's army advancing ever so slowly, allowing Confederate forces to regroup and reinforce into a battle ready positions and strength.

After a battle at Perryville, Kentucky Buell did not pursue the defeated Confederates and on October 24, 1862, this inaction caused frustration in leadership to overboil in Washington. Finally, Buell was relieved of his command and replaced by General Rosecrans. Buell's military career was over.

After Rosecrans inherited the Army of the Ohio, he reorganized it and renamed his force the Army of the Cumberland. By renaming the force, Rosecrans was asserting his authority and distancing himself from Buell's command style and legacy.

Rosecrans was noted for his organizing skills as well as his skills for increasing morale of those under him. He was energetic, thoughtful, and determined to restore Union control over Middle Tennessee. While Rosecrans improved logistics and trained his army in Nashville, General Braxton Bragg reestablished Confederate positions further south around Murfreesboro, Tennessee, a key railway junction and supply hub about 30 miles southeast of Nashville.

Murfreesboro lay astride the Nashville & Chattanooga Railroad, a vital line that connected Union-occupied Nashville with the Confederate heartland and eventually Chattanooga, a key gateway to the Deep South. Control of this railway allowed for the movement of troops and supplies, essential for sustaining military campaigns in Tennessee and beyond. Additionally, the surrounding road network made Murfreesboro a crossroads for movements between eastern and western Tennessee, and between Kentucky and Alabama. This made it an important staging ground for both Union and Confederate armies.

Nashville had been occupied by Union forces since early 1862 and served as a crucial Union logistics base in the Western Theater. Murfreesboro was only about 30 miles to the southeast and was effectively the front line for controlling approaches to and from Nashville. Holding Murfreesboro protected Union control of middle Tennessee and threatened Confederate positions deeper south.

Despite continued pressure from the administration in Washington to move aggressively, Rosecrans deliberately prepared his troops for the next campaign, reinforcing his ranks and waiting until late December to make any kind of advance. He correctly anticipated that Bragg would stand and fight near Murfreesboro to defend Confederate control of Middle Tennessee.

On December 26, 1862, Rosecrans set out from Nashville with about 43,000 men, advancing in three columns toward Murfreesboro. The march was slow, hindered by rain, mud, and resistance from Confederate cavalry under Nathan Bedford Forrest and Joseph Wheeler, who launched raids to disrupt Union supply lines. Rosecrans' mission was to drive the Confederate Army out of Middle Tennessee and secure the region for the Union. Both armies were roughly equal in size, about 43,000 Union troops and 38,000 Confederate troops. They converged on the rocky, winter-dormant fields around Stones River in late December 1862.

By December 29, both armies were positioned along the Stones River, which meandered south to north across the battlefield. It was not a deep river but did form a significant natural barrier. Despite harsh winter conditions, wet roads, and freezing temperatures, both sides prepared for battle. Rosecrans made plans to attack the Confederate right; Bragg planned to strike the Union right first, hoping to destroy Rosecrans's army piecemeal.

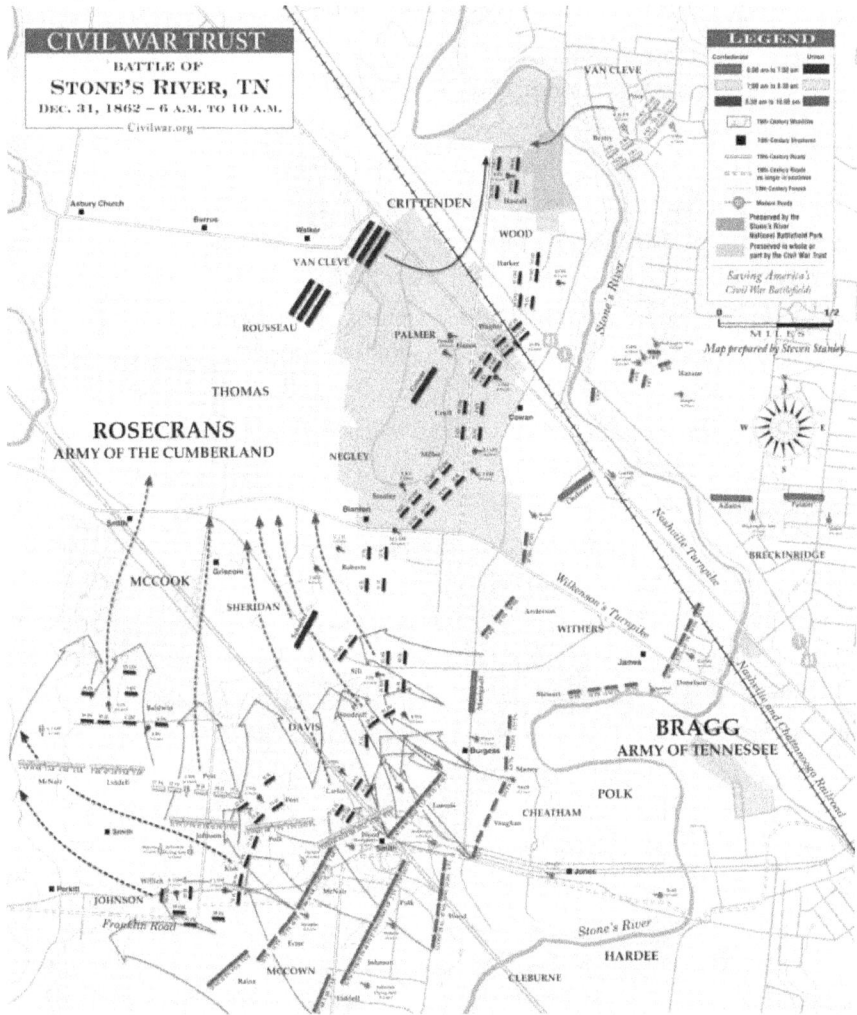

The Union and Confederate forces had troops on both the west and east sides of Stones River. But the majority of both forces were on the west side of the river. The river was no wider than 100 feet and no deeper than six feet with a slow current. But the bottom was rocky and uneven. The water was rather clear, and the bottom could be seen by those crossing. It could be crossed in several locations, but in many spots the bank was steep and slippery, making crossing under fire rather dangerous. On December 29 the armies were facing each other from less than a mile apart in many places along their front lines.

Unbeknown to each other, generals from both sides planned their initial strikes for the next day. Both armies spent December 29 analyzing field conditions and preparing artillery emplacements. Union engineers worked on mapping approaches to Stones River for their anticipated crossing to attack Confederate positions on the east side. As daylight dwindled and campfires were lit, each side saw and heard the other.

On the morning of December 30, both armies completed their deployments and dug in. Neither army made significant movement. But the army of Braxton Bragg managed to strike first. Bragg believed he could win a decisive victory by striking first. His plan called for a strong, coordinated attack against the Union right, where he assumed the enemy was most vulnerable for its line to be broken. That sector, under Major General Alexander McCook, was extended and exposed, anchored along the Wilkinson Pike and bordered by dense cedar woods. Bragg ordered Lieutenant General William Hardee to lead the assault, with divisions under Major General John Breckinridge held in reserve on the Confederate right.

Hardee was to attack with three divisions. The attack was to begin at first light, while Union soldiers were still preparing for the day, eating breakfast, warming by fires, and unaware of what was about to unfold. As the morning fog still clung to the surrounding fields obscuring the sight and sounds of the soon approaching army, Confederate troops silently formed lines in the darkness. In the early morning of December 31, around 6:00 a.m., the Confederate forces surged forward in a massive line catching most of the Union right by surprise. Campfires burned low in the Union lines, their soldiers beginning the day with thoughts of breakfast and routine preparations. Many of the soldiers had stacked arms and were preparing for a scheduled religious service. Intelligence reports had informed them that the South would not attack until New Year's Day.

The Union right was not well anchored in position and still not fully prepared for any kind of combat, let alone what they were facing. The initial attack crumbled their line almost immediately. Entire brigades were overrun within minutes. Many Union soldiers were caught unarmed, eating or warming themselves. Others fought fiercely but were simply outflanked and overwhelmed by the sheer weight of the sudden onslaught. Entire Union brigades were driven from their positions with minimal resistance. Hundreds of Union soldiers were captured or killed within the first hour.

As McCown's men drove forward, Patrick Cleburne's division swept in behind them, adding pressure and disarray. Confederate infantry, many of them hardened veterans, moved with precision firing volleys, screaming the rebel yell, and pressing their advantage through the woods and fields.

Union regiments gave ground reluctantly but were pushed back almost two miles very quickly. The chaos of the rout forced Federal batteries to flee, infantry officers tried to rally their men in mid-retreat, and wounded soldiers were left behind. By mid-morning, the Union right had collapsed, and the line bent sharply back upon itself like a closing door.

In those early hours, the Confederates believed they were on the verge of a complete victory, and indeed they were close. But as the sun continued to rise higher in the sky and the fog began to dissipate, they would encounter fierce resistance from the center and left of the Union line, especially near the rocks and woods that would soon come to be known as the *"Slaughter Pen."*

By mid-morning, the rolling Southern tide had swept nearly two miles across the battlefield, threatening to cut the Union army in two and seize the Nashville Pike, the vital lifeline of Rosecrans' army. But it was in a small, rocky grove just east of the road where the battle took on a desperate, almost primeval character. The Slaughter Pen was a maze of jagged limestone outcroppings and twisted cedar trees near the Union right flank. It was the kind terrain that offered some protection, but which also trapped men in a chaotic vortex of close quarters battle. Here, Colonel William Hazen's brigade, part of Thomas's corps, took a heroic stand against the Confederate onslaught.

Colonel Hazen was defending the Slaughter Pen with about 1,500 men, while the attacking Confederate force was about 7,000 men. Wave after wave of Confederate infantry came crashing into Hazen's lines. The narrow spaces between the rocks became killing grounds where men fought at ranges so close they could see each other's eyes. The rocky terrain made artillery use impossible, forcing both sides into grim, close-quarters combat. Soldiers fell in heaps atop one another; the wounded were unable to crawl to safety. The groves and rockfaces were filled with cries of those looking for safety and those dying.

Despite the relentless attacks and mounting casualties, Hazen's brigade held their ground. The stand they took at the Slaughter Pen was not just gallant; it was essential to the outcome of the battle. Had the Confederates broken through, they would have seized the Nashville Pike and likely forced Rosecrans into a disastrous retreat. Instead, Hazen's men created a stalwart anchor that allowed the Union line to regroup.

By late afternoon, the fury had slackened. The Slaughter Pen, once a peaceful cedar grove, was littered with bodies and blackened by gunpowder.

Hundreds of men had died in the span of just a few hours, and the rocks were stained with blood. But the Union army still held the field. In time, soldiers would speak of the Slaughter Pen with a mixture of horror and awe. It was a place where valor and carnage met in equal measure, where a few hundred men had stood against thousands and, by doing so, may have saved the Union army from annihilation.

Of the 1,500 Union forces at the Slaughter Pen about 113 were killed and over 500 were wounded, accounting for a 40% troop loss. Confederate losses have been estimated at almost 2,000 men.

Rosecrans understood the scope of what Hazen's men were accomplishing. He galloped across the battlefield to rally his troops. He reorganized his forces center and sent reserves to plug the collapsing right. He ordered Major General Philip Sheridan's division to make a determined stand. Sheridan was a relatively new division commander from Ohio with a reputation for energy and precision. He had taken unusual precautions the night before, anticipating the potential of an attack, he had instructed his men to sleep in line for battle, with weapons at the ready. Because of this, his division was one of the few in position to meet the dawn assault with any semblance of order.

When McCown's and Cheatham's Confederate divisions hit the Union right at dawn, Sheridan's troops were waiting. His division occupied ground west of the Nashville Pike, guarding a vital segment of the Union line between Union General Jefferson C. Davis's crumbling division to the south and General James Negley's reserve division further north.

Throughout the morning, Sheridan's three brigades under Colonels Joshua Sill, George Roberts, and Frederick Schaefer conducted a series of disciplined fighting withdrawals, checking the Confederate advance, and giving the Union command time to shore up the rest of the line. Sheridan moved from brigade to brigade, rallying men, adjusting positions, and ensuring that his artillery was well placed and concentrated.

Each time his line began to give way, Sheridan executed a controlled fallback to another prepared position. These defenses were not permanent earthworks but chosen ground, wooded slopes, rocky knolls, and ridgelines, where his infantry could fire and then retreat again under pressure of the Confederate advance. Sheridan's three brigades were positioned in the center-right of the Union line. They fought stubbornly and skillfully, falling back only under pressure but inflicting heavy losses on the Confederate attackers.

The cost of Sheridan's troops holding the line was enormous as all three of Sheridan's brigade commanders were killed: Colonels Sill, Roberts, and Schaefer. Casualties among the rank and file were heavy, particularly from close-range fighting and Confederate artillery. Sheridan lost nearly one-third of his 4,000-man division by noon. But the extraordinary sacrifice had greatly aided the Union effort to turn the Confederate advance. Sheridan's actions bought vital hours for the Union Army. His defense bought enough time for Generals Rosecrans and Thomas to organize a new defensive line near the Nashville Turnpike, supported by the vast artillery that had been amassed there. The Confederate momentum was abated before it could reach the supply lines.

The Confederates had gained two miles of ground, nearly destroying the Union right. The deaths of all three brigade commanders left Sheridan virtually alone in commanding a shattered division, yet he continued to lead his men with determination. By the end of the first day, Sheridan's division had suffered over 1,600 casualties, one of the highest of any division in the battle. This performance, despite devastating losses, began to build Sheridan's reputation as a tenacious and courageous leader, something that would define his later Civil War career.

Sheridan's leadership at Stones River marked his first major recognition of his battlefield brilliance. Rosecrans commended him personally and later described him as *"indomitable."* Though his name was not yet widely known, his poise under fire, his ability to execute fighting withdrawals, and his instinct for holding key terrain would be seen again in later battles from Chickamauga to Cedar Creek. His stand at Stones River did not win the battle outright, but it prevented a rout and, in a campaign, where both sides suffered devastating losses, that act of endurance became the cornerstone of Union survival on December 31.

After the battle that day, General Sheridan's horse was found dead, and his saddle had 3 bullet holes through it. Sheridan himself was unscathed, though he was constantly in the thick of the fighting. He reportedly had three horses shot from under him that day. One of his staff officers said: *"He was like a man possessed, riding up and down the line, urging his men to stand their ground... it seemed that bullets could not find him."*

Despite what had occurred at the Slaughter Pen and the tenaciousness of Sheridan's defense, Bragg still believed that his grand victory was imminent. The Union left and center, anchored by Thomas's men and reinforced by artillery, held firm. The terrain, exhaustion, and Union tenacity, especially from artillery positioned on high ground, blunted the Confederate momentum.

Braxton Bragg's initial attack was well-conceived and well executed. It nearly shattered the Union army. For a few hours on December 31, it seemed as though Rosecrans's army would certainly be routed. But thanks to determined leadership, the resilience of men like Sheridan and Hazen, and the strong defensive fallback position along the Nashville Pike, the Union army survived, what could have been a devastating blow.

The day's savage fighting marked one of the bloodiest single days of the war. Though the first day was a tactical disaster for the Union, the army had not broken completely. On the night of December 31, both armies were exhausted and lay resting in close proximity to one another. Union and Confederate musicians began to play in their camps. One side played *"Home Sweet Home,"* and soon the other picked it up. Soldiers on both sides reportedly wept quietly in the darkness. A soldier recalled: *"There we lay, enemies by daylight and brothers by night, singing the same song under the same stars."*

The morning of New Year's Day dawned cold and foggy, the fields between the opposing lines were littered with dead and wounded. Neither side launched an attack on New Years Day. Instead, the day was marked by repositioning troops, digging entrenchments, engaging in strategizing and tending for the dead and wounded.

Major General Rosecrans, despite sustaining severe losses on December 31, chose to dig in his forces. His army had been driven back, but their morale was still that of a strong fighting force. Union forces remained anchored to the Nashville Turnpike and the railroad, the vital lifelines for Nashville and the rear of the line.

Rosecrans spent the day reorganizing his lines and shifting troops to solidify his new position nearer the river. Artillery was massed near McFadden's Ford and other elevated ground to help guard against the next Confederate attack. Wounded soldiers were moved to makeshift hospitals or field shelters, and supply trains hurried in what food and ammunition could be brought from Nashville. Despite the prior day's devastation, Union morale stiffened with an unusual resolve. Many soldiers now believed they had weathered the worst and could still prevail.

On the Confederate side, Bragg believed he had won a great victory. He had driven the Union right flank nearly two miles and caused thousands of casualties. Bragg even sent a telegram to Richmond that evening announcing that

Rosecrans was retreating, and that the Confederacy had secured a major triumph. But Bragg's perception was badly mistaken. Rosecrans was not retreating. The Union army had consolidated and was now dug in. Worse yet, Bragg's own men had become demoralized due to the significant losses they had incurred, and disorganized due to Bragg's lack of leadership skills.

Bragg did little on January 1 to follow up on his perceived gains. Some Confederate officers, including Generals Hardee and Breckinridge, urged caution, recognizing that the Union now held stronger positions than in the previous battles. Other officers supported a renewed assault, hoping to finish what they thought was a collapsing enemy army. Bragg remained indecisive while ordering only minor attacks, and troop repositioning.

Throughout the day, both sides recovered their wounded and buried their dead. Soldiers on picket lines observed an informal truce in places to allow details to carry off the fallen. As would be expected there was some fighting, but nothing on a major scale. The air was filled with the smell of smoke, gunpowder, and human decay. The sounds of moaning from field hospitals were constant.

The Emancipation Proclamation had taken effect that day. But it was far from the minds of the soldiers from the North or the South amid the carnage that surrounded them. But in Washington and in the press, Lincoln's order to free slaves in rebel territories added profound meaning to the struggle taking place at Stones River, a battle to preserve the Union and now to transform the purpose of the war.

By the morning of January 2, both armies had endured two days of punishing combat, with tens of thousands of casualties already suffered. General Braxton Bragg, still clinging to the belief that Rosecrans was preparing to retreat, thought he saw an opportunity to strike a final and decisive assault on his enemy. His target was the Union left, anchored across the Stones River on a bluff near McFadden's Ford, where Major General Thomas Crittenden's wing had established a strong position. Bragg believed this crossing could be overrun and ordered Major General John Breckinridge to attack.

John Breckinridge was a former U.S. Vice President under James Buchanan and a seasoned but cautious commander. He strongly objected to Braggs order to attack. He had personally scouted the area and saw that the Union position was well-defended, with open ground leading to elevated artillery platforms on the west bank of the river. It seemed to Breckenridge that he was being ordered to have his men slaughtered. He pleaded with Bragg not to order the assault, warning it would be suicidal. Breckenridge was reported to have said to Bragg, *"General, do you mean for my men to attack over that ground? It is murder, not war!"* Bragg was unmoved by the Breckenridge assessment. He ordered Breckinridge to advance by 4:00 p.m.

At 4:00 p.m., Breckinridge launched approximately 4,500 men in two lines across the narrow, open plain east of Stones River. The Confederates advanced with determination and succeeded in routing two Union brigades and briefly captured a portion of the Union line on the east bank. But as they surged forward, they entered a deadly zone of fire from the cannons on high ground.

Waiting for them on the opposite (west) bank of Stones River was a massive concentration of Union artillery, 58 guns, carefully positioned and directed by Captain John Mendenhall, under the supervision of Major General Crittenden. As the Confederates approached the river, Union gunners unleashed a devastating barrage of shell, canister, and solid shot. The guns, arranged hub-to-hub on elevated ground, created what one observer called *"a perfect storm of fire."* As the Confederate lines reached the river and attempted to cross at McFadden's Ford, they were shredded by concentrated fire. Entire ranks quickly collapsed. The riverbanks became choked with the dead and wounded. Officers and couriers were picked off as they tried to rally their men. The slaughter lasted less than an hour but resulted in over 1,800 Confederate casualties.

Breckinridge was both heartbroken and furious. He was seen weeping, crying out, *"My poor boys… my poor boys!"* He had lost many of his best officers and had seen his prediction of disaster fulfilled. It was a senseless, frontal assault in open terrain against overwhelming artillery, and it broke any remaining hope of victory for Bragg's army. Colonel William Preston, Breckinridge's cousin and chief of staff, remembered the general as being visibly shaken and angry after the failed charge, *"It was the only time I ever saw General Breckinridge unnerved. He was pale as death, and the tears ran down his cheeks as he rode among the dead and dying."*

That night, Rosecrans reinforced his positions and prepared for a counteroffensive. Bragg, finally realizing the attack had been a failure, and that Union reinforcements would soon be arriving from Nashville, withdrew his army on the night of January 3. The Confederates retreated southward to Tullahoma, about 40 miles from the battlefield at Stones River, thus ceding Middle Tennessee to the Union.

After the failure of the Breckenridge assault, Bragg's forces were thoroughly demoralized, and Union forces were holding their ground. So, Bragg ordered a retreat on the night of January 3. Many of his subordinate officers were stunned by the order despite the setbacks they had experienced. The Confedcrate army still held considerable ground as well as numerical strength. Some officers, including Breckinridge and General Polk, later accused Bragg of mismanaging the battle and undermining morale.

For all its back and forth, Stones River was considered a Union victory. A victory that was surely snagged from the closing jaws of defeat. Bragg had failed to destroy Rosecrans's army. Rosecrans decided that his own forces remained substantially intact and determined there was no reason for pursuit from the Union forces to cause further harm to the fleeing Army of Bragg. The Union did retain the field and control of Middle Tennessee as Confederate forces retreated southward. Reports of the battle helped lift Union morale at a critical time, especially following the disaster at Fredericksburg and coinciding with the issuance of the Emancipation Proclamation on January 1.

Lincoln later wrote to Rosecrans: *"You gave us a hard-earned victory, which had there been a defeat instead, the nation could scarcely have lived over."*

Bragg had squandered the initiative he had initially secured, and he had subsequently relinquished any chance of winning the battle. The Battle of Stones River was one of the bloodiest battles of the war by percentage of casualties. Of the roughly 81,000 soldiers engaged, nearly 24,000 became casualties. The Union casualties included 13,200 (killed, wounded, or missing) Confederate casualties numbered about 10,200 men. The casualty rate exceeded 29%, which was higher than at Gettysburg or Shiloh.

Despite the terrible losses, the Union considered Stones River a strategic and psychological victory. It gave Lincoln's administration a much-needed confidence boost after the debacle they experienced at Fredericksburg. Strategically the battle ended with the Union having full control of a vital region in Tennessee.

For Braxton Bragg, Stones River marked the beginning of his leadership demise. From that point on, he experienced a long and slow decline in the confidence his officers had in him, a deterioration that would play out disastrously at later battles like Chickamauga and Missionary Ridge. His style was always authoritarian and abrasive, which could be accepted in victory, but not in defeat. He was not a joy to serve under, and his subordinates were now speaking out.

After the Battle of Stones River, Union forces under General Rosecrans were entrenched in Murfreesboro for several months, using it as a base to build strength and prepare for the Tullahoma Campaign and eventually their movement toward Chattanooga.

CHAPTER 15
CHANCELLORSVILLE: TRIUMPH AND TRAGEDY IN THE WILDERNESS

Because of the embarrassing, as well as nearly catastrophic, loss at the Battle of Fredericksburg, General Ambrose Burnside was relieved of his duties in late January 1863, and was replaced by General Joseph Hooker, whose first step was to reshape the Army of the Potomac into a tighter, more disciplined, and more effective fighting force. He rounded up the many thousands of stragglers and deserters and brought them back into the fold of their units, he made sure the men had better food and instituted a furlough lottery so that his troops could go home occasionally.

Hooker got rid of Burnside's cumbersome Grand Divisions and gave each of his corps distinctive insignia, which helped clear up some battlefield confusions while giving his men a certain amount of pride in their own smaller company. He centralized the cavalry into a single unit under Brigadier General George Stoneman and put Colonel George Sharpe in charge of the new Bureau of Military Information, which was responsible for systematic collection of information, cross-referencing for accuracy, and creation of detailed maps and estimates of troop strengths. For the first time in the Army of the Potomac's history, its commander knew more precisely what lay before him. The Union forces appeared to be in good hands under its new leadership.

Joseph Hooker marched alongside his Union Army with a saber at his side as well as a distinct swagger that often burst into unmatched arrogance. Nicknamed "Fighting Joe," a moniker he reportedly disliked but could never quite shake, Hooker embodied the bravado of the early Civil War years. He was tall, broad-shouldered, and sharply dressed, a man who was all too aware of what he perceived to be the value of his presence. But beneath the polish and confidence lay a personality full of tension and contradiction. Hooker was the consummate self-promoter. After the Battle of Antietam, where his corps had suffered heavily but performed relatively well, and he himself was injured, Hooker made sure the press knew of his contributions. He did not hesitate to criticize his superiors, especially George McClellan, whom he regarded as too cautious and indecisive. *"I have the finest army on the planet,"* Hooker once said upon taking command of the Army of the Potomac in early 1863, *"but nobody to command it."*

By April 1863, the Union Army was still reeling from the defeat at Fredericksburg. There had been no major encounters in the east since that fight. The Battle of Fredericksburg was a decisive and demoralizing defeat fought in December 1862. Lee's Confederate Army successfully repelled attacks by the Union army under command of Ambrose Burnside. This battle resulted in significant Union casualties, with the Union losing over 12,500 men compared to the Confederate's losses of 6,000 men. The Union's defeat at Fredericksburg was a major blow to the North's morale and was seen as a major setback in the war effort for the Union.

Following the Battle of Fredericksburg, Ambrose Burnside attempted a winter offensive, which became known as the "Mud March". It was an attempt to do some harm to Lee's army in order to repair morale of his own men and reclaim his reputation after the devastating defeat at Fredericksburg.

The days had been unseasonably warm, and Burnside thought he saw an opportunity to cause some damage to Lee's unsuspecting forces. He positioned his army directly behind that of Lee. The plan was simple but seemingly a good one; to pursue the Army of North Virginia and attack it from the rear. Burnside's army had gotten into place, and morale seemed to be getting better as his men sensed an opportunity to get some manner of revenge. Burnside estimated he was within a two day's march of overcoming Lee. On January 20 the Union Army set out in hot pursuit of Lee. On the evening of January 20, the skies opened up and the rains came, and they were relentless.

It rained all night and into the next morning, in torrents. The dirt road had been turned to dust by the march of thousands of Confederate troops and the movement of their artillery only days before. Now with the rain, the road had turned into a river of water and mud. A logistical nightmare for an army march. The roads became fundamentally impassable. But Burnside remained undaunted in his search for a matter of revenge. The Union Army was commanded to continue its pursuit despite the conditions. Wagons sank in the mud and horses collapsed trying to pull wagons through the deep mire. Men had to physically carry artillery pieces forward, only to have them become stuck again a few yards later. The troops struggled forward, and they were not happy. The rain following relentlessly on them was nearly freezing. They were soaked, chilled to the bone, and ever more demoralized, by the moment. They moved only a few miles in the entire day.

As the rain continued, the pontoons that were to be used for the necessary river crossing lagged far behind. They too were slowed by the effects of the mud. When the Union Army finally reached the banks of the Rappahannock River on January 22, the attempt to deploy the bridges failed miserably. Engineers couldn't assemble the pontoons fast enough in the freezing rain. The river was moving much more swiftly because of the rains. And Confederate cannon fire was further derailing their attempts. Efforts to drive pilings were stymied by the soft soils and mud of the riverbank. Confederate soldiers on the opposite side of the Rappahannock were resting on mostly dry land and could hear, see, and laugh at the comical Union Army.

Any possible surprise of a Union attack had obviously vanished with the confusion at the Rappahannock as Lee moved his men into position to effectively block any further attempt at crossing of the river. The Union Army trudged back to its encampments on January 23 in mud that was often nearly thigh deep. The Mud March was a convergence of poor planning, terrible weather, logistical roadblocks, and ineffective leadership. The ill-fated expedition of the Mud March further eroded what was very low Union morale and was met with considerable Confederate ridicule, and significant damage to Burnside's credibility and reputation.

Captain Charles Johnson of the 100th Pennsylvania Infantry said, *"We moved off in the rain and in the dark, splashing through seas of mud, and bivouacked in the rain and in the mud. Fires were out of the question, and we lay down supperless and shivering. Men cursed and growled, but still pushed on. Horses and mules dropped dead in the traces. Wagons sank axle-deep. Pontoons stuck fast... We were stuck fast too and when the army finally turned back, it was not from the enemy's fire, but from the mud."*

On January 26, 1863, General Burnside was relieved of his duties and was replaced by General Joseph Hooker.

Battle of Chancellorsville

Under Hooker's leadership, morale of the Union forces was mostly very quickly restored with the significant improvements he had made to food and clothing, increase in pay, a better camp life and intelligence gathering. The Army under Hooker was in a place of much better preparation to fight than it had been only a few short months prior under Ambrose Burnside.

But the upcoming battle would again significantly challenge the Union side. Chancellorsville was little more than a crossroads near a large mansion called the Chancellor House. The battlefield lay at the western edge of the region known as the Wilderness of Spotsylvania, a vast expanse of dense second-growth forest, tangled underbrush, and thickets. Because of the conditions of the forest, reasonable fighting visibility was poor. The density of the forest restricted maneuverability, artillery deployment, and line-of-sight, making traditional Civil War Napoleonic battlefield tactics very difficult. The terrain limited the Union's vast advantages in troop numbers and artillery. General Hooker had over 125,000 soldiers at his disposal, while Lee had about 60,000.

Scattered throughout the Wilderness were small farms with clearings for growing their crops, and narrow access roads. These open areas would soon serve as primary battlegrounds during the engagement with names such as Hazel Grove, Fairview, and Catherine Furnace. These relatively small areas of open ground allowed deployment of artillery and clearer lines of engagement.

Opposing General Hooker, General Lee's Army of Northern Virginia was holding firm around Fredericksburg. Lee's forces were smaller, but they were experienced, well led, and operating on familiar terrain.

Hooker had developed a bold plan to initiate the battle. He would flank Lee by moving his main force west through the Wilderness and striking the Confederates from the rear. It was a maneuver that promised to trap Lee and potentially destroy his army. *"My plans are perfect,"* Hooker boasted, *"and when I start to carry them out, may God have mercy on General Lee, for I will have none."* Part of Hooker's confidence may have been because one of Lee's most trusted officers, General James Longstreet, was on a resupply mission in Southern Virginia, and there was no chance the Longstreet could return in time to reinforce Lee.

Lee had also earlier approved Longstreet's plan to attack the North's federal garrison at Suffolk, Virginia some 120 miles from Lee's army making any kind of rapid reinforcement impossible. The Suffolk campaign turned into a siege that lasted for nearly a month and was still in progress when Hooker initiated the Chancellorsville campaign. Longstreet's 12,000 men could have further altered the outcome of the battle of Chancellorsville had they been available to Lee.

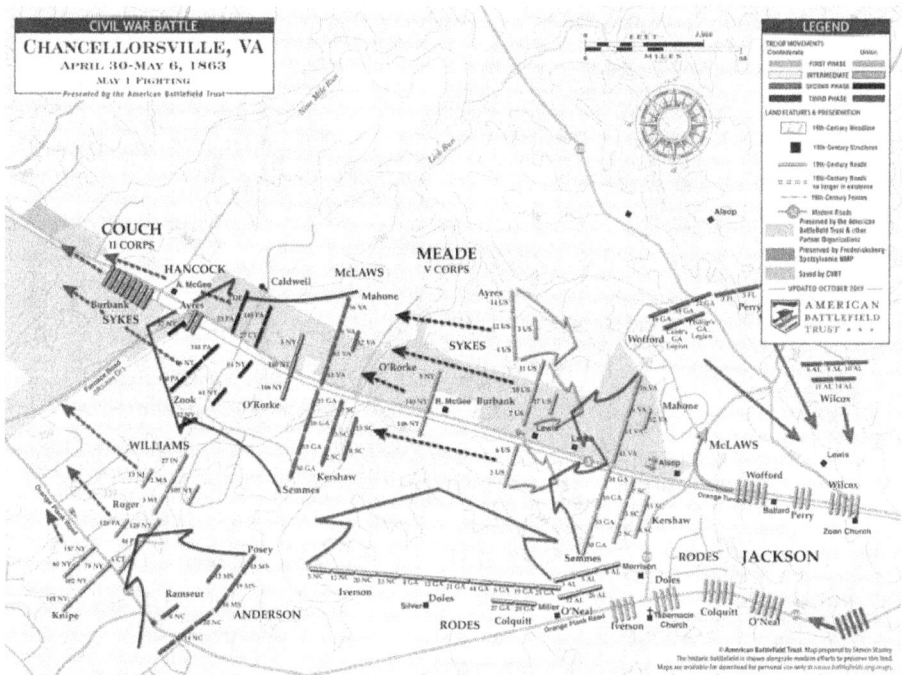

The Chancellorsville Campaign Overview (April 27 – May 6, 1863)

By his own account, Hooker had devised an audacious and brilliant plan to confront Lee. He would send cavalry under General Stoneman deep into Lee's rear to disrupt supply lines, then feint with a portion of his army at Fredericksburg while sending the bulk of his force west to outflank Lee. By all accounts, the plan was sound and in late April, it worked. Hooker's men reached Chancellorsville and Lee's army was caught between two Union forces. Then, on April 30, for some unexplained reason Hooker hesitated to force the attack. *"The enemy must ingloriously fly or come out from behind his defenses and give us battle on our own ground, where certain destruction awaits him."*

He paused at Chancellorsville, entrenching his forces, and waited for Lee to react, relinquishing the initiative. Hooker normally, very aggressive, was seen by his staff as becoming more reserved and cautious as the major engagement drew closer. This hesitation was one of the moments that would define the battle. Rather than push forward aggressively to meet and shatter Lee's divided force, Hooker abruptly halted the advance and ordered his troops to fall back to defensive positions near the Chancellor House, where he intended to let Lee attack him. This decision stunned his subordinates, who had been poised to drive forward. Among them, General George Meade reportedly expressed disbelief, believing that Hooker had *"lost his nerve."*

The precise reasoning for Hooker's decision to fall back is not known. Some suggest that Hooker, a corps commander by temperament rather than a grand strategist, was overwhelmed by the scale of his own plan. Others point to a sense of overconfidence, a belief that Lee, facing a numerically superior and better-positioned foe, would be forced into a desperate, frontal assault.

May 1–2: Lee's Bold Strategy

Combat of the Chancellorsville Campaign began on May 1st, 1863. The battle would soon be renowned for a Confederate flank attack begins with a brilliant flanking movement executed by the Union Army. The fog that clung to the thick trees and further obscured vision in the Virginia Wilderness on the morning of May 1 concealed more than just troop movements, it hid a moment of extraordinary opportunity. General Hooker had outmaneuvered Lee. After instituting a flanking march west of Fredericksburg, Hooker stood behind Lee's lines with over 70,000 men, threatening the Confederate army from the rear. Lee, for all his daring, had fewer than 40,000 men to meet the immediate threat. If ever the Union army had a chance to strike a decisive blow, it was at that time

Hooker moved three of his corps, Slocum's XII Corps in the center, Sykes' division of the V Corps on the right, and Couch's II Corps in support eastward along three roads through the Wilderness. His men were confident, advancing steadily through thick timber and rough terrain. They expected to find Confederate pickets and perhaps scattered resistance, but nothing that could match their overwhelming strength. Spirits were high. Even the usually reserved George Meade believed a breakthrough was within reach.

On the far side of the forest, Lee was confronted with far superior numbers. Despite this obvious fact he made one of the most daring decisions of the war. Rather than fall back, he split his already outnumbered army again. Leaving a portion of his force to guard Fredericksburg, he pressed forward with two divisions under Generals McLaws and Anderson, perhaps 15,000 men at most, to meet Hooker's advance head-on. The terrain favored defense with its twisted paths, thick undergrowth, and poor visibility and made Union artillery nearly useless. In that tangled forest, two small Confederate divisions halted the momentum of a vastly larger foe. The move startled and surprised Hooker.

By mid-afternoon, despite having suffered few casualties and with the bulk of his army yet unengaged, Hooker issued a sudden and fateful order: all forward elements were to withdraw to a defensive position around the Chancellorsville crossroads. Hooker reported, *"I was not willing to jeopardize the advantages I had gained by delivering battle at that point... I deemed it best to select a position and force the enemy to attack me."*

Hooker's generals were dumbfounded. His second-in-command, General Darious Couch thought the order must be a mistake. *"It was incomprehensible to me. He had led us to the very gates of victory and then closed them himself."* Meade protested. *"What was incomprehensible to me was that after having got the enemy on the run, we should stop and not push our advantage."* Slocum hesitated. Yet Hooker insisted. The man who had declared days earlier that the Confederates *"must ingloriously fly"* now chose to yield the initiative again without a major fight.

"I have lost confidence in Joe Hooker," the extremely cautious General Couch confided to a fellow officer. He was not alone. The Union troops fell back through the woods, disheartened, while Lee, still significantly outnumbered realized that his audacity had paid off. Hooker's unexpected retreat allowed the Confederates to consolidate their troops and set the stage for Thomas Stonewall Jackson's legendary flanking march on May 2.

May 1, 1863, could have been the day that Hooker won the war for the Union cause. Instead, it became the day his initiative died, and he lost the full confidence of his staff that he had earlier secured.

The Decision Leading to Jackson's Flank

Lee and Stonewall Jackson stood together around a campfire speaking in hushed tones, separated from their staffs. Nearby aides and couriers waited in silence as the two generals strategized. Their Army was surrounded, and they were in a very dangerous position. The Confederates were wedged between two wings of the Union army. General Sedgwick still sat across from Fredericksburg with 60,000 men, and Hooker's vast flanking force of some 70,000 men, now curled around the Chancellorsville crossroads and held strong positions in the Wilderness. Lee had fewer than 44,000 troops between the two fronts.

Under the Confederate assault of earlier in the day, Hooker had blinked having misjudged Lee. He had quickly secured the advantage and just as quickly had given it up. Now Lee did not want to offer that advantage back. He and his chief adviser needed to draw up a plan that would accomplish the unexpected. The question that lay before them was how to get it done. As he normally would,

Jackson had spent the day studying the terrain. He had ridden the Furnace Road and noted the vulnerability of the Union right. There, far beyond the main Federal defenses, the XI Corps under General O. Howard held a long, exposed flank. It was thin, barely guarded, and shielded by dense woods.

Jackson's idea was as daring as it was dangerous. He would take nearly 30,000 men, two-thirds of Lee's force, and march silently around Hooker's right flank, navigating narrow forest trails to strike the Union rear. Lee would remain behind with just 14,000 men, a threadbare force to hold Hooker's attention and bluff the strength of their line.

As the two generals stood by the fire strategizing, Lee listened carefully, nodding occasionally, his arms crossed and boots kicking at the soft earth. He asked a few quiet questions. What if the march was discovered? What if the Federals attacked while the army was split? Jackson answered with conviction and calm. There was a long pause. Then Lee spoke. *"Go on, then,"* he said. *"Go around."*

It was a decision born not just of tactical calculation, but of unbridled trust, Lee trusted Jackson as he trusted no other. And Jackson, for his part, was eager. *"With God's blessing,"* he whispered to one aide as he mounted his horse, *"we will roll them up like a wet blanket."* That night the two great generals of the Confederacy made a decision that defied logic and reshaped the course of the war, not because they had the stronger army, but because they had the stronger will coupled with incredible daring.

Jackson's corps began their march early in the morning of May 2, using local guides along narrow forested back roads to conceal their movement. The march was scheduled to begin at 4 am, but due to Jackson being sick it did not begin until after 7 am. The flanking maneuver would take Jackson's force on a 12-mile trek that was meant to allow his forces to attack the Union from the west. His column of soldiers stretched for almost five miles, marching four abreast, and moving with an eerie silence through the Virginia wilderness. The road on which they marched was narrow, crude, and often muddy. But the men were veterans of many battles and understood the importance of what they were doing.

Some Union officers observed Jackson's march but mistakenly believed it was Lee's army in retreat. However, some Union officers including General Sickles recognized an opportunity to do some harm to the Confederates. The Union command in the area, however, was in chaos. Communication was almost non-existent, and there were disagreements on how to proceed when communication worked well, now those disagreements were amplified.

Sickles leading the Union III Corps, chased after the Confederates during the afternoon of May 2 and succeeded in caught up to the rear flank of Jackson's column. This move resulted in Sickles capturing of a regiment of Confederate soldiers. But it also deprived Hooker of over 10,000 troops who would otherwise have been in a good position to repulse Jackson's flank attack later that evening.

Believing himself cut off from the rest of the Union Army during the night of May 2, Sickles launched, what he referred to as, a midnight bayonet charge. General Sickles had a way of exaggerating his accomplishments. The charge was little more than a reconnaissance rather than claiming ground. Sickles, with permission from Hooker, withdrew from a high ground around Hazel Grove, and back to the relative safety of the area around the Chancellor House. The Confederates quickly claimed that high ground and fortified it with cannon, from which they would pummel the North's defenses at Fairview and Chancellorsville.

As General Stonewall Jackson's corps rested a bit from its grueling 12-mile march through the tangled Virginia wilderness on the afternoon of May 2, the moment of execution of his daring plan was near at hand. The Confederate soldiers, weary from hours of silent movement along narrow forest roads, now stood in underbrush to the west of the unsuspecting Union right flank. They had marched in near secrecy and in almost total silence screened from view by the thick woods.

Jackson himself had ridden ahead with several officers to survey the terrain and assess Union positions. What he saw confirmed what Lee had hoped. The Union XI Corps, under General Oliver Howard, had made the fatal error of not securing their flank. Their line was aligned north to south, facing the Confederate line to the east, leaving their right flank facing west and completely exposed. Many Union soldiers had stacked their muskets and were preparing supper, or lounging, unaware of the tidal wave about to break upon them.

As his men filed into position, Jackson arranged his brigades in three lines of attack, with General Robert Rodes commanding the lead division. D. H. Hill's and R. E. Colston's divisions would follow in close support. Jackson emphasized speed and surprise. He issued orders to avoid making campfires or any noise that might betray their presence prior to the attack. Officers were warned to keep their commands hushed. The men were hungry, dirty, and exhausted, but the mood was electric with anticipation. The late afternoon hour was nearly perfect for the attack as the sun was at the Confederates' backs and Union vigilance was likely to be at its lowest.

At around 5:15 p.m., the bugles sounded. Jackson's men surged from the woods in waves, shouting their infamous Rebel yell. The assault was sudden, ferocious, and overwhelming. The surprised XI Corps was quickly engulfed in chaos. Private Levi Meyers of the 75th Ohio recalled: *"It was as if the trees exploded. They came howling from the woods. I dropped my rifle and ran until my legs collapsed."*

Panic spread faster than orders, the Union army was in pandemonium. Whole Union regiments fled without firing a shot. Some tried to form hasty resistance, but the Confederates rolled over these pockets quickly, efficiently, and without mercy. Artillery pieces were abandoned and captured. A brigade of German-American soldiers, many of whom had barely been in combat prior to this moment, bore the brunt of the first wave and collapsed under the pressure. Unmanned horses stampeded through the Union lines, adding to the chaos.

As the initial Confederate charge overwhelmed the unsuspecting Union forces, Stonewall Jackson ordered the second and third lines to join the attack to maintain the momentum his original troops had gained. Union units attempted to rally at several points along the Orange Plank Road and near the Wilderness Church, but the confusion, panic, terrain, and difficult communications made it nearly impossible to coordinate a defense.

The Union attempt to gather itself and put up a defense was fruitless. The Southern army had a tremendous advantage gained by its momentum in the close fighting and hand to hand combat. Union soldiers fired blindly into the smoke, often unsure of who was friend or foe. Darkness and exhaustion finally slowed the Confederate onslaught. By nightfall, Jackson's men had driven the Union line back over two miles and captured thousands of prisoners, dozens of artillery pieces, and a large swath of territory. It was a deadly and demoralizing battle for the Northern soldiers.

Hooker's entire right wing was effectively shattered, and his overall position was imperiled.

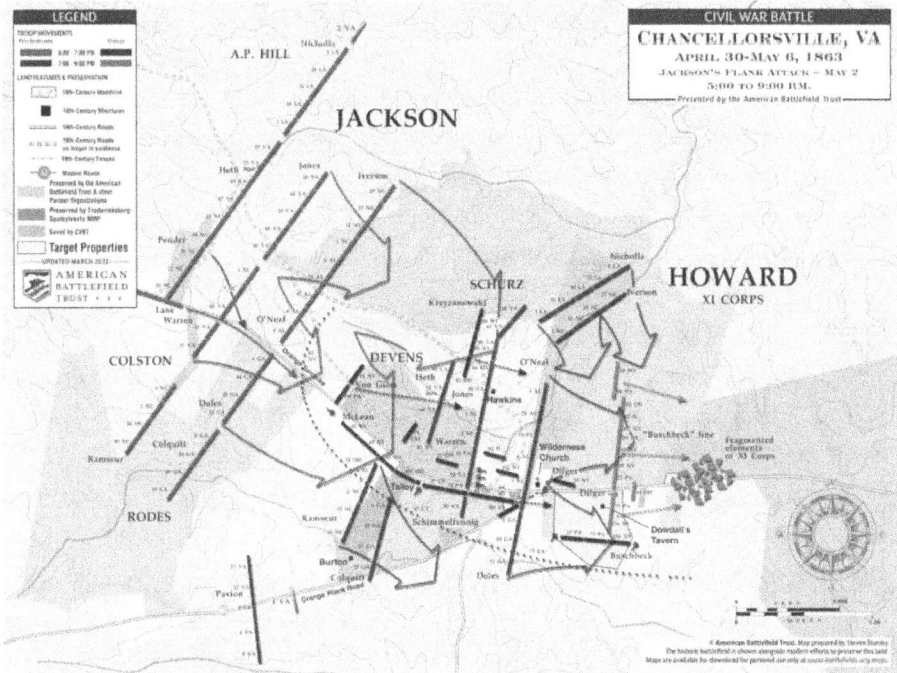

Jackson's Flank March (May 2, 1863)

The Death of Jackson

After the devastating flank attack Jackson had inflicted on the North darkness had fallen and the initial attack had terminated. Around 9:00 p.m., Jackson rode ahead of his own lines, accompanied by members of his staff and a small detachment of couriers. They were scouting the area for a possible nighttime attack. This was classic Jackson strategy. He was aggressive, restless, and eager to capitalize on any gained momentum. But such a ride in the darkness was also highly dangerous.

The 18th North Carolina Infantry, under the command of Brigadier General James Lane, was still very jittery from the battle from which they had just returned. They had no idea that General Jackson was in the vicinity. Their position was very close to Union front lines and Union troops had been probing in the woods in which they were occupying. They were on high alert for a possible full-scale Union counterattack.

The 18th mistook Jackson's party for a Union cavalry unit. Jackson and his entourage of some 14 men rode along the narrow road south of the Plank

Road near the front line without announcing themselves. Confederate soldiers, noticing the intrusion but not knowing who they were shouted, *"Halt! Who goes there?"* Before Jackson's group could respond, the impatient soldiers released a volley of musket fire that ripped through the darkness.

A Jackson aide, Captain James Smith reported, *"It was just at the edge of the thicket… Suddenly the crackle of musketry burst upon us from the left, and a volley was fired by our own men, not 30 yards away. I heard General Jackson exclaim, 'They have shot me!'"* Three bullets struck General Stonewall Jackson. One bullet entered his left arm, shattering the bone below the shoulder. Another passed through his right hand. A third may have grazed his hand or side, though accounts vary.

Later General Lane wrote in his report: *"At the time General Jackson was wounded, my brigade was halted in line of battle in the woods near the Plank Road. I had thrown out skirmishers to the front, and my men were expecting an attack at any moment. Suddenly a body of horsemen approached rapidly through the woods. They failed to answer our challenge, and my men, believing them to be Federal cavalry, fired a volley. Unhappily, this fire struck down General Jackson and several of his staff."*

During the attack, his horse bolted, and Jackson was thrown to the ground. Several of his staff were also hit, and some were killed. Amid the confusion and mounting panic, a second volley was fired. In the chaos, Jackson was left lying in the brush for nearly half an hour, as his staff and litter-bearers tried to retrieve him. A short time later, Union artillery opened fire on the area, further delaying evacuation of the wounded. Eventually, Jackson was placed on a stretcher, though one of the litter bearers was shot during the retreat and dropped his end, causing Jackson to fall and further aggravate his wounds.

Captain R.S. Young of the 28th North Carolina wrote: *"At the time General Jackson was wounded, my brigade was halted in line of battle in the woods near the Plank Road. I had thrown out skirmishers to the front, and my men were expecting an attack at any moment. Suddenly a body of horsemen approached rapidly through the woods. They failed to answer our challenge, and my men, believing them to be Federal cavalry, fired a volley. Unhappily, this fire struck down General Jackson and several of his staff."*

General Jackson was taken to a field hospital near Wilderness Tavern, and Dr. Hunter McGuire, the army's chief surgeon, made the grim decision that Jackson's shattered arm would need to be amputated. The operation was performed in the early hours of May 3. Jackson was moved to the plantation office building at Guinea Station, some 27 miles south of the battlefield, for recovery. Even though the trip was not an easy one, his condition seemed hopeful upon arrival. He was alert and in good spirits, even joking to his chaplain: *"I always wanted to die on a Sunday."*

But over the next several days, Jackson caught pneumonia, likely caused by a combination of shock, exposure, and the rigors of his evacuation. His condition began to worsen. On May 10, 1863, a Sunday, Jackson's breathing became shallow. Dr. McGuire reported that Jackson seemed to be aware of what was happening to him. His final words have become etched in Confederate memory, *"Let us cross over the river, and rest under the shade of the trees."*

The immediate effect of the wounding of Stonewall Jackson was disarray within the Second Corps. A.P. Hill was second in command, but he soon also was wounded. So then command of Jackson's forces fell to J.E.B. Stuart who, though a skilled cavalry commander, had never led infantry in a major engagement.

Through all the doubts he would rise to the occasion, but Jackson's absence marked a turning point for the Confederacy. With Jackson gone, Lee had lost the one general who could consistently execute Lee's boldest strategies and hand him successes. Lee and Jackson had communicated openly and had operated extremely well together. The Army of Northern Virginia would never again strike with such unity and speed as they had under General Stonewall Jackson.

May 3: The Bloodiest Day

With Jackson out of commission Lee launched a massive assault on May 3 to reunite his divided army and further press the attack. Union forces around Chancellorsville were driven back under heavy pressure. The fighting was some of the fiercest of the war. Lee's forces were now a combined reunited force. They were still significantly outnumbered but they maintained the momentum of the battle.

A furious assault struck at Hooker's central position at Chancellorsville. The battlefield was a nightmarish landscape. The terrain was difficult with dense forest limiting mobility. The dense growth that had helped shield Jackson's flanking movement, now trapped men in deadly combat where visibility was reduced to mere feet. Lee's men advanced slowly. Union troops positioned around Chancellorsville, found themselves assaulted from multiple directions. With the terrain rendering formal lines useless, units fought in knots sometimes firing at shadows, often stumbling directly into enemy bayonets.

Union artillery was largely ineffective early in the day due to the confined space. Guns could not be brought to bear effectively, and many cannons were withdrawn from the area. The Confederates, recognizing the importance of Hazel Grove, quickly seized it and turned the ground into an artillery platform. With a commanding view of Union positions, Southern cannons raked the enemy with relentless fire. Corporal Isaac Leeman of the 124th New York wrote: *"The air was filled with branches, bullets, and the screams of wounded men. You fired at sound, not sight."*

Union General Hooker remained at his headquarters near the Chancellor House. He was leaning against a wooden pillar on the porch of the house when a Confederate artillery round slammed into the pillar just above his head. The Union leader fell to the ground and was rendered totally unconscious for about a half hour. A few hours later he had regained reasonable consciousness, and started issuing orders, but he was still not totally coherent. His return to semi-sentience disappointed the veteran corps commanders who had hoped that without him they would be free to employ their army's considerable untapped might.

Prior to the battle, Hooker had not established a clear succession plan in case he was rendered unable to lead. Nor was he willing to relinquish command when he was clearly not competent to lead. But it was obvious that command should have been taken from him. The army became paralyzed in a moment when decisive leadership was most needed. Hooker's designated second-in-command was Major General Darius Couch, a capable but cautious officer. Couch later recalled being deeply frustrated with Hooker's decisions and stunned that no clear orders were being given in the hours after the wounding. Yet Couch did not assert authority. He remained subservient to his superior officer and carried out Hooker's somewhat incoherent orders.

Despite some local counterattacks, including a spirited stand by the Union 12th Corps near Fairview, the Confederates continued their surge forward. The lines shifted like rolling tides, as regiments dissolved into the woods, only to reappear under fresh banners or be absorbed by other commands. The fighting around the Chancellor mansion turned it into a house of horrors with bodies piled in mounds. By midday, the Union center had collapsed entirely under the intense pressure. Some units fell back in good order and others broke entirely. Union soldiers were horrified to find the woods catching fire. Brush fires ignited by shells consumed many of the wounded where they lay. A Union surgeon recalled, *"We could hear them cry out, those poor boys. We could not reach them. The flames moved faster than any stretcher."*

Despite these horrors, many Federal units fought bravely. The 3rd Wisconsin held a ravine for nearly two hours, repulsing three Confederate charges before being overrun. Elsewhere, the 5th Maine Battery fought to the last round before spiking their guns. Confederate General Jubal Early later called May 3 *"a butcher's day."* Union casualties that day exceeded 9,000. Confederate losses were equally staggering with 8,000 or more lost in that single day.

By nightfall, the Union line had reformed near U.S. Ford, as the Confederates paused to regroup. The battlefield was littered with thousands of dead and wounded from both sides with men caught in thickets, sprawled in ditches, and some burned beyond recognition. Major Abner Small of Maine wrote: *"I had seen death before, but not like this. Here death had taken root and flowered in blood."*

Skirmishing continued over the next two days, including a costly but failed Union assault on Fredericksburg's heights. Rain and confusion deepened the misery. On May 6, Hooker ordered a full retreat across the Rappahannock River. His engineering corps had established two pontoon bridges on which the Army could retreat. The bridges had previously been used to garner supplies, now they were used to help a staggered army get back to relative safety. The crossing of the river occurred after nightfall. After six days of fighting Lee decided it would be best not to pursue Hooker further. His men were tired.

During the battle of Chancellorsville, the Union Army had lost nearly 17,000 men. The Confederacy had lost 13,000, including General Stonewall Jackson. Though victorious, Lee had paid dearly. His army was now much smaller but still more emboldened from being victorious.

Chancellorsville may havew been Lee's greatest tactical triumph. Although Jackson was the architect of the plan and implemented it. Lee gave the approval accepting responsibility. Lee's decision was likely both his most triumphant and his most costly. He had faced an enemy twice his size and emerged victorious. Yet the loss of Jackson was incalculable, and the loss of 13,000 men was not sustainable for the future.

For the Union, it was a humiliation. Hooker had begun the battle with brilliance but lost nerve at various times exacerbating critical moments of the battle. Morale in Hooker's army plummeted after the fighting more quickly than it had grown. President Lincoln, anguished, said, *"My God! What will the country say?"*

Many of Hooker's men grew despondent after their commander's decision to stop the fight on May 5. One soldier of the 141st Pennsylvania wondered, *"...must we lose this battle? Have these brave comrades who have fought so bravely and died at their post died in vain?"*

Southerners were also baffled by the Union retreat. Confederate cartographer Jedidiah Hotchkiss who was taking measurements in the area for a map of the campaign, recorded in his journal on May 12, 1863, that he *"had no idea the enemy were so well fortified and wonder they left their works so soon."*

His army was outnumbered more than two-to-one, but Lee had won what many consider his greatest tactical victory. Hooker had held every advantage: troop numbers, supplies, and field position, and yet he still lost the battle. The North was stunned. The South was jubilant.

The seeds of the possibility of the Southern Army moving farther north into Pennsylvania had been planted. Lee and his army were emboldened by what was just accomplished. He was formulating what he hoped to be ultimately a decisive victory, one that might end the war. The Confederate victory over the superior Union force though certain and thorough, carried the burden of overconfidence. Within weeks, Lee would embark on another bold invasion of the North into Gettysburg, Pennsylvania. And at Gettysburg, there would be another chance for the North to master its own fate, or for the South to force an armistice.

Brilliant or Incompetent

The Union defeat at Chancellorsville was both a dazzling display of Lee's strategic genius and a profound failure of Union leadership under Joseph Hooker, as well as much of his command. Both factors were so deeply entwined that the outcome cannot be fully understood without acknowledging both.

Lee's Strategic Brilliance

- Lee faced daunting odds: he was outnumbered roughly 2 to 1, with around 60,000 Confederate troops to Hooker's 130,000. Yet he made a series of bold, risky moves: Dividing his army in the face of a superior force, two times. First, he left a small force to attack a portion of Hooker's army and marched the rest west to confront the Union's right flank. Then, even more daringly, he split his forces again and sent

Stonewall Jackson on a 12-mile flanking march through the woods to strike Hooker's exposed right.

- Jackson's surprise attack at dusk on May 2nd completely unraveled the Union XI Corps, creating chaos in Hooker's lines and further seized the initiative.
- Lee's aggressive posture throughout the battle kept Union forces off balance despite inferior numbers and the devastating loss of Jackson, who was mortally wounded by friendly fire that night.

Hooker's Failures

On the other side of the conflict, Hooker started with a strong strategic position:

- He had moved the Army of the Potomac across the Rappahannock River and outflanked Lee.
- He had far greater numbers and interior lines.
- His initial movements had even forced Lee into retreat. But then Hooker hesitated, lost nerve, and abandoned the offensive:
- On May 1, instead of pressing the attack as planned, he pulled his army back into defensive positions around Chancellorsville, giving up the initiative.
- He was stunned by Jackson's flank attack and failed to respond decisively even when he had significant reserves.
- Hooker was injured when a Confederate shell struck a column on the porch of the Chancellorsville house, affecting his command capacity, but he refused to relinquish control
- He ignored his corps commanders' advice, including that of Generals Meade and Reynolds, who urged counterattacks at key moments.

In short, Hooker gave Lee opportunities, and Lee seized them with remarkable daring and skill.

Conclusion

Chancellorsville was not just a Southern victory or a Union defeat, it was Lee's masterpiece. The battle was fought with a level of audacity that few generals would dare attempt. But it could not have succeeded to the extent it did without Hooker's collapse in confidence and command. The South won the battle, with grave costs, not least of which was the death of General Jackson, which Lee described as losing his *"right arm."*

CHAPTER 16
GETTYSBURG, TURNING OF THE TIDE

After his triumph at Chancellorsville in his home state of Virgina, Robert E. Lee sought to carry the war onto Northern soil for only the second time in the entire war. Until that point, the South had been nearly totally on the defensive. But with his last two major engagements decisive victories, confidence was growing, and opportunities seemed to be unfolding.

The Army of Northern Virginia began marching toward Pennsylvania in June 1863. Lee had marched his forces into the north one other time for the Maryland Campaign in September 1862. That march had ended in the one-day Battle of Antietam, the bloodiest single day of fighting in United States history. That first battle on Union soil was not a strategic for the South.

Lee marched his forces through the Virginia Shenandoah Valley, then into the fields of the North to engage the enemy on its own lands. As Lee's army crossed into Maryland and then into Pennsylvania, he gave strict orders that there would be no looting and no destruction of civilian property. His army was to be respectful to the locals. Although the orders were not totally obeyed, they were intended to show a superiority of the Confederacy army and perhaps plant a seed that negotiation might be possible to end the war.

The one area where the Confederate commanders totally failed Lee's orders was in the taking of free black persons. General Richard Ewell's men, along with other Confederate units captured hundreds of free African Americans in Pennsylvania and sent them into slavery in the South, primarily Virginia. This action was not officially sanctioned by Confederate policy, but it was in line with the general racial attitudes of the Confederate army and its leadership. Soldiers rounded up African Americans in the countryside and from within towns. Some had lived freely for generations. Others were children.

This was effectively a reverse Underground Railroad, Confederate forces forcibly transporting people into bondage, despite their legal status as free citizens of Pennsylvania. Apparently, Lee was aware of the actions of Ewell and

Early and did nothing to squelch them. These captures were systematic and widespread, not isolated incidents.

Lee had previously condoned the capture and return of fugitive slaves during the 1862 Maryland Campaign and saw African Americans as legitimate war spoils in many cases. There's no record of Lee disciplining officers like Ewell or Jubal Early for these kidnappings, even when they were reported by Southern newspapers and Union observers. In effect, Lee silently approved of these actions as a means of disrupting Northern communities, claiming black citizens as enslaved people, and striking psychological blows.

After defeating Hooker at Chancellorsville, Lee rightly believed that momentum was on his side. He had successfully repelled three major Union offensives in Virginia. He thought the Union Army to be disorganized and demoralized. Lee saw this as an opportunity to further the momentum he had gained and force the Union to react to him, rather than remaining on the defensive in Virginia.

The Virginia countryside, especially the Shenandoah Valley, had been heavily used to supply food to Lee's army in the past. But by the summer of 1863, local resources were mostly depleted and incapable of sustaining his army. Invading Pennsylvania, especially fertile south-central counties like Franklin, Adams, and Cumberland, meant Lee could feed his army off the bounty of Northern farms. Seizing supplies like horses, cattle, shoes, cloth and grain were undertaken but paid for with Confederate currency, which had little value in the South and essentially no value in the North. Ransoms were randomly required from Northern towns, mostly by Jubal Early. In a certain sense, moving north was a massive foraging expedition with military teeth.

It was also a chance to potentially outmaneuver the Union and threaten Washington or Baltimore from the north, potentially forcing a battle on ground of his choosing. In addition, Lee was acutely aware of the political calendar. The Northern public was weary of war, and dissatisfaction with Lincoln's management of the war was growing. By bringing the war onto Northern soil, Lee hoped to increase political pressure on Lincoln to negotiate for peace, especially if he could win a decisive victory.

Though unlikely by mid-1863, Confederate hopes for recognition by Britain or France had not entirely faded. Lee had expressed that a resounding Confederate victory on Union territory might strengthen their case for legitimacy or at least renewed interest in negotiation. European powers were watching the war closely, and a triumph in Pennsylvania might give the impression that the Confederacy was both viable and ascendant.

Lee also fully appreciated the psychological effect of war. A Confederate army operating deep in Northern territory could shake Union confidence and stir panic among civilians. It would mark a dramatic shift, an offensive threat rather than a defensive struggle. Moreover, the symbolism of invading Pennsylvania, especially so close to Independence Day, was not lost on either side. A Confederate victory on or near July 4 could have dramatically altered the tone of the war and the national narrative.

Perhaps most importantly, Lee believed that the key to Confederate victory was the destruction of the Union Army of the Potomac. He had repeatedly outmaneuvered the Union Army in Virginia. As Lee later stated in his official report: *"The enemy was depressed by the reverse which he had recently sustained, his numbers diminished by the expiration of the term of service of a portion of his troops… and we were therefore justified in entertaining reasonable expectations of success."*

Following the Battle of Chancellorsville, Union General-in-Chief Hallack instructed General Hooker to engage in the pursuit of Lee's army. By mid-June, the Army of Northern Virginia was poised to cross the Potomac River and enter Maryland. After defeating the Union garrisons at Winchester and Martinsburg, General Ewell's Second Corps began crossing the river on June 15. Hill's and Longstreet's corps followed on June 24 and 25. Hooker's army pursued from close behind, keeping themselves between Washington and Lee's army. The Union army crossed the Potomac on June 27.

On June 26, elements of Major General Jubal Early's division of Ewell's corps occupied the town of Gettysburg after chasing off the newly raised 26th Pennsylvania emergency militia in a series of minor skirmishes. General Jubal Early laid the borough under tribute but did not collect any significant supplies. Soldiers burned several railroad cars and a covered bridge, and destroyed nearby rail and telegraph lines.

The following morning, General Early departed for nearby York County. Lee ordered him to move toward Harrisburg and to scout or secure bridges across the Susquehanna River. Early's assignment was part of the effort to advance east from the Gettysburg area, seize supplies, and threaten the state capital at Harrisburg from the south. While in York County, Jubal Early demanded $100,000 in tribute from the town of York (which he never collected in full), as well as shoes, clothing, and food. His men took control of railroads, cut telegraph lines, and disrupted Union logistics in the region.

Hooker wanted to abandon Harper's Ferry and assimilate the troops stationed there into his army. General-in-Chief Henry Halleck denied that request. Feeling unsupported and insulted, on June 28 General Hooker offered his resignation, which Lincoln readily accepted.

Lincoln and the high command had most often been unimpressed with Hooker, mostly due to his overconfidence and his indecision. Both faults were magnified by his embarrassing defeat at Chancellorsville. And now he had shown his inability to stop Lee's invasion onto Union soil. Lincoln, Secretary of War Stanton, and Halleck had agreed after Chancellorsville that while it may be politically damaging to fire Hooker, they would quickly accept his resignation if he ever offered it.

In choosing a suitable replacement for Hooker, Lincoln ignored pleas to reinstate the still publicly popular George McClellan. Lincoln also ignored urgings from Radical Republicans to install their favorite, Major General John Fremont. Two of Hooker's corps commanders, John Reynolds and George Meade, were the top candidates, and after Reynolds strongly sought to remove himself from consideration, Meade was chosen. Secretary Stanton noted that Meade had no real enemies, *"and as a Pennsylvanian, he has patriotism enough to draw out all the latent energies of his nature."* Lincoln added, *"And will fight well on his own dunghill."* Changing army commanders while a major confrontation loomed was an extraordinary gamble.

In the pre-dawn of June 28, 1863, a mounted officer approached the camp of the Union Army's V Corps near Frederick, Maryland. Inside his tent, Major General George Gordon Meade was roused from sleep by the unexpected arrival of a messenger bearing orders from Washington. The letter, signed by General-in-Chief Henry Halleck, informed him that, effective immediately, Meade was to assume command of the entire Army of the Potomac. General Joseph Hooker had been relieved after his resignation was accepted.

Meade was both startled and reluctant. He read the orders twice to be sure that what he assumed it said was accurate. He was not seeking glory nor command. *"This is an honor I neither sought nor desired,"* he wrote to his wife. *"As a soldier, I had nothing to do but accept and exert my utmost abilities to command success."* The weight of command had come to him in the dark, unannounced and unwelcome, with Lee's army deep in Pennsylvania and the potential of a decisive battle looming.

With barely three days before the first shots would be fired at Gettysburg, Meade inherited an army on the move. He had only a vague understanding of the enemy's position. He inherited a war-weary command structure whose loyalty had been shaken by a series of changing leaders. He knew only a fraction of the army's total whereabouts, but knew he had to quickly consolidate his troops. Several Union corps were on the march mimicking the movement of Southern troops. Many of the North's officers he had never commanded, others he barely knew. Supply lines were in motion, and information was fragmentary at best. The Confederate army, somewhere to the north, remained with its intentions unclear, its strength uncertain.

Meade's instinct was typically cautious. But he was very aware of what would happen to the war effort if he were to effect command leading to the results that had been suffered by Burnside and Hooker. That type of loss would put major Northern cities at major risk and would likely lose the war for the North. The pressure on Meade was intense.

He drafted a plan to establish a strong defensive line along Pipe Creek in Maryland, where he could anchor his army and compel Lee to attack him on ground of his choosing. But events overtook intention. On July 1, a skirmish erupted near the crossroads town of Gettysburg between Union cavalry under General John Buford and advancing Confederate infantry under Henry Heth. The encounter escalated rapidly. By afternoon, the hills and ridges south of town were contested ground, and the passage to a great looming battle had opened without any formal order.

Meade responded with precision and resolve. Abandoning the Pipe Creek strategy, he ordered his scattered corps to concentrate at Gettysburg. Within 24 hours, he had reinforced the position, establishing a strong, fishhook-shaped line anchored on Cemetery Hill, Culp's Hill, and Cemetery Ridge.

He had assumed command with little notice, less preparation, and an army still in motion. Yet in three days, George Meade had staged himself and those under his command to lead the Union Army through its greatest trial.

Hooker issued a farewell order in which he called Meade "*a brave and accomplished officer, who has nobly earned the confidence and esteem of this army on many a well-fought field.*" A colonel wrote, "*His farewell order is excellent, the most modest of all his productions.*" At one time, Hooker had done well to revive the demoralized

Army of the Potomac, but he ultimately proved incapable of achieving any kind of victory.

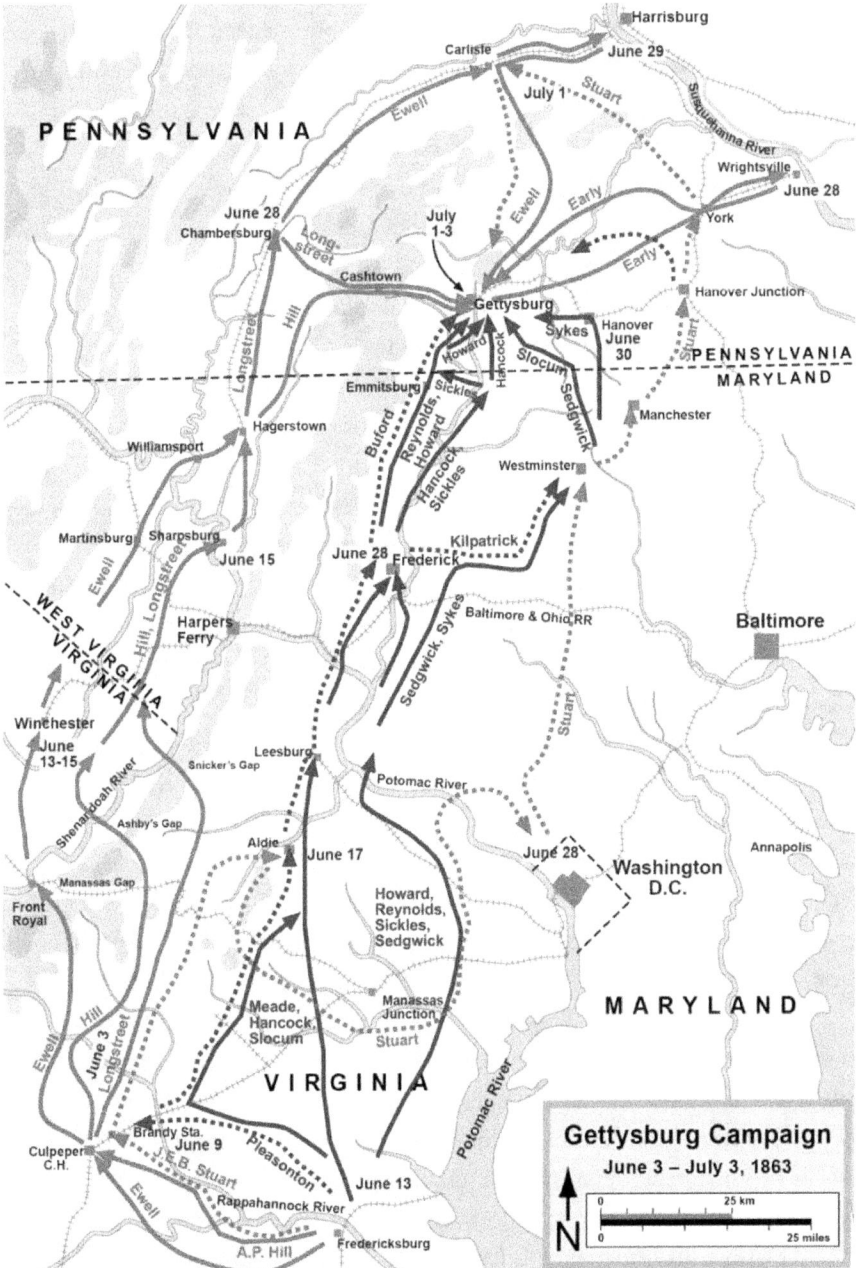

Gettysburg Campaign Overview (June–July 1863)

July 1, The Clash Begins

The small crossroads town of Gettysburg, nestled among the rolling hills of southern Pennsylvania, held no particular military significance, at least not at the outset. But on the morning of July 1, 1863, it would become the site of a clash that neither army had planned, yet both would be drawn into with unrelenting force. The first day of the Battle of Gettysburg was marked by chance encounters, escalating engagement, and ultimately, a Confederate tactical victory at the cost of disorganization and missed opportunity.

Major General John Reynolds was among the Union Army's most respected and capable commanders. He had flatly turned down the commission that was eventually forced upon Meade. On July 1, 1863, Reynolds was leading the left wing of the Army of the Potomac, comprising the I, III, and XI Corps, as it rushed toward Gettysburg to meet the advancing Confederate forces.

Union cavalry under General John Buford had engaged the Confederate forces west of the town earlier that morning and was being pressed hard. Buford was holding out for infantry reinforcements. Reynolds, recognizing the strategic importance of the high ground south of town, galloped forward and reached the scene around 10:15 a.m. He quickly approved Buford's decision to stand and fight and began deploying the I Corps infantry as it arrived.

Reynolds was helping to position elements of the 2nd Wisconsin Infantry in McPherson's Woods, west of town. While mounted on his horse and giving directions, Reynolds was likely turning to look over his shoulder when he was struck by a bullet, probably from a Confederate sharpshooter. The bullet entered behind his right ear and killed him almost instantly. He was the highest ranked Union officer killed at that point during the war. He was one of the only commanders in the Union Army that Lincoln implicitly trusted.

I Corps leadership then fell to Major General Abner Doubleday who was the highest ranking remaining officer in that field. Doubleday directed the battle through the remainder of the day including the heavy fighting at McPhersons Ridge and Seminary Ridge. Under his command, the I Corps fought skillfully but suffered grievous losses, gradually falling back through the town of Gettysburg to take defensive positions on Cemetery Hill by evening.

Despite his leadership under extreme pressure, Doubleday was not confirmed as permanent corps commander by Meade. On July 2, Meade replaced him with Major General John Newton, a less senior officer. Doubleday was deeply offended by this, seeing it as an insult to his conduct and seniority.

Throughout the late morning, fierce fighting erupted along McPherson's Ridge and into Herbst Woods, with Union troops repelling repeated assaults by Heth's division. Union lines bent but held, reinforced by additional brigades.

What began as a skirmish turned into a full-scale battle as Confederate and Union forces collided northwest of Gettysburg. Low ridges to the northwest of Gettysburg were initially defended by a Union cavalry division under Brigadier General John Buford soon reinforced with two corps of Union infantry.

By 4:00 p.m. Union forces were collapsing on both flanks with many soldiers retreating through the streets of Gettysburg, some engaging in house-to-house skirmishes as civilians took shelter in basements and root cellars. The retreat was chaotic, but a portion of the force managed to rally on Cemetery Hill, where General Oliver Howard had prudently placed reserves earlier in the day. Private Charles Wainwright wrote in his diary: "*We fell back through the streets, firing as we went. The rebels surged forward like a dark wave.*"

Lee arrived on the field late in the day and surveyed the unfolding scene. His army had clearly won the field that day, Union forces had been driven from their positions west and north of town, thousands were taken prisoner, and the enemy had fallen back in disarray. Yet Cemetery Hill, the key to the southern defenses of the town, remained in Union hands.

Lee believed the hill should be taken before the Union could fortify it. He sent word to General Ewell, whose corps had just executed a successful attack, to press forward *"if practicable."* Ewell, perhaps fatigued, uncertain of what lay ahead, and lacking support, chose not to press the attack. That hesitation, though understandable, would prove costly. By nightfall, Union reinforcements from II and III Corps were already arriving, and the high ground would soon be bristling with artillery and fortified infantry.

On the first day of the battle at Gettysburg, Union casualties were about 9,000 men and Confederate casualties included about 7,000 men. There were no significant breakthroughs for either side. The worst of the casualty numbers were yet to come.

July 2, Battling for High Ground

The second day at Gettysburg dawned as a hot and quiet day. The thunder and smoke of the first day's clash had ended with Confederate forces in control of the town of Gettysburg, and Union troops entrenched on the high ridges to the south, forming a defensive *"fishhook"* line from Culp's Hill and Cemetery Hill, sweeping down Cemetery Ridge, and curving around to Little Round Top at the southern end. The line provided the Union a favorable position on high ground that would be difficult to break from below.

How the battle would be fought on July 2, was far more than just a continuation of the previous day. It was a vast escalation, a ferocious, chaotic struggle across rocky hills, wheat fields, and peach orchards, etched into memory by names of individual fierce battles like those at Devil's Den, the Wheatfield, and Little Round Top. The day would test the Union line to its limits and further reveal the aggressive daring, and the human cost of Robert E. Lee's overall war strategy.

Lee's Plan: Hammering the Flanks

Lee, buoyed by the Confederate success on Day 1, sought to deliver a crushing blow on Day 2 by attacking both Union flanks simultaneously. His plan relied on coordination. James Longstreet's corps would strike the Union left, to roll up their line from south to north, while Richard Ewell's corps would attack the Union at Culp's Hill and Cemetery Hill.

Lee believed he could break the Army of the Potomac and perhaps finally bring the North to its knees, possibly even finally forcing recognition of the Confederacy. But coordination between his two generals proved elusive on day 2. Longstreet's men were delayed by poor maps, miscommunication, and a reluctance to act hastily without full readiness. Longstreet didn't launch his assault until around 4 p.m., giving Union forces just enough time to reinforce critical positions before the strike.

The Union Left: A Race for the High Ground

At the extreme left of the Union line sat Little Round Top, a boulder-strewn hill that overlooked the entire Union position. It was undefended for a what could have been a crucial window of time. Fortunately for the Union cause, Brigadier General Gouverneur Warren, Meade's chief engineer had climbed the hill and surveyed the ground. He quickly realized with horror that if Confederates seized it, the Union line could be rolled up like a carpet. Warren urgently called for reinforcements, and they were delivered in the form of Colonel Strong Vincent's brigade, which climbed the hill just minutes ahead of a Confederate assault to do the same. What followed was one of the most dramatic encounters of the entire war. On the far left of Vincent's line was Little Round

Top under the control of the 20th Maine Regiment, commanded by Colonel Joshua Lawrence Chamberlain.

Devil's Den and the Wheatfield: The Middle Mayhem

To the right of Little Round Top, the Union line twisted through a region of open fields and rocky outcrops that would soon become known in legend and horror as Devil's Den, the Wheatfield, and the Peach Orchard. Confederate General Longstreet had sent in John Bell Hood's division to assault Devil's Den and the southern end of the Union line. Hood's men surged up the rocky slopes under withering fire, shouting the Rebel yell, pushing through boulders and tree stumps. The Union defenders, part of the 3rd Corps under General Daniel Sickles, fought valiantly but were soon overwhelmed and Devil's Den fell into Confederate hands.

To the north, General Lafayette McLaws' division attacked the Union center-left, where Sickles had moved his corps. Sickles orders were to cover the Union left flank. As he sometimes did, Sickles decided he knew best and moved his men to the Peach Orchard. The result was that the Third Corps under his command was once again overrun and driven from the field. The move exposed his flanks and created a dangerously thin line of defense. Confederate artillery and infantry tore into it. Sickles himself was horribly wounded, losing his right leg to a cannonball (he would later donate the amputated leg to the Army Medical Museum in Washington and visit it annually, with a card saying *"With the Compliments of Major General D.E.S."*). His corps disintegrated under intense Confederate pressure.

The Wheatfield changed hands six times in a chaotic series of attacks and counterattacks that left the field carpeted with dead and wounded, many of the injured were too hurt to crawl away, crying out through the night. Union reinforcements from Pennsylvania and New York eventually stabilized the line, but at a ghastly cost of life.

Little Round Top and the 20th Maine

The afternoon of July 2, 1863, was slipping into dusk, but for the men of the 20th Maine Infantry, time was about to freeze in a desperate, defining moment. Perched atop the rocky slope of Little Round Top, they held the extreme left flank of the Union line, and they held it alone.

The commandeer of the 20th Maine, Colonel Joshua Chamberlain, was a man fluent in six languages, a scholarly professor from Bowdoin College who turned soldier as the Civil War unfolded. Because of his desire to serve in the War, he wrote to Maine's Governor Israel Washburn, Jr., *"I fear, this war, so costly of blood and treasure, will not cease until men of the North are willing to leave good positions, and sacrifice the dearest personal interests, to rescue our country from desolation, and defend the national existence against treachery."* He was given a leave from the college under the pretense of studying in Europe. Instead, he enlisted in the army with no previous military experience. He was appointed by the governor as Lieutenant Colonel of the 20th Maine regiment where he and his men first fought at Fredericksburg. He was promoted to Colonel upon the promotion of the former Colonel Adelbert Ames who was asked to join the staff of Major General George Mead.

On July 2, 1863, at the Little Round Top on the field of battle at Gettysburg, Chamberlain was ill with both dysentery and malaria. Despite his physical condition he was given a simple but chilling order by his brigade commander: *"This is the left of the Union line. You are to hold this ground at all hazards."* He could expect no reinforcements, and he was not to retreat. There would be no excuses for bad results. If the line of the 20th Maine were to be broken, the entire Union line could be easily outflanked, and the battle, perhaps the war, could be lost. As Chamberlain wrote *"We knew well what that meant. It was to die on the line, if needs be, to hold that position at any cost, for if that point were turned, the entire line would be taken in flank and rolled up."*

On the Confederate side, Colonel William Oates led the 15th and 47th Alabama up the steep, wooded slope, unaware that they were about to face the 20th Maine Infantry, which had been hastily positioned at the extreme left of the Union line. The Alabamians had marched 20 miles earlier that morning with little water and little food. Their canteens were empty, their throats dry, and still they climbed the hill toward Little Roundtop.

"Fix bayonets!" Oates ordered, as his men fanned out and began probing the Union line. The fighting was brutal, close, and often hand-to-hand, until the troops from Alabama were ordered to fall back in a temporary retreat. Time and again, the 15th and 47th Alabama launched charges up the slope, only to be repulsed by the disciplined volleys and fierce determination of the Maine men. The terrain was against them, favoring the defenders. It was slippery granite, thick underbrush, combined with the type of July Pennsylvania heat that choked one's breath away.

The battle for Little Round Top was not a single, grand assault but a series of desperate thrusts, fall backs, and counterthrusts. As Oates recalled later,

198

"There never were harder fighters than the 15th Alabama, but the enemy had the advantage of position, and it told in the end."

Colonel Chamberlain's men of the 20th Maine were a voluntary group, dedicated to the Union cause. As a group, they were very well educated. Many were, in fact, teachers themselves. They had almost no military training before being thrust into the war. But they had been in several engagements prior to Gettysburg. They were disciplined and prepared for almost anything they had to face. The 20th Maine had already responded bravely and effectively at Little Round Top by repelling several ferocious charges from the 15th and 47th Alabama regiments. These men were a part of Law's Brigade, under the command of Brigadier General Evander Law.

At the top of the hill the Union soldiers were determined to hold their position, but also, they were exhausted and in a very difficult situation. Ammunition was running dangerously low for the 20th Maine. Colonel Chamberlain walked the line, physically debilitatingly sick but repeatedly encouraging his exhausted men to hold their line at all costs. Many of his men had been wounded but still refused to leave their posts. They were aware of the importance of the mission they were conducting.

In all there were about 386 men in the 20th Maine, many healthy, many sick, many wounded. As they awaited the next charge of Confederates from below, they removed cartridges of their fallen comrades and put them into their own belts, getting as ready as possible for yet another assault from the men of Alabama. All the Maine men knew that there was an increasing reality that another Confederate charge might break their exhausted line and they would all die for the Union cause. They were willing to do whatever they could to repel another attack. And then that charge they had been expecting started their advance back up the hill.

The Alabamians too were a tough and determined group of fighters. They had a brief chance to recuperated and became even more determined to take the hill from the Union. The path up the hill was not an easy one, it was climbing under very difficult conditions. As Colonel Oates would later write, *"It was the roughest, rockiest, most stony and bushy place I ever saw on a battlefield. It was uphill too. A goat could hardly climb it."* And as Joshua Chamberlain would later say from a defensive position, *"It was like fighting on the roof of a house."*

There were almost 700 men in the combined Alabama 15th and 47th. They were fatigued from the long day's march and their four earlier charges up the hill. Each of those charges covered a straight path of about a quarter mile. But their path up the hill was never a straight line. Those four charges had all taken place in less than two hours. These brave men were being entrusted to take the high ground that would give the Confederacy tactical advantage. They remained fiercely undaunted and determined to get the job done in the next attempt. The order was given and back toward the top they went.

As the sight of 700 or so Confederate soldiers again charging up the hill met the eye of Joshua Chamberlain, he knew his options were limited. Chamberlain saw the inevitability of the situation. His men could not hold another defensive line. They were not only well outnumbered, but they also had little ammunition, and moreover there were almost no options of a positive outcome. Then, from somewhere deep in his instinct, or perhaps from the depths of his soul, Chamberlain made a decision as audacious as it was desperate - *"Bayonets!"*

The command snapped down the line of the 386 men of the Twentieth Maine like lightning. Officers echoed the cry. Men fixed bayonets to their rifles, some fixing them for the first time in battle. Without sufficient ammunition, their rifles would soon serve only as spears. The Confederates were once again confidently climbing the hill just as the sun was setting across the field. And then astonishing the attackers below, Chamberlain gave his final order: *"Charge!"*

With a left-wheel maneuver, the 20th Maine swung forward like a door hinge, pivoting off their anchored right flank and sweeping down the hill toward the stunned Confederates below. The sudden fury of the bayonet charge caught the Alabamians completely off guard. They had expected to attack, not to be attacked. Seeing the charging wall of screaming Union soldiers, many of the Confederates soldiers threw down their rifles and fled, some falling and rolling down the hill. Others tried to stand their ground, but the sheer momentum of the charge overwhelmed them. Some Union soldiers tackled their enemies bodily; others used the butts of their rifles like clubs. A few, too wounded to run, advanced anyway, limping, crawling, shouting to keep their line intact and their momentum flowing.

The charge of the 20th Maine broke the Confederate attack on the Union left. In the space of a few chaotic minutes, Chamberlain and his men had not only held the line, but they had also pushed the enemy back down the hill and captured dozens of prisoners in the process. Out of about 386 men, the 20th Maine had over 130 killed, wounded, or missing in the charge. But they had held the flank. Little Round Top remained in Union hands. And with it, the high ground of Gettysburg.

Sergeant Elisha Hunt Rhodes recorded, *"The air was thick with lead and smoke. The groans of the wounded were constant, even in victory."*

Joshua Chamberlain would later write: *"In great deeds, something abides. On great fields, something stays. Forms change and pass… but spirits linger, to consecrate ground for the vision-place of souls."* That day, Chamberlain and the men of Maine consecrated that ground with courage, discipline, and an unwavering commitment to duty. Their bayonet charge remains one of the most heroic actions in American military history.

It is interesting in history how one small decision, oftentimes made on a whim, can have such impactful consequences for so many people, for an entire county, for history. The desperate and instantaneous decision of Colonel Chamberlain to throw out common defense tactics and go on the offensive was not just an act of bravery, it was a decision made in the moment, that helped decide the fate of a battle and in a large measure the fate of a nation. A moment in time that totally altered history.

Colonel Chamberlain was eventually awarded the Medal of Honor for his leadership and bravery at Little Round Top, and rightfully so. There may not have been one single brief moment during the entire Civil War that made such an impact on which one army would eventually be victorious.

Below are some remembrances of the soldiers involved in the battle.

Union Perspective	Confederate Perspective
Col. Joshua L. Chamberlain (20th Maine): *"We had never before seen the grim visage of war so close. The order was simple: hold the ground at all hazards. When the moment came, we fixed bayonets and swung down like a door on its hinge — and the enemy broke."*	Col. William C. Oates (15th Alabama): *"There never were harder fighters than the Twentieth Maine men and their gallant colonel… He did not retire, and he would not surrender… and then he charged."*
Sgt. Andrew Tozier (20th Maine Medal of Honor recipient): *"We were nearly out of ammunition. I told*	Private Elijah Harman (47th Alabama): *"They came down at us screamin' like devils*

Union Perspective	Confederate Perspective

my boys, 'We go with steel now.' And we did. No one ran."

with bayonets shinin' in the sun... We weren't ready for them to come down. We broke."

Pvt. Theodore Gerrish (20th Maine):
"It seemed we were all part of one single body surging down the hill. I've never seen such ferocity. We were farmers, clerks, schoolboys — but that day, we were warriors."

Anonymous Confederate veteran:
"We had fought them nearly an hour and thought they were beat. But they came yellin' down like madmen. Some of our boys didn't even have time to reload."

Joshua Chamberlain (postwar):
"In great deeds, something abides... spirits linger to consecrate ground for the vision-place of souls."

Colonel Oates (years later):
"Had we been able to turn their left, we would have gained the top of the hill... There was no better regiment in the whole Union army than the Twentieth Maine."

Other High Ground

On the Union right, Confederate General Ewell, commanding the Second Corps, was supposed to assault Culp's Hill and Cemetery Hill, but delays and vague orders caused his men to launch their attacks much later than Lee had intended.

Cemetery Hill was a knob just south of the town of Gettysburg. It was a vital artillery position. Losing Cemetery Hill would open the Union line to a direct assault from the town. When they did attack, Brigadier General Harry Hays' *"Louisiana Tigers"* charged Cemetery Hill in a storm of gunfire and hand-to-hand combat, temporarily breaching Union lines. The Union troops on Cemetery Hill received reinforcements just in time and the Confederates attackers were repelled by counterattacks and artillery fire. As night fell the Union stubbornly controlled the hill.

Culp's Hill was a steep, wooded rise that anchored the Union right flank. On Culp's Hill. The Confederates were commanded by Major General Edwaard Johnson. During their first assault up the hill the Confederates had gained a foothold in the lower trenches and earthworks that had been constructed and subsequently abandoned by the Union during troop redeployments. The hill was defended by about 1,400 men trying to repel 4,500 Confederate troops. But defending the high ground held significant advantage. The defenders at the crest of the hill would not be overtaken. The failure of coordination between his

Generals cost Lee dearly. His attempt to collapse the Union line by striking both flanks ended in tactical stalemate.

By nightfall, the fields and hills of Gettysburg were strewn with nearly 20,000 additional casualties. On Day 2 alone, the casualty toll nearly matched that of entire major battles earlier in the war. The Confederates had come close, at multiple points, to breaking through during the day. Union lines had bent but mostly remained unbroken.

A Pennsylvania soldier later recalled: *"The Wheatfield was a terrible place...you could walk from one end to the other without stepping on the ground."*

Lee was naturally frustrated, but he was still not deterred. He began planning an all-out assault on the Union center for the next day, an audacious gamble that would become legend as Pickett's Charge.

July 3, Pickett's Charge

By the evening of July 2, 1863, General Lee believed he still had a chance to break the Union Army once and for all. Though the Confederate assaults on both Union flanks had failed to control any of the high ground that day, most notably at Little Round Top on one side and Culp Hill on the other, Lee was convinced that the Union center on Cemetery Ridge might be a soft spot in their defenses. It was uncharacteristic, but his intelligence was poorly gathered. In addition, as did Napoleon, Lee preferred frontal assaults on the enemy, having faith in the superiority of his infantry. The obvious risk was the great loss of manpower, attacking from low ground to high, when the enemy was well entrenched above.

Lee discussed his battle plan of July 3 with the *"Old War Horse"*, James Longstreet, who had become Lee's senior corps commander, following the death of Stonewall Jackson. Longstreet preferred maneuver over frontal assaults and strongly disagreed with his commander's plan. Longstreet argued for swinging his forces around the Union left again to outmaneuver the enemy. He believed the frontal assault to be suicidal. He wanted to flank the enemy to get to high ground, form a defensive line and encourage the Union to attack Confederate forces that were dug in and protected. Lee listened to Longstreet but remained unconvinced of his strategy. Lee decided to stick with his original plan of a frontal assault...

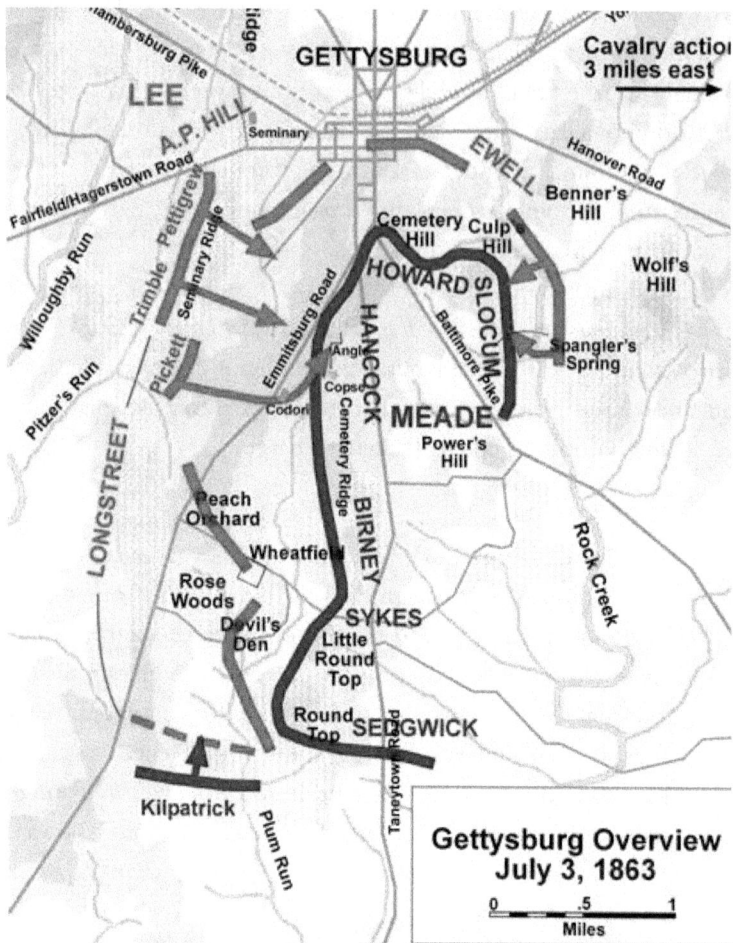

**Gettysburg Overview
July 3, 1863**

0   .5   1

Miles

On the afternoon of July 3, 1863, as the summer heat shimmered over the fields of Pennsylvania, General Lee made one of the most fateful decisions of the Civil War. Mistakenly believing the Union center on Cemetery Ridge had been significantly weakened, he ordered a massive frontal assault across open ground. The attack was meant to break the back of the Union Army and end the war on the North's own territory.

The assault would go down in history as Pickett's Charge, though in truth it involved far more than just General George Pickett's division. In addition, General Pickett was shown the plan by Longstreet, under chain-of-command, before it was enacted and expressed his opinion that it could not be effective. Lee made the order, and the assault was scheduled.

It was the third day of the Battle of Gettysburg. After two days of costly fighting, Lee's army had failed in their attacks on the Union flanks, the Confederate commander looked to the center of George Meade's line. There, along a gentle rise known as Cemetery Ridge, the Union army had entrenched itself behind stone walls and shallow earthworks. Lee believed, based on mixed reconnaissance information and reports from his subordinates, that this position could be pierced.

Lee's plan called for an assault by approximately 12,500 men drawn from three divisions: Pickett's Division of Virginians, newly arrived and fresh, forming the right, Major General Isaac Trimble, replacing the wounded Dorsey Pender, commanding a division from A.P. Hill's corps on the left. Major General Johnston Pettigrew's Division, largely composed of North Carolinians, taking the center.

Starting at Seminary Ridge, these forces were to march about ¾ of a mile across open fields, under artillery and rifle fire, to strike the Union line between a copse of trees and a small rise known as the Angle, a subtle bend in the stone wall that formed a natural target. They would move from low ground toward the higher ground of the Union Forces along Cemetery Ridge.

On the gently rising slope of Cemetery Ridge, near the center of the Union line at Gettysburg, stood a small, seemingly inconspicuous clump of trees, mostly oaks, perhaps thirty yards across, dark against the summer sky. To the average eye, it was a patch of shade from the oppressive sun in a Pennsylvania field. But on the third day of the Battle of Gettysburg, it became the most famous aiming point in American military history. Confederate artillery officers, preparing for Pickett's Charge, chose the copse of trees as the visual guide for the ensuing infantry assault. From their position on Seminary Ridge ¾ of a mile away, the small clump of trees provided a visible landmark that could be used to guide thousands of men across open ground toward the Union center. In the rolling fields of Pennsylvania, where uniformity was rare and visibility was everything, this dark silhouette became a target of both geography and intention.

General Lee believed that the Union center had been weakened by fighting on the flanks during the previous two days. He ordered an assault that would drive straight through the heart of the enemy line, right where those trees stood.

Lee assigned General James Longstreet to oversee the assault. Longstreet, deeply skeptical of the plan, pleaded for reconsideration, arguing that the Union position was too strong and the ground too exposed. *"General, I have been a soldier my entire life. It is my opinion that no fifteen thousand men ever arrayed for battle can take that position,"* he said. But Lee, convinced that the Union army was weakened and demoralized, insisted the attack would take place. Reluctantly, Longstreet gave the orders required of him.

Picket's division had just arrived the day before. They started gathering in their attack lines shortly before 11:00 a.m. The blazing late-morning sun and high humidity was taking its toll the men, standing and waiting for the call to charge. Shortly after 1:00 p.m. the calmness was shattered by a sound so deafening it seemed to rip the heavens open. For nearly two hours, the ridges of southern Pennsylvania trembled under the weight of the largest artillery barrage ever unleashed in the Western Hemisphere up to that time. This was not mere prelude; it was intended as destruction. General Lee believed that by unleashing the full fury of his artillery upon the Union center, he could shatter its remaining defenses and pave the way for a victorious infantry assault.

Lee's chief of artillery, Colonel Edward Alexander, was given the responsibility of coordinating the fire. He amassed over 150 Confederate guns, lining them up across Seminary Ridge, cannon muzzle to muzzle, stretching nearly a mile. It was an impressive display of firepower, manned by gunners from Virginia, Georgia, South Carolina, and elsewhere. Their barrels had been carefully sighted toward a stretch of low ground in the Union line, Cemetery Ridge, particularly near a slight bend in the stone wall now called the Angle, just south of the copse of trees.

The earth shook, and soldiers on both sides covered their ears and pressed themselves flat against the ground. The Confederate guns were aiming uphill to the tops of the slopes, which significantly complicate hitting any target accurately. The Union response came swiftly. Brigadier General Henry Hunt, commanding the Union artillery, had over 80 guns positioned along Cemetery Ridge. Though initially surprised by the ferocity of the Confederate bombardment, Union gunners began returning fire. Soon, both ridges, Seminary and Cemetery, erupted in a return of cannon fire.

The sound could be heard thirty miles away. In Gettysburg, windows shattered. Residents cowered in cellars. Horses went wild and fled. Union soldiers, crouching behind stone walls, endured the unrelenting blast without significant harm. Some began to wonder if this day would be their last.

The South's objective was clear: to pulverize the Union artillery and infantry positions, to unnerve the defenders, and to create a rupture in the line that could be exploited by the massive infantry charge that would follow. Many of the Confederate shells overshot the Union lines.

The Union artillery commander had carefully conserved his ammunition and kept much of its strength intact. At around 3:00 p.m., the cannonade from both sides began to die down. That wait in the heat, with cannon booming around them and no shade or escape, was mentally punishing for the Confederate soldiers. For many, it was a form of torment in itself, before even taking a step toward Cemetery Ridge. One Confederate soldier later wrote: *"We had waited so long, the suspense was worse than the charge."*

Longstreet, still not convinced of any potentiality of success, gave the final nod to initiate the assault. A line of gray emerged from the trees on Seminary Ridge, first one division, then another, and another. Banners fluttered; bayonets caught the sun and shined forward. Nearly a mile long line of Confederate infantry stepped forward in disciplined ranks. The men were calm and resolute. One Union observer would later write: *"It was the most magnificent sight of the war."*

As they advanced, Pickett's Virginians were on the right, Pettigrew's men in the center, and Trimble's division on the left. They moved slowly at first, then quickened their pace, their ranks aligned like a parade. As they drew close enough the Union guns opened up. From Cemetery Hill to Little Round Top, batteries unleashed a storm of shot, shell, and canister. As the Confederates approached the Emmitsburg Road, they were exposed to plunging fire from Union infantry behind stone walls and massed artillery above them. Men fell in great swaths, entire companies wiped out in seconds. The carefully formed lines began to waver, then regroup, then totally dissipate. Still, many came on as best they could as General Lee had commanded.

As they neared the Union position, flanking fire from Vermont and Ohio regiments to the north tore into their left. Generals Trimble and Pettigrew both had horses shot out from under them. Their divisions faltered in the slaughter. On the right, Armistead's Brigade of Pickett's division pushed hardest toward the center. At the copse of trees, a small number of Virginians breached the Union line, this would later be called the *High-Water Mark of the Confederacy*. Brigadier General Lewis Armistead, waving his hat atop his sword, led the charge over the wall. He reached a Union cannon and placed his hand on it before being struck down by musket fire. The Confederate breakthrough lasted only minutes, perhaps less, and was quickly crushed by Union reinforcements. The entire charge had lasted under 30 minutes.

A little-recognized confrontation on the day of Picket's Charge that was successful and partially allowed the Union rout of the South was attributed to General George Armstrong Custer, who was only 23 years old at the time of the Battle of Gettysburg. He had just been promoted to brigadier general of volunteers as one of the youngest generals in the Union Army. He commanded the Michigan Cavalry Brigade, part of General Alfred Pleasonton's Cavalry Corps.

Confederate General J.E.B. Stuart attempted a large cavalry sweep to flank and strike the Union rear. Custer's role was critical. Along with Union cavalry under General David Gregg, Custer helped intercept Stuart's forces near the Rummel Farm, in a fight now known as the Battle of East Cavalry Field. At a key moment, Custer is said to have galloped to the head of his brigade shouting, *"Come on, you Wolverines!"*, leading a charge that met Confederate cavalry head-on. The fighting was intense and chaotic, saber-to-saber, with repeated charges and countercharges. Ultimately, Stuart was repelled, and his attempt to reach the Union rear was thwarted, ensuring that Pickett's Charge would not be supported from behind.

The Aftermath of the Charge

The survivors of the charge staggered back across the field, many crawling, many simply left behind. Of the 12,500 Confederates who began the assault, over 6,000 were killed, wounded, or captured, which was a truly catastrophic loss. Pickett's Division alone lost more than half its men. All three of Picket's commanders were killed or mortally wounded. This was the first major combat in which Pickett's men had been involved.

Picket had retreated with what remained of his troops, which was very little. Some of his brigades had lost two thirds of their men. Lee asked Pickett to rally his division. *"General Picket, you must look to your division."* Pickett replied with bitter sorrow, *"General, I have no division now."*

As the last waves of Confederate infantry collapsed near the stone wall at the Angle and the smoke began to clear, the battlefield fell into a surreal and eerie silence. The charge had lasted about half an hour, and in such a short time, its human cost was overwhelming. Where there had been ordered lines and battle cries, there were now crumpled bloodied bodies, remnants retreating as best they could, and men being carried, crawling or staggering back toward Seminary Ridge.

Union artillerymen, many of whom had fired their last canister shot into the tightly packed Confederate ranks just minutes earlier, stood by their guns and watched the shattered remnants of the Confederate ranks retreat down the slope. What they saw was not an army withdrawing with discipline, but a mass of bloodied, stunned survivors, many without weapons, uniforms torn, faces blackened with powder and streaked with tears. Some dragged wounded comrades behind them, others simply collapsed.

One Union officer observed that no cheers rose from the Union lines. There was only silence. The spectacle was too terrible, too inhumane. The defenders, who just moments before had poured fire into the advancing ranks, felt no elation. What had come across the field was not just a military force, it had been thousands of young men, and now so many of them were gone or were left with their lives in ruin.

It is said that some Union gunners, overcome by the horror and bravery of what they had just witnessed, lowered their eyes and turned away. Others wept openly. More than one officer is reported to have ordered his men to cease fire without waiting for commands, recognizing the futility and cruelty of shooting at broken men in retreat.

Union Major Thomas Chamberlin later wrote: *"The sight of those men, torn and bleeding, stumbling back across the field they had so bravely crossed, struck me like a blow. It was not a victory I could cheer."*

The battered ranks of the brave Confederate soldiers slowly melted back into the trees of Seminary Ridge, and the field between the two armies was left quiet but for the moans and cries of the wounded. The thunder of the brief battle had given way to the cries of the wounded. For both sides, the moment marked a sobering realization that whatever glory had once been imagined in war had, in the previous hour, been obliterated in the heat, smoke, and slaughter of the open Pennsylvania field.

As those retreating from the charge made their way back across the field between Cemetery Ridge and Seminary Ridge, General Robert E. Lee mounted his horse and rode forward to meet them. He did not send aides. He did not remain behind lines. He went himself calm, composed, but clearly burdened by the weight of the moment. The men he encountered were not in formation. They were beaten, they were broken, they were bloody. Some limped, others wept, and many looked dazed, stunned by the scale of the slaughter they had just endured. Entire brigades had been reduced to clusters of survivors. Some regiments had lost over 70 percent of their men in less than an hour. Officers were dead, standards lost, friends and brothers left behind on the field.

Lee addressed them directly not with false encouragement, but with deep solemnity and honor. Again and again, those who survived the encounter recalled hearing the same words from him:

"It is all my fault. I am responsible."

"You have done all your duty could require."

"This has been my mistake, and mine alone."

He spoke to privates, captains, and colonels alike. His voice, always firm and composed, carried the full weight of command but now with sorrow, not command's pride. Men who could barely stand removed their caps in his presence. Some broke down in tears. One officer recalled, *"He looked upon us as a father upon his children... He reproached himself while praising us. We loved him more in that moment than ever before."*

Lee's assumption of responsibility was not rhetorical. He truly believed the failure of the charge, and perhaps the entire campaign, rested on his shoulders alone. Though he had hesitated only briefly before ordering the assault, convinced that a hard blow at the Union center would break Meade's line, he had ignored the reservations of Longstreet and others. He had chosen to press forward, and the result was thousands of his men lie dead and wounded in the fields above him. It was a miscalculation of enormity.

That evening, as he met with his generals in the woods behind Seminary Ridge, Lee was subdued. He made no effort to deflect blame. He spoke not of glory, but of preparing for a Union counterattack and how best to secure a retreat across the Potomac. Longstreet, who had opposed the charge, reportedly said little. He later wrote that Lee *was "more depressed than I have ever seen him."*

Lee sent a dispatch to President Jefferson Davis after the defeat and offered to resign, but the President of the Confederate States refused. Picket's Charge was a rare but calamitous, ill-informed, and disastrous decision from Lee, and a key decision that sent him back home to Virginia. Making the war once again a defensive effort. The extraordinary loss at Gettysburg started to slowly turn the war in the favor of the North.

The Union victory at Gettysburg, and the failure of Pickett's Charge, was marked as a much-needed victory for the North. But it did not stop the war, it only stopped the momentum that Lee had gathered in his two previous victories over the North in Virginia. Nevertheless, Lee would never again attempt a major offensive into Northern territory. The myth of Confederate invincibility was shattered in the fields and ridges outside of Gettysburg, Pennsylvania.

For generations to come, the attempted assault of Pickett's men would symbolize both the valor and tragedy of the Southern cause, a moment of doomed glory, at least as haunting as it was potentially heroic.

In the Northern press and in the governmental halls of Washington, Gettysburg was celebrated as a much-needed victory after a string of disastrous Union defeats. News of Meade's victory over Lee arrived almost simultaneously with Grant's victory at Vicksburg on July 4, making early July 1863 arguably the most hopeful period for the Union since the war began.

Newspapers like the *New York Times* and *Harper's Weekly* hailed the Gettysburg victory as a sign that the Confederacy's strength was waning. But there was also criticism. Many asked why General Meade had not pursued Lee's retreating army more aggressively. President Lincoln himself was deeply disappointed that Meade did not press the advantage, believing that with more initiative, the Army of Northern Virginia might have been crushed entirely.

Immediately following the battle, public mood in the North, turned nearly euphoric. Church bells rang from every town, fireworks lit the skies, and editorials declared that the tide of the war had finally turned. There was, however, a growing sense of dread. The defeat ended Lee's second and final attempt to bring the war to Northern soil, and many Confederate leaders and soldiers understood that from this point on, the South would again be largely on the defensive.

Gettysburg was certainly a turning point toward a potential North victory, but an end was nowhere within sight. The war would continue for nearly two more years. The battle severely depleted Lee's army, both in manpower and morale it was true. But there were many battles left to fight and countless more casualties that would be inflicted.

Gettysburg became a psychological blow to Confederate hopes. For the Union, it was a major morale boost and helped blunt growing calls in the North to negotiate peace. In the 1864 election, the battle became a symbolic reminder of the sacrifices needed to preserve the Union. Lincoln's *Gettysburg Address,* delivered in November 1863 months after the battle itself, elevated the battle's significance from a tactical victory to a moral turning point in American history.

Lee's army began its retreat on July 4 from Pennsylvania. Meade did not pursue aggressively, certainly not aggressively enough for Lincoln and his cabinet. There was a sense that the weakened Army of the Potomac was ripe for destruction. Meade, having suffered heavy casualties and wary of a possible Confederate counterattack, decided not to launch an aggressive pursuit. His army was also badly bloodied and exhausted, and he faced logistical difficulties. Still, he did follow Lee's army, only at a rather deliberate pace, first gathering reinforcements and then assessing Lee's direction.

By July 12, Lee was entrenched near Williamsport, Maryland, with the Potomac still too high to cross. Meade's forces established their lines behind the Confederate encampment. A major engagement might have occurred, but Meade again hesitated. He convened a council of his top officer, who advised caution. Meade prepared for an attack on July 14, but the previous evening Lee's army had slipped across the river on pontoon bridges and ferries.

Casualties in the engagement totaled over a 51,000 men between the North and the South, making Gettysburg the bloodiest battle in American history. The fields surrounding the town became a vast graveyard. The stench of death filled the air for months to come. Local civilians helped bury the dead where they fell, mostly in very shallow graves to expedite the process. Horses lay bloated in the sun.

Lincoln would later consecrate the battlefield with a brief but immortal address. But the cost was already etched in blood. *"That government of the people, by the people, for the people, shall not perish from the earth."*

CHAPTER 17
LINCOLN AT GETTYSBURG, THE SPEECH

The war had already claimed hundreds of thousands of lives when the guns finally fell silent in the small Pennsylvania crossroads town of Gettysburg in early July 1863. For three days, the hills and fields had exploded with fire, smoke, cannon, and blood. More than 51,000 men were killed, wounded, or missing, making it the bloodiest single battle ever fought on American soil. The landscape was mutilated, orchards shattered, fences and buildings burned, with bodies strewn in an incredibly morbid scene in the hot July sun. Makeshift graves dotted the countryside, many so shallow that rain exposed arms or legs. The townspeople were mostly overwhelmed. They were left to care for many of the wounded and to bury the dead. There was barely room for the living amid the dead.

The government knew this ground could not simply return to pasture or to agriculture. A national cemetery was proposed, something sacred and permanent to honor the Union soldiers who had died to preserve the republic. The idea came from David Wills, a local Gettysburg attorney who was appointed to oversee the project. It was Wills who sent the invitation to President Abraham Lincoln, requesting that he attend the dedication ceremony on November 19, 1863, and offer *"a few appropriate remarks."*

Lincoln was not the headliner of the event proposed for that day. The principal speaker was Edward Everett, one of the most renowned orators of his time. Everett was asked if he would deliver an address concerning the dedication for an October 13 date, but replied that he was so busy, the earliest he could be in Gettysburg would be November 19. His availability is what set the date for the dedication of the cemetery. It was a bit late in the year to expect favorable weather in western Pennsylvania. Lincoln's role, as described, was ceremonial. There were no expectations that he would deliver anything memorable.

Lincoln's official calendar leading up to the dedication was filled with domestic, military and foreign affairs, leaving him very little time to concentrate on the *"few appropriate remarks"* he would deliver at Gettysburg. The President was in the midst of preparing to issue his Proclamation of Amnesty and Reconstruction (issued on December 8) and was working on his annual message to Congress, to be submitted on December 9. Lincoln was also waiting for military operations to commence around Chattanooga and Knoxville, Tennessee, as well as events along Mine Run near Culpeper in northern Virginia, all of which had the potential to be setbacks.

The president of the B&O railroad prepared a special car for the President, and made sure the route was free of traffic. The train itself left Washington at noon on November 18. The President's car was in the lead, but several other cars were attached. They contained dignitaries of various sorts, as well as military protection for the President and a military band. The train made numerous stops along its journey, and at each, Lincoln was asked to give a short speech.

Lincoln had given much thought to what he wanted to say at Gettysburg but nearly missed his chance to say it. Shortly before the trip, Lincoln's son, Tad, became ill with a fever. The president and his wife Mary Todd Lincoln were no strangers to juvenile illness. They had already lost two sons to disease. Prone to fits of hysteria, Mary Lincoln panicked when her husband prepared to leave. However, Lincoln felt the opportunity to speak at Gettysburg and present his defense of the war was too important to miss, so he boarded the train and headed to Pennsylvania. His mind was occupied with the looming speech, matters of state, and the health of his son.

Crafting the Words

There is a popular myth that Lincoln scribbled the Gettysburg Address on the back of an envelope on the train from Washington to Pennsylvania. It's a poetic image but untrue. In reality, Lincoln began forming his thoughts well before the journey. He understood the gravity of the moment, not just as a memorial, but as a defining point in the war and in American history. His message would not be merely about the cause they had died for, but for the living, and for the Nation.

His language drew on scripture, classical rhetoric, and the Declaration of Independence. His law partner, William Herndon, said Lincoln believed the Declaration, not the Constitution, was the *"sheet anchor"* of American liberty, and that belief runs through every line of the address. The final edits were made at the Wills house in Gettysburg, where Lincoln stayed the night before the ceremony. He read drafts aloud to his aides, pacing, revising, distilling. The speech would be just 271 words, but he labored over every one.

The Speech and the Crowd

The morning of November 19 was cold, overcast, and raw, with a stiff wind sweeping across the open fields. A parade of dignitaries began at the Wills house, with Lincoln the center of attention. As the parade rode through town hundreds of persons lined the streets to cheer. Between 10,000 and 20,000 people gathered to witness the dedication in the fields outside of town. The platform for the speakers was built on Cemetery Hill, overlooking the rows of freshly dug graves. The scene was solemn and disordered at the same time. Soldiers stood ranks in the mud, music played from brass bands, spectators crowded onto wagons and rooftops hoping to get a view of the proceedings. Some clutched photographs of loved ones buried nearby. The smell of damp earth and the faint rot of decay still lingered from the battle still fresh in the minds of all present. It was a day soaked in sorrow.

Edward Everett was the featured speaker at the event and gave his speech before Lincoln. His reputation as one America's greatest orators was the primary drawing card for the large crowd. He was, quite simply, the man you invited when you wanted the best speech possible. His orations were long, scholarly, and full of classical references. Before Lincoln, Everett was considered the model of rhetorical power. He had been president of Harvard, a congressman, senator, and governor, as well as a Secretary of State. Everett represented the apex of American oratory and education. He was well-respected across party lines and had no military ties. He would bring a moral, civic, and classical gravitas to the occasion.

He prepared thoroughly, as was his custom, and delivered a two-hour address to the gathered crows, who listened intently. His speech traced the history of the war, paid tribute to the dead, and reflected on the values of the American republic. It was considered a masterclass in formal oratory. But it was also overshadowed, not because it was a poor speech, it was very good by the standards of the time, but because Lincoln's speech was so brief, so clear, and so enduring in its meaning and elegance.

The dignitaries on the podium and in the front rows were many. Alongside Lincoln and Edward Everett stood Governor Andrew Curtin of Pennsylvania, a few of Lincoln's Cabinet members, foreign diplomats, Supreme

Court justices, military leaders, and members of Congress. The newly elected Governor of Ohio, John Brough, and Secretary of State William Seward were among them. Everett spoke eloquently, learned, and exhaustive. He recounted the causes of the war, the strategic movements of the armies, the nobility of the soldiers. His speech, masterful in form, stretched to nearly 13,000 words.

The introduction for the second speaker of the event was brief and respectful, but not dramatic. Reports vary slightly, but most agree that the master of ceremonies, Judge David Wills, offered a simple and formal introduction along these lines: "Ladies and gentlemen, the President of the United States." There was no rousing ovation or grand buildup

Then Lincoln rose.

He wore a simple black suit, a black silk stovepipe hat, and white gloves. He stood awkwardly on the platform, taller than all around him, and looked out at the weary, wind-chilled crowd. No trumpet announced him. No fanfare followed. He began to speak in his quiet, reedy voice, difficult to hear at the back of the crowd. There were no dramatic gestures, no rhetorical flourishes. But his words sliced through time and space, anchoring the nation in both its founding ideals and its war-torn present.

The Gettysburg Address

Four score and seven years ago our fathers brought forth on this continent, a new nation, conceived in Liberty, and dedicated to the proposition that all men are created equal.

Now we are engaged in a great civil war, testing whether that nation, or any nation so conceived and so dedicated, can long endure. We are met on a great battlefield of that war. We have come to dedicate a portion of that field, as a final resting place for those who here gave their lives that that nation might live. It is altogether fitting and proper that we should do this.

But, in a larger sense, we can not dedicate—we can not consecrate—we can not hallow this ground. The brave men, living and dead, who struggled here, have consecrated it, far above our poor power to add or detract. The world will little note, nor long remember what we say here, but it can never forget what they did here. It is for us the living, rather, to be dedicated here to the unfinished work which they who fought here have thus far so nobly advanced.

It is rather for us to be here dedicated to the great task remaining before us—that from these honored dead we take increased devotion to that cause for which they gave the last full measure of devotion—that we here highly resolve that these dead shall not have died in vain— that this nation, under God, shall have a new birth of freedom—and that government of the people, by the people, for the people, shall not perish from the earth.

The Reaction

As Lincoln finished and started back to his chair, the audience stood in stunned silence. Some were unaware that it could possibly be over because of its brevity, especially after Everett's long oration. A few people applauded. Lincoln, believing he had failed, reportedly told his friend Ward Lamon, *"That speech won't scour. It is a flat failure, and the people are disappointed."*

But Edward Everett knew better. The next day, he wrote to Lincoln: *"I should be glad if I could flatter myself that I came as near to the central idea of the occasion in two hours as you did in two minutes."*

After the dedication ceremony, both Everett's and President Lincoln's speeches were reprinted in newspapers around the country. Reactions to the speech were, unsurprisingly, divided on political grounds.

The Chicago Times (a Democratic paper) *"The cheek of every American must tingle with shame as he reads the silly, flat and dishwatery utterances of the man who has to be pointed out to intelligent foreigners as the President of the United States."* The Chicago times was in deep political opposition to Lincoln.

The Springfield Republican (Massachusetts) *"President Lincoln's speech at Gettysburg will live among the annals of man. The few words of solemn consecration to the dead and of inspiration to the living will not be forgotten. It is a perfect gem; deep in feeling, compact in thought and expression, and tasteful and elegant in every word and comma."*

The New York Times appreciated Lincoln's solemn tone and moral clarity, Lincoln's *"brief address was delivered in a clear, loud tone of voice, which could be distinctly heard at the extreme limits of the large assemblage."* The paper described his manner as *"very deliberate,"* with *"strong emphasis,"* and characterized his demeanor as having *"a most business-like air"* .

The Philadelphia Evening Bulletin wrote that Lincoln's remarks were *"brief but exceedingly appropriate… Thousands who would not read the elaborate oration of Mr. Everett will read the President's few words, and not many will do it without a moistening of the eye and a swelling of the heart."*

Among soldiers and attendees, reactions were generally more positive. Many recognized the solemn gravity in Lincoln's simple words, though the power of the message was not immediately universally understood. Some veterans later wrote that they were moved, even if the crowd had seemed quiet and confused at the time.

In the days and weeks following the speech, southern newspapers attacked it, while northern opinions largely reflected party lines with Republicans praising and Democrats rebuking the speech.

The speech would grow in stature with time, eventually becoming the most iconic expression of American ideals, quoted at battlefields, schools, and presidential inaugurations for generations to come.

What made Lincoln's remarks immortal was not their length or their poetry, but their clarity of moral vision. In a war that had become mechanized in its slaughter of soldiers, and disorienting in its scale, Lincoln reframed the purpose of the conflict. The war was no longer merely a rebellion to be crushed. It was a test of democracy, a re-founding of the nation on the principle of equality.

His gallantry was not just in words but in his presence. He came not as a conqueror or a showman, but as a mourner-in-chief. He walked among the graves. He comforted parents and children. He carried on his back the burden of every man buried beneath the soil of Gettysburg, and those yet to die.

At Gettysburg, Abraham Lincoln did not merely dedicate a cemetery. He re-dedicated a nation.

CHAPTER 18
VICTORY AT VICKSBURG, DIVIDING THE CONFEDERACY

Ulysses S. Grant was born as Hiram Ulysses Grant in 1822 in Ohio. His father Jesse provided for his family as a tanner. Jesse was a devout abolitionist. Hiram Grant's name would eventually be changed due to a clerical error made by his Congressman on papers submitted for his entrance to West Point. Grant liked the new name better than his own and decided to stick with it. But to his friends he was called neither, he was known as "Sam." Grant was not a man that seemed to be destined for glory. He graduated twenty first out of the 39 cadets in the West Point class of 1843. He was known as an exceptional horseman, but he was not known for his exceptional academic skills.

After graduating from West Point, Grant was first stationed in Jefferson Barracks south of Saint Louis, and then in 1846 he was sent to Corpus Cristi, Texas. Soon thereafter, he was commanded to march south into Mexico serving as a lieutenant in the Mexican-American War under Zachary Taylor and Winfield Scott. While in that war he gained valuable fighting experience under excellent leadership, and was twice cited for bravery, mainly due to his expert horsemanship navigating the narrow streets of Monterrey, Mexico. His citations reportedly were granted when he was riding through the streets of Monterey clinging the left side of his horse protecting himself from the enemy on his right. He also received two temporary battlefield promotions: as a First Lieutenant, and then as a Captain, based on his leadership and bravery.

"For myself," Grant wrote later about the United States war against Mexico, *"I was bitterly opposed to the measure, and to this day regard the war, which resulted, as one of the most unjust ever waged by a stronger against a weaker nation."*

In 1848, after the Mexican-American war he returned to Saint Louis where he met and married Julia Dent. Shortly thereafter he was assigned to posts in Monterrey, Mexico, Detroit and Sackets Harbor, New York. He was accompanied by his wife in each of these posts. He then went to Fort Colombus,

Texas before traveling to New Orleans and then to Corpus Christi, all with his wife.

Then his military service took him to various remote outposts far from his family. Julia could not go with him, as was custom for an officer's wife, because of her pregnancy. The 1852 trip from Corpus Cristi was a difficult one. Grant sailed to Colon, Panama and travelled overland to the Pacific Coast, during which several of his party died from yellow fever, malaria, and dysentery, including the wives and children of fellow soldiers...

From Panama City, he and his men took the sailing ship "Golden Gate." Grant himself caught cholera as did many of the other men on the ship. The 4th Infantry and Grant sailed to Benicia (just north of San Francisco) mostly to recuperate with almost no official duties to conduct there. In the far west he was sick and far separated from his pregnant wife. He started to become despondent and took to whiskey as a crutch.

During his short time in Benicia was where he first met William Tecumseh Sherman, who was to become instrumental in Grants rise to power and his eventual success navigating the war to its conclusion.

From California Grant was shipped, not closer to his family, but to Fort Vancouver in present day Washington. He had still not recovered from the cholera he contracted in Panama and was becoming more depressed. He was then transferred to a new post at Fort Humbolt in California, not only a desolate place but also very dreary, cold, rainy, and cloudy. At Fort Humbolt he was drinking more heavily. Due to being drunk during a pay call, his commanding officer gave him the choice of resigning or being court martialed.

Grant resigned from the army in 1854 under a cloud of insobriety and insubordination that provided a respite for his grief of being separated from his family. He had a two-year old son that he first met after his resignation from the army and return home to the family of his wife in Illinois. He settled into ineptitude quickly and quietly. Grant was never intended for civilian life. He could not maintain reasonable work to support his family and eventually moved to the plantation of his wife's family. Grant drifted between jobs, farming, bill collecting, and clerking in his father's leather goods store in Galena, Illinois. He was greatly struggling financially and was largely a forgotten man by the time Civil War broke out in 1861.

When the Civil War erupted in April 1861, Grant was 39 years old. He strongly supported the Union cause, but at the time no one else really cared. He wrote: *"Whatever may have been my political opinions before, I have but one sentiment now, that is, we have a government, and laws, and a flag, and they must all be sustained."* In attempting to join the war Grant initially wrote to the Adjutant General but did not receive a response. So, he travelled to Cincinnati trying to speak in person to General McClellan, in whose hallway he waited for days, never receiving a meeting. He was essentially a nobody, and his West Point and subsequent military record had long faded from relevance. But he was anxious to get back to the life he knew well and wanted more.

He applied for staff positions, even as a drill instructor, still nothing came through. He volunteered to train local volunteer companies in Galena, Illinois informally and helped organize them for federal service. People began to take notice of his competence and calm leadership style.

At last, congressman Elihu Washburne, a Republican from Illinois, advocated for him. Through Washburne's efforts and at the direction of Governor Richard Yates, Grant was appointed Colonel of the 21st Illinois Volunteer Infantry in June 1861. It was a ragtag group of untrained and unpolished volunteer boys and men. He trained these men as quickly as possible into a reasonably reliable fighting force and led them competently in skirmishes with the enemy in Missouri. Grant and his troops displayed a calm under fire. Grant proved to have a relentless focus on objectives. In a very short amount of time success on the battlefield garnered Grant the notoriety he deserved.

His success in battle coupled with politics initiated on his behalf helped Grant to be promoted to Brigadier General in August 1861. His early victories at Fort Donelson, Shilo, Fort Henry, and eventually Vicksburg propelled him toward high command. By 1862 he had surprised many, especially when he demanded, and received, unconditional surrender from the enemy at Fort Henry and Fort Donelson. He gained the nickname *"Unconditional Surrender"* Grant from his troops. Following these two battles, he was recognized for his success and leadership by the President who advanced Grant's rank to Major General of volunteers. His dogged stand at Shiloh, despite enormous casualties, confirmed to the President that he was a commander who would not retreat from adversity.

Grant certainly lacked the polish of many of his contemporaries, but he possessed clarity of purpose like no other. He was modest, even appearing humble, honest, and fair. He had a remarkable intellect for the battlefield and a bulldog-like determination. Where other generals hesitated, he advanced. Where others doubted, he pressed forward. He was able to assess a situation, decide to affect the situation, and then follow through quickly. He rarely gave speeches or sought personal glory. His military philosophy was brutally simple: find the enemy, engage, and destroy their capacity to fight.

By early 1863, Grant had earned his promotion to command the Union forces of the Western Theater of the war. He had learned valuable lessons from every failure as well as from each success and fought forward through every doubt. He had achieved victories in each of his initial battles, even though sometimes with significant casualties. He was a leader who would not easily accept defeat. He was aggressive. He was decisive. He was a conqueror. His next challenge would be Vicksburg, and this engagement would test every lesson he had learned, and every ounce of resolve he possessed. Except for a lack of flair, Grant could be compared favorably to Napoleon.

Vicksburg Siege

Early in the year, Ulysses S. Grant stood on the west bank of the Mississippi River, eyeing the Confederate fortress of Vicksburg from across the water. The city sat on high bluffs, commanding a long stretch of the river and presenting what seemed to be an impregnable position. For months, Union forces had attempted to take it through direct assaults, diversions, and engineering schemes, but every effort had failed.

Grant had considered several plans to capture Vicksburg before he settled on a long siege. Initially he had planned to assault Vicksburg head-on from the north in a typical land campaign. But from the north, the terrain was swampy and well-defended. This plan became far too risky. He then considered a river-based assault but found such an assault to be principally unmanageable. He also considered engineering efforts to divert the river to flank Vicksburg. Grant's engineers started this effort by digging a canal directly opposite Vicksburg so Union vessels could bypass the city's guns. Thousands of men worked on this effort, until it was found to not be feasible.

Grant also considered and attempted engineering a navigable waterway to link the Mississippi River to the Red River through a system of bayous and lakes, this too was found to be impractical. Two different routes were considered for this attempt, but neither would work out. Grant was under pressure from Washington, which encouraged him try as many options as possible in as short of time as possible.

Finally, he decided to move his entire army down the west side of the Mississippi, cross the river and attempt to cut Vicksburg off from their supply chains from the east side. This movement would require cooperation from the Union Navy. The final decision demanded use of his engineering acumen learned at West Point, as well as difficult logistics, and a lot of creativity.

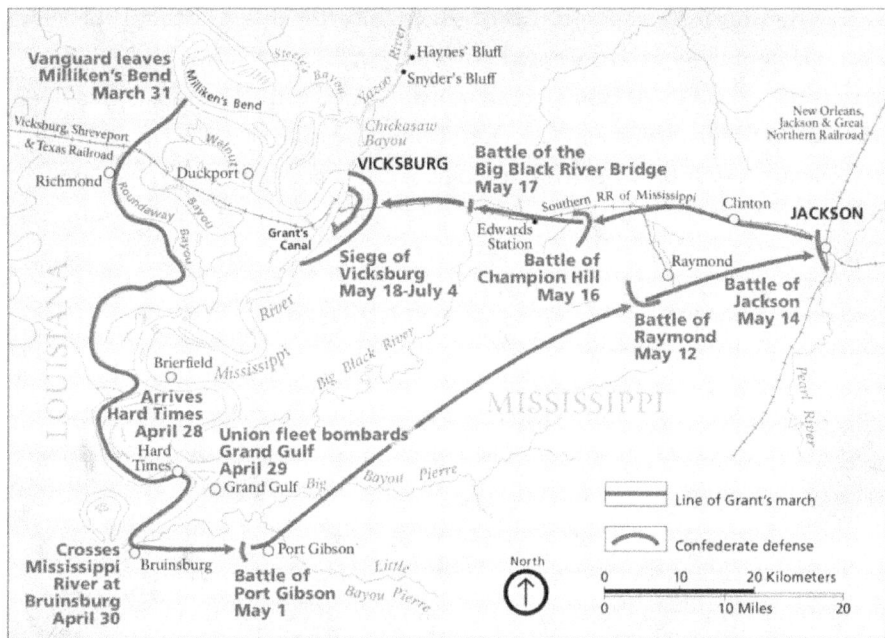

The Vicksburg Campaign, April–July 1863

On April 16, 1863, Admiral Porter of the Union Navy, in conjunction with a request from Grant ordered seven ironclad boats, one armed ram, three army transports, and a tug to start downriver past Vicksburg. Porter urged his men to take *"every precaution possible to protect the hull and machinery"* of their ships. To shield against shellfire, each vessel had its port side, which would face the Vicksburg guns in passage, piled high with bales of cotton, hay, and grain. Coal barges were lashed alongside as an additional defense. As they rounded the bend toward Vicksburg, the Navy vessels came under heavy fire from the city, with the Union gunboats returning fire soon thereafter.

There was no moon on that night, forcing the Confederates to light bonfires alongside the bank to guide their guns, but it was not enough. One of the three transports was sunk but the gunboats sailed through. Through this daring engagement, Grant was able to secure transports to cross the river further to the south away from Vicksburg. His transfer and landing of 17,000 soldiers was the largest amphibious operation in United States military history until the Normandy Invasion of World War II. Porter's navy continued to support Grant's men during the siege, providing cover from Confederate fire and ferrying food and supplies to entrenched soldiers during the siege.

On April 30, Union forces began crossing the Mississippi at Bruinsburg, a landing point about 60 miles south of Vicksburg. Grant's army, now numbering nearly 45,000 men, began moving inland with surprising speed. His plan was to eventually attack Vicksburg from the east, isolate the city, and prevent any reinforcements from reaching it. Most daring of all, Grant cut his army loose from their supply lines, telling his men to forage from the countryside as they marched. This was a radical move, but it made the army lighter, faster, and more mobile than any the Western Theater had yet seen.

What followed was a dazzling campaign of movement. Grant's forces defeated Confederate troops at Port Gibson (May 1), Raymond (May 12), and Jackson, Mississippi (May 14), effectively pushing General Johnston and his reinforcements out of the region. Then Grant turned west toward his ultimate prize of Vicksburg.

After weeks of maneuvering through Mississippi, Grant's army stood between the Confederate forces of General John Pemberton and their only hope of reinforcement from the army of Joe Johnston to the east. Grant had already cut inland from the Mississippi River, severed the rail lines at Jackson, and had driven Johnston out of the state capital. Now, as of mid-May 1863, Grant's attention turned toward the Confederate forces retreating westward toward Vicksburg. Their path of retreat followed the Southern Railroad of Mississippi and passed over a commanding ridge known as Champion Hill.

On the morning of May 16, the hills east of Vicksburg were thick in fog. Pemberton had positioned his roughly 29,000 troops in a defensive arc near the crest of Champion Hill, hoping to delay or perhaps repel Grant's advance. Pemberton had been indecisive about whether to move south in attempt to cut Union supply lines or retreat to Vicksburg. At Johnston's urging, he had belatedly chosen to retreat, but it was already too late because Grant's forces were closing in quickly.

Grant's plan that morning was straightforward. With his three corps of men under Generals McClernand, McPherson, and Sherman, he would push forward with speed and coordination. McPherson's corps struck first, approaching from the northeast and making contact with the Confederate left flank near Champion Hill. The terrain was rugged with thick woods, deep ravines, and the high ground of the hill itself. Union skirmishers were engaged early in the morning, and soon the battle erupted into a full engagement.

By midmorning, McPherson's men surged up the slopes of Champion Hill, engaging in close-quarters combat. Union regiments from Illinois and Iowa, under Logan and Crocker, pushed hard against the Confederate left, eventually turning it and threatening to roll up Pemberton's entire line. Panic began to spread through the Confederate ranks. In response, Pemberton ordered a desperate counterattack using troops under General Bowen. For a brief time, Bowen's men succeeded in retaking parts of the hill and halting the Union momentum. But that success did not last long. Reinforcements from Union Generals McPherson and McClernand arrived just as the Confederate assault began to falter. Superior numbers and firepower turned the flow against the Confederates.

By late afternoon, the Confederate line was broken. With Union troops pressing from multiple directions, Pemberton ordered a retreat toward the Big Black River, the last natural barrier between Grant's army and Vicksburg. The withdrawal quickly descended into a disorganized retreat. Thousands of Confederate soldiers threw down their weapons and fled. Ammunition wagons and artillery pieces were abandoned. Grant's troops pursued the fleeing enemy relentlessly, capturing many.

The battle of Champion Hill was a decisive Union victory. Grant later called it *"the decisive battle of the campaign."* In terms of tactical movement, terrain, and coordination, it showcased the maturation of Grant as a field commander. And this was the first real feel that the Rebel army commanders had about the style of Grant's leadership. Grant's ability to maintain pressure, shift forces as needed, and exploit weaknesses in real time left the Confederate army in full retreat and left Vicksburg vulnerable.

At the skirmish of the Big Black River Bridge on the following day some 1,800 Confederate troops were captured, and General Pemberton and his remaining soldiers were forced to take refuge in Vicksburg, where there would be no escape without defeat of the enemy. The bridge over the Big Black River was burned by the Rebels, which prevented Union troops from following Pemberton's army and routing their adversaries before they reached Vicksburg.

By May 18 the entire army of General Pemberton had retreated within the walls of Vicksburg and its outside battlements. The battered Confederates made their stand along a seven-mile defensive perimeter surrounding the city.

Vicksburg itself sat on high bluffs overlooking the river, encircled by rugged ravines and dense forest, terrain ideal for defense. The Confederate trenches formed a series of fortifications, redoubts, and rifle pits strung along ridges and valleys. Inside the city were some 29,000 Confederate soldiers, along with thousands of civilians who soon found themselves trapped in what would become a long hellish siege.

With the Confederates now having retreated to the hilltop city, Grant prepared for the next stage of his campaign, the siege of Vicksburg itself. The road to that siege had been cleared by the hard-won fight on the steep, bloodied slopes of Champion Hill.

Grant initially believed the Confederates were disorganized and demoralized, so he launched two direct assaults on the city, one on May 19, and a second, larger one on May 22. Both were repelled with heavy Union casualties. The Union soldiers, attacking steep ridges under intense fire, found themselves mowed down in the open. After these costly failures, Grant changed tactics. He would not try to storm the city again. Instead, he would encircle it and starve it into submission.

By late May, Grant's army had fully surrounded Vicksburg. Sherman's corps blocked the city from the north, McPherson from the east, and McClernand (later replaced by Edward Ord) to the south. The Mississippi River was to the west, controlled for the most part by the Union Navy. Union engineers began digging approach trenches, moving their lines steadily closer to Confederate defenses. Batteries of artillery were positioned across the front. Gunboats in the river shelled the city from below. Nothing could enter or leave the city.

Inside Vicksburg, the population of about 4,600 citizens and 29,000 soldiers soon faced dire shortages of food, medicine, and clean water. Civilians took to living in dugouts carved into the hillsides to escape the shelling, creating an eerie honeycomb of earthen shelters. People ate dogs, rats, mule meat, and anything else they could scavenge. Disease spread rapidly. Despite their suffering, morale among the civilians and soldiers remained stubbornly resilient for weeks.

The siege would last an additional six weeks. During the siege, Vicksburg was under constant bombardment with heavy artillery, there were occasional sorties to capture outposts, movements of artillery and men forward to the newly captured positions and then resumption of bombardment from closer range. The Army of Grant was moving forward almost inch by inch.

The Union army-maintained pressure from all sides and slowly choked the life out of the garrison. Sharpshooters picked off anyone who dared to show themselves above the parapets. Artillery fire was nearly constant. The Third Louisiana Redan was an earthwork defensive line of Vicksburg. It helped protect a key sector of the Confederate line, and was a focus of Union attacks, most of which failed with heavy casualties.

On June 25, Union engineers detonated a massive mine beneath a Confederate earthwork, using 2,200 pounds of black powder. The explosion threw men, artillery, and debris into the air and created a crater some 12 feet deep. Union troops followed that explosion with a charge, briefly breaking through, but Confederate forces quickly counterattacked, and the breach could not be exploited. The encounter lasted some 12 hours of mostly hand to hand combat. After that skirmish ended, the Union soldiers continued efforts of digging trenches, inching their way closer to the city.

By late June the siege had taken its toll on the city. Pemberton's army was on the brink of collapse. Rations had all but disappeared. Ammunition was low. Morale had significantly eroded. The hope that Johnston might return to lift the siege had faded. On July 3, Pemberton met with his officers and decided to seek terms of surrender. Grant was normally determined to accept only unconditional surrender. He initially refused negotiations. But soon he came to the realization that further bloodshed was unnecessary.

Grant and Pemberton met at the river's bank and Grant agreed to parole the Confederate army rather than take thousands of prisoners that he could not easily feed or guard. On July 4, 1863, the day after the Lee surrender at Gettysburg, General Pemberton officially surrendered to General Grant at Vicksburg. The 23,000 men that remained of Pemberton's troops, sick and hungry, laid down their arms and began their journey back home. The effect of the parole was a gentleman's agreement that these men would not re-enter the war.

The fall of Vicksburg was a monumental moment in the war for both the North and the South. The Union now controlled the entire Mississippi River, fulfilling a major part of General Scott's Anaconda Plan and effectively cutting the Confederacy in two. The western states of Arkansas, Texas, and part of

Louisiana were now isolated from the rest of the Southern war effort. The Anaconda Plan was a strategy imagined as a serpent coiled and slowly crushing the enemy from the outside in, chocked by a combination of naval blockade and territorial encirclement. It was a plan of slow suffocation rather than quick conquest. By the end of 1863 it was starting to take its full effect.

The Vicksburg surrender came one day after the Confederate defeat at Gettysburg. Together, these twin Union victories marked a turning point in the Civil War. With Vicksburg and the fall of Port Hudson five days later, the interior rivers were free and in control of the Union from Pittsburg to New Orleans. In the words of President Lincoln: *"The Father of Waters again goes unvexed to the sea."*

Grant, who had risen from relative obscurity, was now a celebrated hero across the North. The Vicksburg campaign was a masterpiece of operational strategy and a brutal demonstration of how war could be waged through logistics, patience, and relentless pressure. The Confederate stronghold that had once seemed untouchable had been brought to its knees not with spectacle, but with steady, grinding determination.

A Confederate diarist wrote*: "Our children no longer cry. They are too weak. We pray the Yankees end it soon, one way or another."*

Private Caleb Young of the Union's 31st Illinois regiment remembered, *"We advanced by shovel and rifle. The air was powder and sweat. Every day, the trenches grew closer."*

Private Lemuel Ford of Missouri wrote in a letter home: *"I have not seen the moon for seven nights. We dig and fire, dig and fire. The boys say the rats are better meat than the mule meat we stew."*

Nurse Clarissa Hill, caring for the wounded in a field tent, noted: *"They come in by the dozen. Fevered, filthy, frightened. Many cry out not from pain, but from homesickness. One lad clutched my hand and begged me to sing him a hymn. He died before the chorus."*

Lincoln had watched Grant's military rise with cautious optimism. Despite rumors of drunkenness and a rough demeanor, Grant delivered victories where others faltered. When one senator urged Lincoln to dismiss him, the President reportedly replied: *"I can't spare this man. He fights."* To a cabinet member who voiced concern, Lincoln quipped, *"If Grant is drinking, find out what it is and send a case to the rest of my generals."* The victory at Vicksburg catapulted Grant into national fame. Quiet, tenacious, and unflinching, he had done what others could not.

The Human Cost

Union artillery pounded Vicksburg day and night from land and river. The booming guns of Admiral David Porter's fleet on the Mississippi, combined with Grant's siege batteries, created a relentless cacophony. The city was struck by over 22,000 artillery shells, flattening homes, splintering churches, and tearing into public buildings. Residents and soldiers alike described the experience as living under a *"hailstorm of iron."* It was not safe to walk the streets in daylight. By the end, much of the city was reduced to rubble, with buildings shattered and smoke hanging constantly in the humid air.

To escape the shelling, citizens of Vicksburg dug caves into the clay hillsides surrounding the city. These makeshift shelters, known as *"bombproofs,"* became the homes of many for weeks. The caves were damp, dark, stifling, and infested with insects. Entire families, wealthy and poor, huddled in these earthen holes, cooking over small fires, sleeping on the ground, and emerging only at night as the shelling subsided. Some caves collapsed from nearby explosions, killing their occupants. Southern diarist Mary Loughborough wrote of *"living in a tomb,"* with *"a fearful, clinging sense of doom."* Babies cried endlessly. Fresh air was a luxury. Sanitation was almost non-existent.

As Union forces cut off supply lines, food quickly ran out. At first, rations were reduced. Then the people of Vicksburg and its defenders began eating mules, dogs, rats, and even boiled shoe leather. Flour was rare to non-existent. Corn meal became the staple, when it was available. Soldiers were issued limited amounts of coarse meal, bacon grease, and peas, when they could be found. Civilians traded jewelry for scraps of food. Accounts tell of Confederate soldiers boiling weeds for stew and mothers weeping as their children cried from hunger. The Confederate commander, General Pemberton, attempted to assure the population that relief was on the way, and indeed he was under the impression that it was. But as weeks passed, that hope faded and was soon replaced by resignation.

Overcrowding, poor nutrition, and extreme summer heat led to outbreaks of disease that spread quickly, particularly dysentery, malaria, typhoid, and scurvy. The city's makeshift hospitals overflowed. The water supply was contaminated, and latrines were inadequate. Soldiers weakened by hunger were unable to resist even minor illnesses. Medical care was rudimentary at best. Medicines were scarce, and surgical tools were often reused without sterilization. It was common for a soldier to lie wounded for days with minimal care or none at all.

The civilians of Vicksburg, including women and children, showed remarkable endurance in the face of horror. But as the siege wore on and supplies became unattainable, morale steadily declined. People began blaming Confederate leadership for putting the city in harm's way without adequate defense.

Church services were held in the caves. Some clergy tried to comfort the people with promises of divine purpose, while others turned bitter, questioning whether God had abandoned the South. Diaries tell of increasing hopelessness, bitterness, and fatigue.

On July 4, 1863, after exhausting all options and with starvation rampant, Pemberton surrendered Vicksburg to Grant. Pemberton chose that date hoping for more generous terms from the Union on the national holiday. Union soldiers, upon entering the city, were shocked by what they saw. ghostly figures in rags, children with distended bellies, houses turned to rubble, and the sick too weak to stand. The civilian population was left to slowly recover, but the psychological trauma lingered for years.

The Siege of Vicksburg became a symbol of Union resolve and Confederate suffering. Its capture split the Confederacy in two and gave the Union full control of the Mississippi River. But for those inside, the memory was of deprivation, terror, and the collapse of hope.

The siege left scars, on the landscape and on the men who survived it. Union and Confederate soldiers alike suffered from dysentery, dehydration, and heat exhaustion. The Union army suffered nearly 5,000 casualties of men killed and wounded. The Confederate army had 3,200 killed or wounded and another 26,000 captured and sent home.

Private Elijah Barnes of Ohio recalled, *"The smell never left us, sulfur, blood, and rot. We buried friends in silence and then had to shoot again by nightfall."* Civilians in Vicksburg wrote of living like moles, emerging only at night. *"I have forgotten the color of the sky,"* one woman wrote.

General Grant himself wrote *"…I found that many of the citizens had been living under ground. The ridges upon which Vicksburg is built, and those back to the Big Black, are composed of a deep yellow clay of great tenacity. Where roads and streets are cut through perpendicular banks are left and stand as well as if composed of stone. The magazines of the enemy were made by running passage-ways into this clay at places where there are deep cuts. Many citizens secured places of safety for their families by carving rooms in these embankments…. Some of these were carpeted and furnished with considerable elaboration. In these the occupants were fully secure from the shells of the navy, which were dropped into the city night and day without interruption."*

After the surrender, a Union soldier named George LeClaire described the silence that followed: *"We expected cheers or gunfire, but there was nothing. Just the sound of men laying down their weapons like they were laying down their burdens. It was over, and we didn't know how to feel."*

Vicksburg marked a turning point in strategy for how the war was fought from that point on. Grant's campaign of maneuver, encirclement, and siege would be echoed later in Chattanooga, Petersburg, and beyond. More importantly, it gave Lincoln a general he could trust to pursue the war to its end. A soldier who fought not for glory but for results. The Confederacy was no longer whole. And Ulysses S. Grant was no longer just a Western commander. He was the rising star of the Union war effort, and the man who would one day finish what others could not.

CHAPTER 19
PORT HUDSON AND CONTROLLING THE MISSISSIPPI RIVER

In the spring of 1863, as the Union was tightening its grip on control of the Mississippi River, two Confederate strongholds still barred the way to complete control: Vicksburg in Mississippi, and Port Hudson in Louisiana. Both were in strong positions with almost identical fortifications. They were both perched on high ground overlooking the river. The tenacious Grant was engaging the larger of the two forts at Vicksburg.

There was another vital campaign unfolding further south. Port Hudson, a heavily fortified bluff overlooking a sharp bend in the Mississippi, stood as one of the two obstacles preventing the Union from severing the Confederacy. The Union was attacking both simultaneously.

The Confederate forces at Port Hudson were commanded by Major General Franklin Gardner who was a West Point graduate and veteran of the Mexican-American War. Gardner was originally from New York but married into a Louisiana family and chose to serve in the Confederate Army. Gardner was not a battlefield star prior to Port Hudson, but he was considered a solid and loyal officer who could be trusted with a critical defensive assignment. His performance during the siege, though ultimately ending in surrender was seen as one of determined resistance under impossible conditions, and it significantly enhanced his military reputation. He took command of Port Hudson in 1862 and immediately began strengthening its defenses in anticipation of an eventual Union assault.

During the siege of Port Hudson, Gardner led a garrison of roughly 7,000 men, facing a vastly larger Union force. Despite being outnumbered and under constant bombardment, Gardner and his men held out for 48 days, making it one of the longest sieges in American history. They endured severe shortages of food, ammunition, and medical supplies.

The Confederacy understood the value of Port Hudson as the southern anchor of its control over shipping activity on the Mississippi River, its loss would result in severed supply lines and were it to be under Union control the southern Confederacy would be isolated from Texas, Arkansas, and much of Louisiana. This would cause a stoppage of the much used and needed supply lines from the west.

To the Union high command, capturing Port Hudson was essential to fulfilling General Winfield Scott's Anaconda Plan. Port Hudson was a town of less than 1,000 inhabitants and by the time the battle was looming, and Confederate forces were occupying the town, all the permanent citizens had moved out, leaving the town to their Confederate troops who overwhelmed the buildings with their 7,000 men.

Union commander, Nathaniel Banks was a political appointment as a Major General, He was a prominent figure in mid-19th century American politics. Born into a working-class family in Massachusetts, Banks had little formal education and worked in a textile mill during his youth. Despite humble beginnings, he developed strong oratory skills and an interest in politics. Banks first rose to national prominence as a member of the Democratic Party but soon aligned with the emerging Free Soil party and later the Republican Party, opposing the expansion of slavery. He served in the U.S. House of Representatives and became Speaker of the House (1856–1857), backed by a coalition of anti-slavery factions. He later served as governor of Massachusetts from 1858 to 1861.

He commanded Union forces in several key operations before being assigned to Louisiana, including in the Shenandoah Valley, where he suffered a major defeat by Stonewall Jackson in 1862. To put it mildly, Banks was a much better politician than he was a military commander

The Union forces under General Banks' command were an assembled mixed contingent of regular troops, newly enlisted volunteers, and the first significant deployment of African American soldiers in combat roles. These soldiers, many of them formerly enslaved, would find themselves at the center of one of the longest and most grueling sieges of the Civil War. While the more famous siege of Vicksburg unfolded upstream, Port Hudson tested endurance and strategy, grit and resolve under the very difficult circumstances of inadequate leadership. Here, the Union not only fought for territory, but it also fought for the future it had only begun to define following the Emancipation Proclamation.

The most feasible and logical position to anchor the Confederate line was on the 80-foot high bluffs at the small Louisiana town which was situated on a 150-degree bend of the Mississippi River. The navigation of the bend was slow and tedious work for any ship traveling up or down river. There the Rebels built a high-bastioned fortress in almost the exact configuration of Vicksburg. Located 25 miles north of Baton Rouge, 150 miles upriver from New Orleans, and 110 miles downriver from Vicksburg, a series of tiered and fortified batteries covered the river approach below the town. The 21 heavy guns placed there could methodically rake passing ships with concentrated fire as there was need.

Together, these two fortresses, Vicksburg and Port Hudson allowed the Confederacy to maintain contact with the Trans-Mississippi West keeping open vital supply routes for food, livestock, armaments and troops. By the end of 1862, Port Hudson employed over 9,000 Confederate soldiers. The Union, under the guidance of President Lincoln and General-in-Chief Henry Halleck, had long emphasized the importance of gaining control of the entire Mississippi River to remove the bulk of the Confederacy from western supply sources. The Mississippi River was the most important inland waterway in the country, providing the major transportation and communication route. The fall of New Orleans in April 1862 had been a step in that direction, and now only Vicksburg and Port Hudson remained.

In late spring of 1863, Ulysses S. Grant laid siege to Vicksburg. At the same time General Banks, commanding the Department of the Gulf, began his campaign to take Port Hudson. Nathaniel Banks was not a West Point graduate. He was a former millworker and then a successful politician. After his defeat in the Shenandoah Valley, he was assigned as commander of the Department of the Gulf and charged with gaining control of the Mississippi River. He was sent to reinforce Grant at Vicksburg but intentionally failed to reach that area, as he instead attempted the siege of Port Hudson.

There was a strategic relationship, but not a personal one, between Nathaniel Banks and Ulysses S. Grant regarding operations along the Mississippi River. While the two generals had separate commands, their efforts were strategically coordinated but not integrally entwined as part of the Union's overarching goal to gain full control of the river.

Banks had been expected to make his way upriver from New Orleans to affect a juncture with Grant at Vicksburg. But Banks had his own campaign in mind. He was focused on capturing Port Hudson. He was politically ambitious and believed that the independent capture of Port Hudson would bring him the

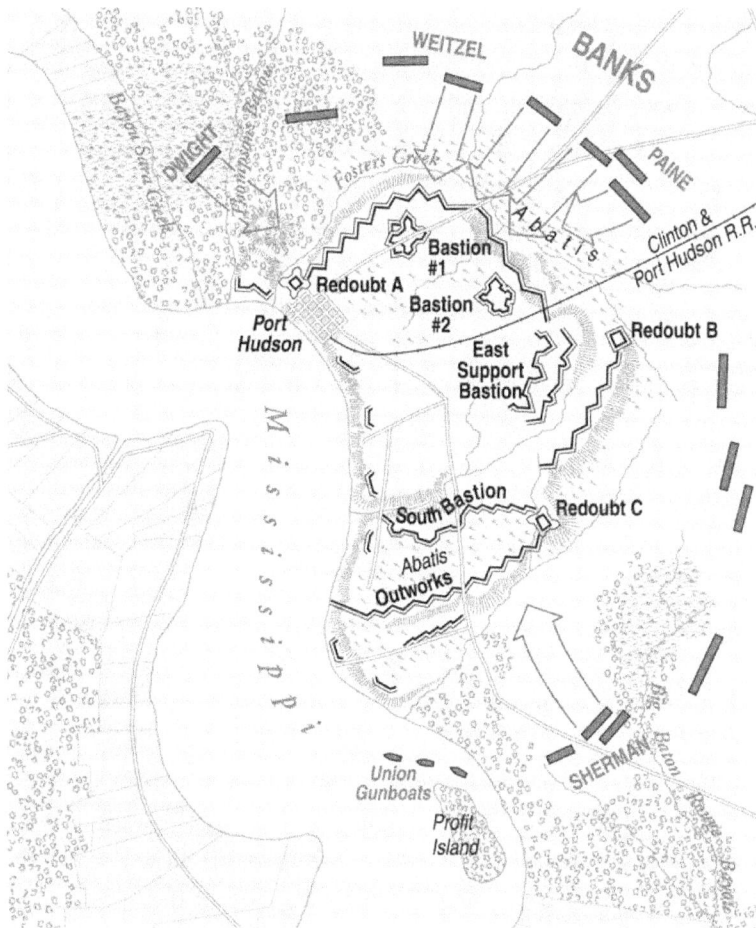

military glory that would align with his greater political goals. He gave excuses for not supporting Grant arguing the logistical obstacles of marching across swampy terrain were too great, and his army was not well prepared for rapid deployment, also suggesting that going to Grant would leave New Orleans exposed.

The major prize now confronting him then was Port Hudson, and by early April he had decided to attempt to take it. Moving up Bayou Teche to Alexandria in central Louisiana, Banks marched his army down the Red River to its confluence with the Mississippi. By May 22, his army was stationed across the river and confronting Port Hudson from the north, while Federal troops from Baton Rouge sealed off the fortress from the south.

A cordon of Union forces encircled Port Hudson for nearly six miles from one bank of the Mississippi River to the other. The Army of the Gulf was comprised of about 20,000 men and coupled with their numerical superiority they possessed 90 pieces of artillery. The Union Navy had the power to pound the fortress, as over a dozen gunboats and mortar boats roamed the river and maintained a regular bombardment. On May 26, Banks sent a formal request of surrender. The request was flatly refused. Gardner's strength was that he was holding the advantage of high ground and had significant fortifications.

Banks' force soon grew to about 30,000 troops, including United States Colored Troops, many of whom were formerly enslaved men from Louisiana. The Confederate garrison at Port Hudson had no recent reinforcements and still numbered around 7,000 men.

Eager to strike a decisive blow, Banks ordered a frontal assault on May 27, the first significant fighting of the battle. The Union troops advanced through dense underbrush and up steep ridges under a blazing summer Louisiana sun. The assault was met with fierce resistance. Confederate artillery and rifle fire from behind earthworks of the fort cut down wave after wave of attackers.

The Union advance was made by two brigades. Banks had planned the infantry assault to be synchronized, but the plan soon fell apart due to a series of badly coordinated and disjointed attacks. Pressing forward at a run in broken terrain laced with fallen timber, the bluecoats sent the enemy back into their works. Meanwhile, a Confederate battery on Commissary Hill erupted with murderous effect at point-blank range. Men were swept off their feet, and gaping holes appeared in the Union lines. The advance slowed as the Federal troops hugged the ground and sought whatever cover they could find. Southern commanders could be heard barking out orders, *"Take good aim, boys, and break their legs."* Still Union troops advanced as they could, crawling where they were able and sprinting forward as they could, through the difficult terrain.

Of historical importance, this day also saw the first large-scale use of Black troops in a Union assault. The 1st and 3rd Louisiana Native Guard were African American regiments that had formed for the Confederacy in New Orleans in 1862 before the Emancipation Proclamation. When the Union captured New Orleans, many offered their services to the Union, and were welcomed by General Butler.

These units charged bravely against the entrenched Confederate positions of Port Hudson. Despite suffering heavy casualties, they fought with remarkable determination and courage, proving their worth to skeptical white Union commanders. This engagement by Union Black troops predated the 54th Massachusetts charge on Fort Wagner, but it was just not as well known.

Banks' assault was horribly mismanaged by himself as well as a group of incompetent staff officers and was repelled with severe losses. There were nearly 2,000 Union casualties in that first day of fighting. Gardner's men held firm in their fortified high positions with very few losses.

After weeks of shelling, trench-digging, and probing attacks, Banks ordered another general assault on June 14. Once again, Union forces advanced under withering fire. Once again, they were driven back. The terrain was composed of dense woods, steep ravines, and fortified heights, which made coordinated attacks nearly impossible. Among the casualties was Union General Halbert Paine, who lost a leg in the fighting. Thousands more Union troops fell wounded or killed. If the first assault had not, the second failure made it clear that the Confederate defenses could not be overtaken by ground advances of Union soldiers, especially under incompetent command.

After the second failed assault of the fort, Banks settled in for a prolonged siege. Union engineers dug approach trenches, gradually tightening the noose around Port Hudson, similar to what Grant was doing upriver at Vicksburg. Artillery batteries rained down fire day and night. The Union Navy, with gunboats positioned on the Mississippi, added to the bombardment. Inside the town, Confederate soldiers inside the city fortifications endured worsening conditions. Food supplies dwindled, water sources became polluted, and morale declined by the day. Starvation and disease spread throughout the garrison.

The bombardment was bothersome to a vast extent but there were very few deaths from that action. Gardner's men continued to resist as best they could under the conditions, they found themselves in. They held their positions, believing that help might yet arrive. They had been promised reinforcements by General Joseph Johnston who was preoccupied with an attempted relief at Vicksburg, but he was so hesitant and indecisive that he was unable to relieve conditions at either fortress.

Since the initial days of the late-May assault, Union confidence had given way to doubt. The two attempted frontal assaults were absolute failures. Union leadership was substantially incompetent. Although the Union had access to supplies; sickness, and fatigue, were affecting the morale of the troops. The high command itself was fragmented with personality clashes over bureaucratic assignments and petty jealousies. An impatient and frustrated Nathaniel Banks decided to attempt a third assault. This time they would try an attack in dark of the pre-dawn morning of June 11, that he hoped might somehow change the course of the engagement.

The operation was doomed from the start by ambiguous orders and further inept leadership from Banks as well as his staff. *"The futility and foolhardiness of the thing was clear to all, we looked upon our instructions as simple madness,"* one Union captain reported. At 1 am, accompanied by a stepped-up naval bombardment, Union infantry crept forward in the misty darkness and found the enemy pickets well prepared for their advance. The alarm was sounded, and Gardner's main line poured gun fire at anything that moved. Some Federal troops made it through the hail of fire, and up to the Confederate lines. Many were captured and many retreated. A torrential rainstorm burst through the clouds shortly after the assault, drenching soldiers and slowing any potential advance. Confederates taunted their counterparts: *"What's keeping you fellas? Come on over. We're waiting for you."*

The Confederate soldiers were to a man sick as well as tired. But they had held again and had defeated another Union surge of their fortifications, with very few casualties. Buoyed again by the success of his men, General Gardner sent couriers through enemy lines with coded messages advising General Johnson of the garrison's predicament, but it was a forlorn hope. Johnson was focused on aiding Vicksburg, but even in that effort he was too cautious to be effective. Although, it was substantially unknown by Gardner there was absolutely no chance of saving his army, even from a mostly bungling Union command.

Banks' final attempt at attacking his enemy head on resulted in another devastatingly unsuccessful attack. His losses were significant and obviously very demoralizing to his remaining troops. Total Union casualties were estimated at almost 2,000 men. While total Confederate casualties were estimated at about 235. The Union command was continuously formulating plans destined for extreme failure with significant losses and the Confederates had relatively been unaffected, remaining cocky and comparatively unharmed but for the effects of the siege.

Meanwhile, a few Confederate soldiers deserted their posts and surrendered themselves to General Banks with claims that the garrison at Fort Hudson was just about played out, and the men there were staring starvation directly in the face. To test the validity of the reports, Banks ordered a wickedly intense bombardment on June 13, to be followed by a summons to surrender.

The same war strategy that marked the dismal failures of May 27 and June 11 continued to propel the army on its hapless course. As dawn broke on June 14, Banks initiated yet another assault on the Confederate stronghold. The ground shook and the sky exploded with a vigorous one-hour volley of cannon fire, which served little purpose except to warn the Confederates that the Union army was about to surge forward. The primary effort was stopped shortly thereafter when it was demonstrated that no man could clear the fire-swept ridge along their front and live. More Union soldiers died needlessly at the whim of their commander.

The decisive moment in the Port Hudson battle for Union victory came not from any action of the Union commanders at Port Hudson, but from the outcome of the parallel campaign to the north at Vicksburg. On July 4, 1863, General Grant accepted the surrender of Vicksburg. The strongest Confederate stronghold on the Mississippi River had fallen. Confederate General Gardner recognized the futility of continued resistance, with Grant's forces only a hundred miles to the north there was no hope of being reinforced. His men were starving, exhausted, encircled, and there was literally no hope for victory. On July 9, 1863, General Gardner surrendered Port Hudson to General Banks. One Confederate soldier said later that he and his comrades eventually ate *"all the beef, all the mules, all the dogs, and all the rats"* before the surrender of the fort.

General Gardner surrendered the entire garrison that included 5,500 soldiers, most of whom were sick or wounded. All the arms, ammunition, and fortifications were turned over to the Union. Banks did not take the Confederate soldiers as prisoners; they were allowed to return home on the promise that they would not continue in the Confederate war effort. The wounded were treated by Union doctors.

The fall of Port Hudson, just five days after Vicksburg, was the final blow to any Confederate hopes of retaining any semblance of control of the Mississippi River. Union gunboats and supply ships now had access from St. Louis to New Orleans.

CHAPTER 20
CHICKAMAUGA, A STREAM OF DEATH

It had been a little over six months since Major General William Rosecrans and his Army of the Cumberland had checked the Confederates at the Battle of Stones River (December 31,1862–January 2,1863). Fought 30 miles southeast of Nashville, Stones River secured the Tennessee capital for the North as a base of supply. From there the Federal advance southward could continue to the next vital strategic objective in the state, Chattanooga. Its capture would unlock the door to a march into Georgia, thus bringing the South one step closer to ultimate defeat.

Chattanooga was a very important military objective for the North because of its position as a gateway through the Appalachian Mountains and into the heartland of the South. It had a population of about 2,500 people, and was a central rail hub from Memphis, Charleston, Nashville, Atlanta, and west to the Mississippi River. The single most important obstacle to the Union designs on Chattanooga in the summer of 1863 was the principal Rebel army in the West, the Army of Tennessee. Battle hardened and determined, the *"second army of the Confederacy"* had been dogged by ill fortune and a lack of manpower and equipment. As telling as these problems were, they were compounded by the poor leadership of its army commander, Braxton Bragg.

Few Confederate generals inspired as much frustration, among both their men and their superiors, as Braxton Bragg. A native of North Carolina and a career soldier, Bragg had distinguished himself in the Mexican-American War, earning praise for his bravery and artillery skill. Yet in the Civil War, his rigid leadership style, abrasive personality, and frequent feuds with fellow officers made him one of the most controversial figures in the Southern high command.

The Union victory at Vicksburg coupled with the taking of Port Hudson in early July 1863 had opened the Mississippi River, dividing the Confederacy into two parts, with neither being accessible to the other, severely weakening its grip on the Trans-Mississippi West. But the war was primarily being fought in the east. It was the heart of the Confederacy. In the hilly country of northern

Georgia and eastern Tennessee, the South was very strong, and the war was far from over. Northern Georgia was crisscrossed by rivers, railroads, and rugged terrain, and it remained vital to both sides. Chattanooga, nestled along the Tennessee River and framed by steep ridges, emerged as the next key prize if the Union were to obtain a final victory.

For the Confederacy, Chattanooga was the gateway to Georgia, a vital hub connecting the Deep South to the embattled west. For the Union, it offered the chance to cut deeper into Southern infrastructure, threaten Atlanta, and perhaps deliver a decisive blow to end the war. After the fall of Vicksburg, Union attention shifted eastward with fresh determination. It would not be long before the rolling hills and dense woods of northern Georgia would run red with blood.

Commanding the Union's Army of the Cumberland was Major General William Rosecrans, a West Point graduate known as much for his intellect as his obstinacy. A skilled strategist and an energetic officer, Rosecrans had earned praise for his earlier campaign at Stones River at the beginning of the year. It was a morale boost following the Union debacle at Fredericksburg. But his tendency to challenge superiors, particularly Secretary of War Stanton, made him a controversial figure in Washington. Nevertheless, Lincoln and Stanton had little choice but to rely on him to dislodge the Confederates from their stronghold in Chattanooga. Rosecrans' chief of staff was a future president of the United States, James Garfield.

Opposing Rosecrans was General Braxton Bragg, commander of the Confederate Army of Tennessee. Bragg was a deeply unpopular officer among his own subordinates. He was abrasive, rigid, and quick to blame others for missteps. Despite this, he remained in command due largely to his personal political loyalty to Jefferson Davis. Many of Bragg's officers, including James Longstreet and D.H. Hill, openly distrusted his judgment, and this atmosphere of distrust would have lasting consequences in the days ahead.

The Chattanooga campaign began in earnest in late summer 1863. Rosecrans devised a bold and complicated maneuver to entrap the Confederates. Rather than attack Chattanooga directly, he sought to outflank Bragg by moving south, crossing the Tennessee River downstream, deep within Alabama. He divided his army in three parts hoping to press Bragg out of Chattanooga.

Rosecrans executed the movement with precision. His three corps, the XIV under George Thomas, the XX under Alexander McCook, and the XXI under Thomas Crittenden, fanned out across the mountainous terrain. The Army of the Cumberland advanced over difficult roads, cut across rivers, and wound through narrow gaps. Rosecrans believed Bragg was in full retreat and that a rapid pursuit might trap the Confederates before they could regroup. But Bragg, recognizing the threat, evacuated Chattanooga on September 8 and moved his army south. He took up a new defensive position near LaFayette, Georgia on September 8. He had the intention of striking Rosecrans when the Union army was most vulnerable, as it was spread across the hills and valleys in pursuit.

As Rosecrans pressed forward, his army became dangerously stretched. His forces were separated by ridges and miles of dense wilderness, each corps predominately isolated from the others. Bragg saw an opportunity to strike at the unorganized foe. Reinforcements were already enroute to his command from Mississippi and Virginia, including the divisions of Nathan Bedford Forrest and the long-anticipated arrival of James Longstreet's men from Lee's Army of Northern Virginia.

Still, though recognizing the enemy's weakness, Bragg hesitated. Despite having superior knowledge of the terrain and the advantage of concentration of resources, his own inability to inspire confidence in his subordinates delayed a cohesive offensive. Several planned attacks were postponed or mismanaged, giving the Union forces time to close their lines and establish a more defensible posture.

The Battle of Chickamauga took place on a battlefield of less than four square miles in area. There were to be approximately 130,000 soldiers engaged in that battle, on that field.

Rosecrans, still convinced that Bragg was retreating further south, ordered his men to press on. On September 18, his columns were moving through the dense forests of northern Georgia, crossing Chickamauga Creek, which was not a large water body. The creek was about 30 feet wide at its widest and mostly two to four feet deep. It was a gently flowing meandering stream. But soon it would enter the lore of the war.

The roads were poor, communication between corps was difficult, and maps were vague as well as inaccurate. The Confederates, meanwhile, were converging rapidly, planning a coordinated assault to cut off and destroy part of the Union army.

Although there is some discrepancy, some say the name "Chickamauga" comes from a Cherokee word often translated as "River of Death," and that moniker would prove to be a dark prophecy. By the evening of September 18,

Confederate forces had nearly fully massed for an attack. They now outnumbered Rosecrans' forces, who remained unaware of the scale of the Confederate concentration. Confederate cavalry under General Forrest and infantry under D.H. Hill began to probe the Union lines, especially near Jay's Mill and Reed's Bridge. Union forces resisted but soon realized that the Confederates were not retreating, they were laying preparations for an all-out assault. The woods echoed with skirmish fire. As darkness fell, soldiers on both sides bivouacked nervously, becoming aware that something ominous was about to occur.

The initial engagements began on the afternoon of September 18. Bragg's objective was to cross Chickamauga Creek and cut off Rosecrans from Chattanooga. Skirmishes flared around Reed's Bridge and Alexander's Bridge as Confederate cavalry and infantry attempted to force crossings. Union troops under Colonel Robert Minty and Brigadier General John Wilder's *"Lightning Brigade,"* armed with Spencer repeating rifles (capable of shooting 20 rounds a minute), put up fierce resistance, delaying Bragg's advance and buying valuable time for the Union army.

The day before the full fury of battle erupted at Chickamauga, both Union and Confederate forces were already locked in a desperate race, a race not for territory, but for position. At dawn on September 18, the fields and thick forests of northern Georgia were heavy with mist. Bragg was determined to cut off Rosecrans's Army from Chattanooga, ordered his Confederates to force crossings over Chickamauga Creek. His plan was to strike Rosecrans's left flank, wedge the Union army apart, and destroy it piecemeal before it could concentrate. With his recent reinforcements, Bragg commanded a significant numerical advantage.

Early that morning, Confederate cavalry under Nathan Bedford Forrest clashed with Union cavalry at Reed's Bridge and Alexander's Bridge, vital crossings over the winding creek. Union cavalry fought stubbornly to delay them, but under pressure, they fell back. Confederate infantry columns, crossing behind the cavalry, began to move westward through the thick woods, setting the stage for a major attack on Rosecrans's vulnerable flank.

Meanwhile, the Union army was still dangerously stretched. Rosecrans had divided his forces across miles of rough country to cover potential Confederate approaches. Communications were slow. The threat of being attacked and defeated was real, and growing. Recognizing the mounting danger, General George Thomas took critical initiative. Studying the reports of Confederate movements and feeling the urgency of the moment, Thomas urged Rosecrans to immediately concentrate the army. Thomas understood that if the Confederates struck before the Union army pulled together, disaster would certainly follow.

Communication between the commander and his subordinates had been very difficult throughout their time in Georgia. The terrain and narrow roads lead to difficulties in getting requests and orders delivered effectively. However, luck was on the Union side with this request. Rosecrans received the request from Thomas, understood the urgency, and responded quickly by ordering his corps, scattered between Lee and Gordon's Mill to Crawfish Springs to shift northward toward LaFayette Road, forming a defensive front that could potentially block or delay Confederate advances.

Throughout the afternoon and evening of September 18, Union troops marched through the dust and darkness. Division after division stumbled along narrow forest paths, struggling to find their designated places in a landscape of dense underbrush and confusing landmarks. Artillery rumbled past fields still green with late-summer crops. Infantrymen, weary from the heat and the long marches of the campaign established plugs in lines hastily formed along the roadways and fields near Kelly Field and Brotherton Road.

Clashes between the two sides slowly intensified as Union pickets traded shots with Confederate scouts probing westward from the creek. At dusk, soldiers on both sides fired blindly into the darkening night. Flares were sent skyward lighting the mist and dark woods with brief flashes of fire. Though no great battle erupted that day, the maneuvers of September 18 shaped the days that followed. Thomas's urgency, Rosecrans's orders, and the weary night marches of the Union Army meant that when Bragg launched his full assault the next morning, the Union army was battered, tired and somewhat confused but was more cohesive and willing to repel their adversaries.

The Battle of Chickamauga, September 19

As the sun rose over northern Georgia on September 19, light started filtering through heavy mist in thick stands of pine trees. Neither army had fully grasped how close they were to one another until that morning. What began as scattered skirmishing quickly erupted into a brutal, confused, and grinding fight. At dawn, Union cavalry under Colonel Robert Minty and Colonel John

Wilder fought desperately to slow the Confederate crossings of Chickamauga Creek at Reed's and Alexander's bridges. Meanwhile, Bragg's Confederate forces, having successfully crossed the creek the day before, began to push westward, seeking to drive between the divided Union corps.

The fighting opened in earnest when Union troops under Brigadier General John Croxton, part of Thomas's division, stumbled into Confederate

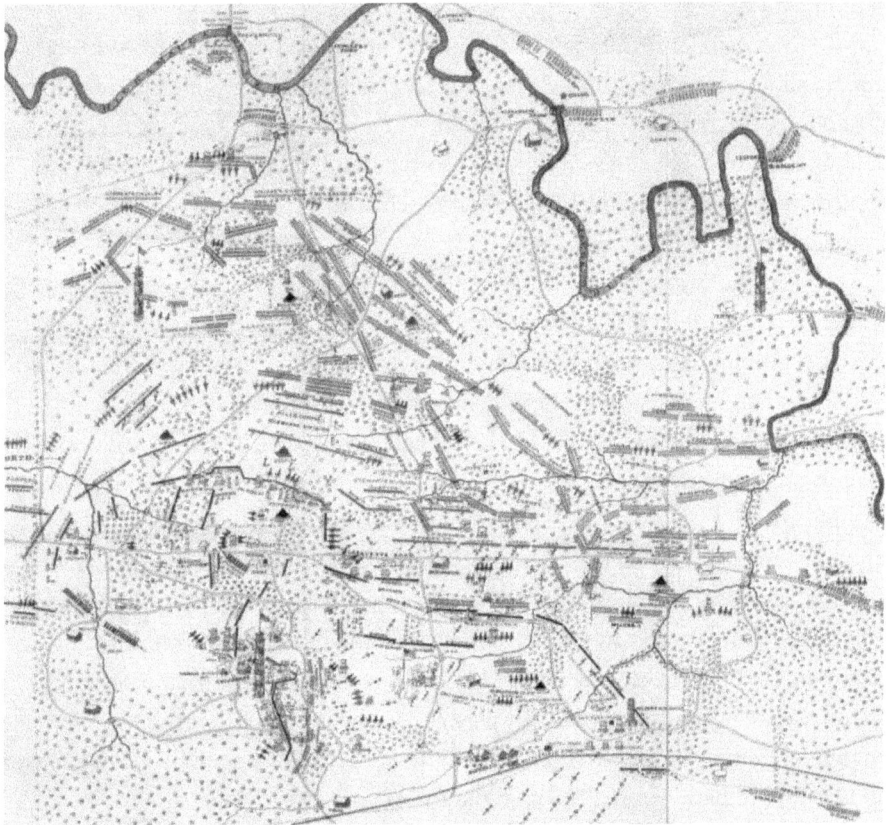

brigades advancing west of Reed's Bridge. A sharp engagement broke out in the woods. Shots cracked through the early morning mist as soldiers fired blindly in the dense undergrowth. Reinforcements quickly fed into the fray from both sides, and what had begun as a skirmish swelled into a roaring battle.

By midmorning, both armies were fully engaged across a chaotic front that stretched for miles. The terrain was difficult with units fighting without being able to see more than a few dozen yards ahead. Visibility was so poor that commanders frequently lost control of their regiments, and battle lines bent, buckled, and at times were reformed with little coherence.

George Thomas was alert to the danger of Confederate massing on the Union left and so he moved his forces steadily to reinforce vulnerable sectors. His brigades formed along LaFayette Road, anchoring the Union's northern flank near Kelly Field, and absorbed repeated Confederate attacks with gritty determination.

Meanwhile, further south along the line, Rosecrans committed more troops, albeit piecemeal at times, into the growing maelstrom. He was reacting to Confederate movements as best he could, often based on conflicting and outdated reports. There was no grand coordinated Union attack plan on September 19, only a desperate series of patchwork defenses to meet each new Confederate thrust.

On the Confederate side, Braxton Bragg's leadership as was sometimes typical, was fragmented and indecisive. Though he had more men on the field and opportunities to concentrate them for decisive attacks, the orders he issued were most often unclear and subsequently poorly coordinated. Subordinate generals like Leonidas Polk and D.H. Hill acted sluggishly, allowing Union forces time to plug gaps in their defenses. If these gaps had not been plugged, any ensuing charge by the South could have been disastrous for the North.

Throughout the afternoon, the woods erupted again in spasms of violent fighting. Units collided head-on, often with little warning. Some of the bloodiest fighting occurred near Viniard Farm, where Confederate forces smashed into Union lines. Union General Thomas Wood had moved his division eastward, attempting to support units already clashing in the dense undergrowth. What he encountered instead was a wave of Confederate brigades under Bushrod Johnson and Ben Cheatham surging through the forest.

The open ground of Viniard Field became a bloody corridor. It was a small area of open ground, less than 40 acres in size. But it quickly became a place where men emerged from the woods only to be raked by artillery and musket fire, and where formations dissolved in the face of ferocious resistance. Between the two sides there were almost 3,000 casualties at Viniard Field, one of which was Confederate Brigadier General Ben Helm, who was married to the half-sister of Mary Todd Lincoln. Ben Helm was shot in the stomach and died later that day.

Wood's brigades, particularly those under Nathan Kimball and George Buell, tried to hold the tree line on the eastern edge of the field. But Johnson's men came on hard, crossing the open space, absorbing casualties and returning fire in kind. Orders were shouted and misunderstood or never heard. Units tangled in the woods; some fired on friends, mistaking them for the enemy in the difficult vision of twilight, gunpowder haze and broken lines.

As the sun was setting the battle only intensified. General Preston Smith, a Confederate brigade commander, led his men into the maelstrom with characteristic boldness. But his boldness quickly proved fatal. In the confused confrontation at the edge of the field, Smith was struck by musket fire as he tried to rally his troops. His fall momentarily disrupted the Confederate advance and added to the uncertainty and confusion the battlefield.

Reinforcements poured into the confrontation from both armies. Union brigades under John Beatty tried to stabilize the line, while Cheatham's men pressed harder from the south. The clearing changed hands more than once as control slipped from one side to the other. At times, the same patch of ground was contested three or four times within the hour, littered with the dead and wounded from both armies.

As darkness overcame the battered landscape, the Confederates finally secured the field, though at great cost. The Union pulled back toward the Lafayette Road, still holding key positions but shaken by the intensity of the combat. The fighting at Viniard Field stood as a grim foretelling of the bloodshed yet to come. The field had become a symbol of the savagery that Chickamauga would represent, dense woods, confused orders, brave men fighting in near blindness, and a price in human sacrifice for every yard gained or lost. One Union soldier later wrote of the first day: *"We could hear them before we could see them — a roar in the trees, and then they were on us, and the whole world turned into smoke and thunder."*

Darkness allowed a cease of fighting and exhaustion gave way to regrouping. Fires on both sides of the line dimly in the darkened woods, wounded men cried out from thickets and hollows, and the ground was littered with the dead and dying. Both armies had suffered heavily, and neither had achieved a clear advantage. But there remained a confidence in the Confederate camp. The Confederates had gained ground, especially along the Union left, and Bragg sensed another opportunity for a definitive victory. Plans were already underway for a massive Confederate assault the following morning, one that would include James Longstreet's newly arrived veterans from the Army of Northern Virginia.

The Union army was battered but still mostly cohesive thanks to Thomas's calm leadership. They readied themselves for the onslaught to come. The bloodiest day of the Battle of Chickamauga would be coming in the morning. An officer from the 21st Ohio wrote: *"The smoke hung so thick we could only tell our lines by the screams. The forest became a slaughterhouse."*

As the quiet of the night engulfed the battlefield, some may have been able to sleep, but not many. Both armies were dug into hastily organized defensive positions, but mostly less than 200 yards apart and in some areas as little as 75 yards apart. Fires flickered in the dark. Wounded men cried out. Neither side held a decisive advantage, but casualties already numbered in the thousands.

September 20

Dawn seamed to brake more slowly than normal over the fields and forests of Chickamauga on September 20, 1863, with another heavy mist clinging to the ground. The smell of gunpowder was still hanging in the damp air from the previous day's fighting. Exhausted men on both sides stiffened in the chill, knowing that the first day's brutal, confused fighting had likely only set the stage for something that could be far worse. And there was an awareness that the far worse would soon be upon them.

On the Confederate side, General Bragg, with an ego that had been buoyed by modest gains from the day before, had developed yet another ambitious plan. He divided his army into two wings: Leonidas Polk would command the right and attack the Union left at dawn, while James Longstreet, freshly arrived from Virginia, would command the left and drive into the Union right. Bragg envisioned a crushing blow that would shatter the Union Army and recapture Chattanooga for the Confederacy.

The morning of September 20 began as the previous day had ended, with chaos and confusion on both sides. Bragg intended to launch a coordinated attack at dawn, but delays, miscommunication, and poorly executed orders fragmented his plan yet again. Despite this uncoordinated effort fortune favored the Confederacy. Shortly before 11:00 a.m., Union General Thomas Wood, acting on a misunderstood order from Rosecrans, pulled his division out of line to reposition it elsewhere, creating an unexpected gap in the center of the Union defense along the Lafayette Road.

At nearly the same moment, Confederate General Longstreet launched a massive attack with a newly assembled strike force of around 10,000 men that struck directly into the gap left open by Wood. The move shattered Union cohesion. Entire brigades were engulfed in panic. Confederate divisions under Bushrod Johnson and John Bell Hood swept through the Union center, turning what had been a sturdy defense into a route of the Union troops occupying the area. General Rosecrans was caught in the wave of retreating troops and was physically swept from the field.

In a panic, he later reported to Washington, incorrectly, that his army had been destroyed. The Confederate advance was swift, and it was brutal. General Hood was seriously wounded by an artillery shell, but his men pressed forward, routing the Union Army as they proceeded. The road to Chattanooga lay open, but the South could not negotiate an immediate breakthrough.

As the Union right collapsed, only the left, anchored by General George Thomas near Snodgrass Hill and Horseshoe Ridge, stood firm. Recognizing the danger that lay ahead, Thomas organized a defensive line and refused to retreat. Throughout the afternoon, Confederate forces launched wave after wave of attacks. Fierce close-range combat ensued in the forested high ground, with regiments often engaging at point-blank range. Thomas's men, reinforced by elements of Granger's reserve corps, fought with heroic tenacity. Soldiers from the 21st Ohio, 89th Illinois, and 18th U.S. Infantry held the line under immense pressure from attacking forces. Union artillery had been dragged by hand up the slopes to higher ground and now blasted the dense formations below.

Private Alonzo Bartlett of the 89th Illinois later wrote: *"It was like holding the earth itself against the heavens. We fired until our barrels were too hot to touch, and still they came."* By 5:30 p.m., after six hours of sustained combat, Thomas began a slow, orderly withdrawal of his troops. The battlefield finally and mercifully fell silent. Snodgrass Hill was littered with bodies, broken cannon, and shattered trees. George Thomas had earned his place in history, forever known as the Rock of Chickamauga.

By the night of September 20, the battered Army of the Cumberland clung desperately to a defensive line around Snodgrass Hill and Horseshoe Ridge, where General Thomas had held off wave after wave of Confederate assaults. His determined stand had bought precious time for Union troops to regroup and withdraw. By nightfall, it was clear that the position could no longer be held. The men under Thomas began their own withdrawal.

General Rosecrans had already left the battlefield earlier in the day, retreating to Chattanooga after a massive Confederate breakthrough had shattered the center of the Union line. With him were portions of the army that had been swept from the field. The burden of holding the enemy at bay and organizing the retreat fell to Thomas and a few key subordinates who remained behind to prevent total collapse. The retreat began around 7:30 p.m. under cover of darkness. Thomas carefully orchestrated a rear guard action, pulling units off the ridge one brigade at a time, while maintaining enough pressure on the Confederates to discourage pursuit. He employed quiet withdrawals, skirmish screens, and used the rugged terrain to conceal his movements. The withdrawal was made all the more difficult by exhausted troops, wounded men, and the disorienting thickets and ravines.

Wagons and artillery had already been moving back toward Rossville Gap, and the army funneled through this key pass during the night. While there were moments of bewilderment and the column stretched thin, the retreat never disintegrated into panic. The Confederate army did not aggressively pursue, due in part to exhaustion, lack of coordination, and their own heavy losses.

By the next day, the remnants of the Union army were safely inside the fortifications at Chattanooga. Rosecrans's failure to destroy Bragg's army had turned into a near disaster, saved only by the stubborn defense led by Thomas. The retreat to Chattanooga was a tactical withdrawal under extreme duress, carried out with a degree of professionalism that prevented total annihilation.

Though technically a Confederate victory, Chickamauga was marred by Bragg's indecision and command disputes. It revealed the South's resilience, but also its inability to capitalize fully on battlefield success. For the North, Chickamauga was a sobering defeat. But it might had been far worse without the heroism of George Thomas. He gave the army a rallying point despite the Union's loss.

Conclusion

The Battle of Chickamauga was the most significant Confederate victory in the Western Theater, boosting Southern morale after a string of setbacks, particularly the fall of Vicksburg and Gettysburg in July. In the two days of chaotic, close-quarters fighting, the Union Army of the Cumberland suffered approximately 16,170 casualties, including around 1,657 killed, 9,756 wounded, and 4,757 missing or captured. Confederate losses were even heavier, with an estimated 18,454 casualties, including about 2,312 killed, 14,674 wounded, and 1,468 missing.

The scale of the bloodshed was once again almost intolerable for both North and South, in a war in which immense bloodshed was common. Chickamauga became the second bloodiest battle of the Civil War and left vast sections of the woods and fields of northern Georgia carpeted with the dead. Surgeons worked day and night in makeshift hospitals; wounded men lay for hours or days where they fell, crying out for water or rescue. Dead horses and destroyed cannons littered the ground alongside the fallen men.

Though the South's General Bragg technically held the field, his failure to pursue and possibly destroy Rosecrans's army allowed the Union Army to retreat to the well-fortified city of Chattanooga, a strategic rail hub whose possession would prove decisive in the months ahead. Meanwhile, George Thomas's heroic stand at Snodgrass Hill preserved the heart of the Union army and prevented a catastrophe. Chickamauga proved that bravery alone could not guarantee victory, and that poor communication, misunderstanding, and the chaos of battle often decided the fate of armies more than strategy and bravery.

The fields of Chickamauga fell silent on the evening of September 20, but the war in the West was far from over. A new, even more critical struggle loomed on the horizon. The fight for Chattanooga the *"Gateway to the Deep South"* would soon unfold.

CHAPTER 21
CHATTANOOGA AND THE ASCENDANCE OF SHERMAN

With its major victories at Gettysburg and Vicksburg in early July, the North had limited the Confederate offensive operations. Having control of the Mississippi River was vital to the ultimate success of the Union. In the Western Theater, the situation was more fluid and more precarious. The Union's hold on Chattanooga, Tennessee, a critical rail hub and transportation gateway to the Deep South, would soon be challenged in one of the most dramatic episodes of the war.

Union General William Rosecrans had led a successful campaign through Tennessee, culminating in the capture of Chattanooga in early September 1863. Chattanooga was vital to Union plans, it sat at the junction of several railroads, offered access to Georgia and the Confederate heartland, and provided a staging ground for future operations that included capturing Atlanta.

To defend the city, Rosecrans pursued Confederate General Bragg and his Army of Tennessee southward into northern Georgia. There, Bragg was reinforced by troops with those from Mississippi and Virginia, including forces from Lee's army. The Confederates turned on the pursuing Union forces at Chickamauga and fought an intense battle on September 19 and 20. The result was a defeat of the Union forces there and the most significant Confederate victory in the Western Theater.

After their setback in Chickamauga, the beaten and demoralized Union army had retreated into Chattanooga. Bragg followed, without attacking, and took up strong positions on the surrounding high ground. The Southern army camped on Lookout Mountain to the southwest, Missionary Ridge to the east, and Raccoon Mountain to the west. The Confederate army effectively besieged the city, cutting off most supply lines and pushing the Union forces to the brink of starvation, taking from the Union playbook used at Vicksburg and Port Hudson.

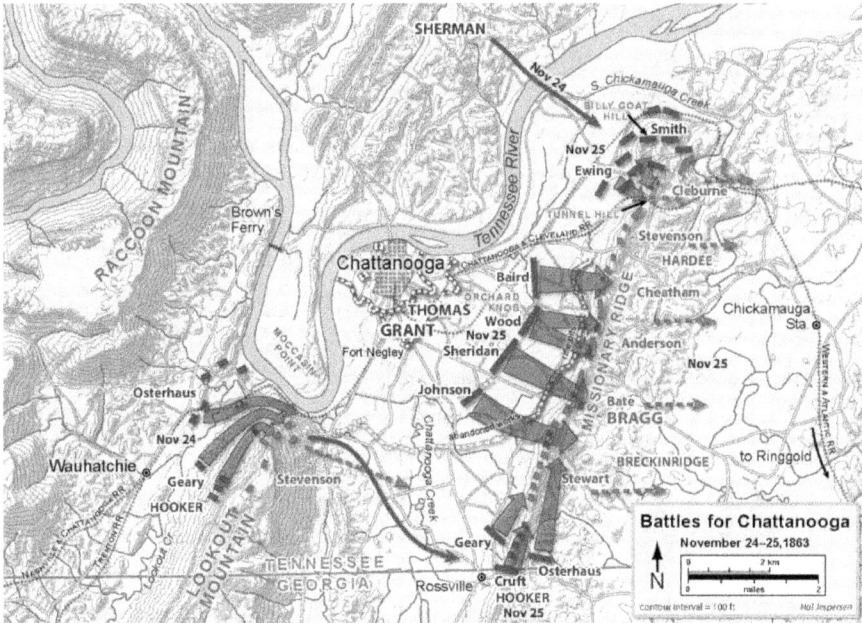

Battles for Chattanooga
November 24–25, 1863

Within a month of the start of the siege, morale in the Union camps was growing very low, as supplies started to dwindle and with that hopes began to fade. Rosecrans had failed his men when he was caught up in a chaotic retreat from Chickamauga to Chattanooga initiating the decline in morale, and at the same time he had lost the confidence of Washington. President Lincoln remarked that he was *"confused and stunned like a duck hit on the head."* Rosecrans had failed to secure supply lines into the city and had effectively put an end to any momentum his forces had gained from their initial occupation of the city.

To rescue his besieged army in Chattanooga, Lincoln turned to a man whose name had become synonymous with success in the West, Ulysses S. Grant. After his victory at Vicksburg, Grant had been placed in command of the newly created Military Division of the Mississippi, giving him control of all Union forces from the Mississippi River to the Appalachian Mountains. As was his manner, Grant moved quickly. Upon receiving his new assignment, Grant relieved Rosecrans of his command in Chattanooga and appointed General Thomas, to command the Army of the Cumberland. He also ordered reinforcements from the Army of the Tennessee under General Sherman, and from the Army of the Potomac under Joseph Hooker, to join the effort to relieve the Union forces in Chattanooga.

With remarkable speed and ingenuity, Union engineers opened what would soon be called the *"Cracker Line."* This was a supply route along the Tennessee River that created an avenue allowing food, ammunition, and reinforcements to come into the city. The Cracker Line was so named because Union troops besieged in Chattanooga had been subsisting on four crackers a day, and whatever they could forage from the nearby countryside.

Grant approved an aggressive plan developed by Brigadier General William F. "Baldy" Smith, the Union's chief engineer. On the night of October 26, 1863, Union troops floated silently down the Tennessee River in pontoon boats under cover of darkness. They landed at Brown's Ferry, surprising and overwhelming the Confederate pickets stationed there. Almost simultaneously, another force under Joseph Hooker began marching from Lookout Valley, west of Chattanooga, after crossing the river at Bridgeport.

By October 28, the two Union forces had linked up, securing the river and road routes through Lookout Valley and opening a narrow gap along the Tennessee River at Brown's Ferry offered the possibility of creating a supply corridor linking Chattanooga to the Union-held town of Bridgeport, Alabama, where rail and river supplies could be brought in. The key to this maneuver was to outflank the Confederate siege lines without drawing attention, by using a combination of stealth, speed, and coordination.

The supply route started in Union controlled Bridgeport, Alabama, where they were loaded onto riverboats travelling up the Tennessee River to Browns Ferry and carried by wagons by roads newly controlled by Grant's army. Many tons of food, ammunition and medical supplies now flowed into the city of Chattanooga, literally overnight. With the arrival of their new provisions morale of the men immediately improved. Grant had not broken Bragg's siege through brute force, but by bold maneuvering and riverine ingenuity. Grant had transformed a desperate, hungry, demoralized Union force into an energized and nearly exuberant army.

Grant later remarked, *"The breaking of the enemy's lines of communication and the opening of our own, at Chattanooga, was the turning point of the campaign."* Within weeks, Chattanooga was not only secure, but a staging ground for Union offensives that would soon sweep through the heart of the South.

By mid-November the dire situation inside the city had been totally reversed. The besieged Union army had become an armed, well-fed juggernaut again. There were nearly 60,000 men, now nourished, rearmed, and ready to fight as needed, which lead to a soaring of moral. Across the ridges, Bragg's army of about 40,000 men was still demoralized, divided by internal disputes among officers, and spread thin. Much of their morale problems were due to the uneven leadership of their general. The stage was now set for one of the most dramatic and unexpected Union victories of the war: the Battle of Chattanooga, fought over three days, November 23 to 25, 1863, across the mountains, rivers, and ridgelines that dominated the landscape.

Grant and Sherman: Brothers in War

Before their wartime partnership, William Tecumseh Sherman and Ulysses S. Grant had followed strikingly different paths shaped by early promise followed by military failure, personal hardship, and personal failure.

Sherman was born in 1820 in Lancaster, Ohio. After the early death of his father, he was raised in the household of U.S. Senator Thomas Ewing. He graduated sixth in his class from West Point in 1840 and served with distinction in Florida and California but saw little combat during the Mexican-American War, an absence that would leave him feeling inferior to many of his peers. After leaving the army in 1853, like Grant, Sherman struggled in civilian life. He worked as a banker in San Francisco, a lawyer in Kansas, and eventually as superintendent of the Louisiana State Seminary of Learning and Military Academy (now LSU). He resigned from that post at the outbreak of war, refusing to fight for the Confederacy. It marked a moral line Sherman would never cross.

Despite his patriotism and training, Sherman's early Civil War career could be considered at best - rocky. In October 1861 he was appointed commander of the Department of Cumberland, which put him in charge of the Union forces in Kentucky. He was reported to have suffered a nervous breakdown after early assignments, prompting newspapers to call him "insane." Sherman had requested 200,000 men to secure his region, and his superiors saw this as a gross exaggeration, a sign of panic and mental instability. Today his "insane" diagnosis might more accurately be called stress or burnout.

As it turned out, Sherman saw the war for what it really was, a long and brutal campaign, well before others accepted that reality. Nonetheless he had been extraordinarily stressed and had suffered from extended bouts of melancholy. Sherman was quickly reassigned to administrative roles back home in Ohio, where he reportedly regained his stability with the help of his wife and his brother Senator John Sherman. General Halleck soon placed him in a command subordinate role to General Grant in February 1862. He faced his first major test at the Battle of Shiloh in early April, where he performed admirably.

It was during the campaigns of 1862, particularly in Tennessee and Mississippi, that Sherman and Grant truly bonded. Grant recognized Sherman's organizational brilliance, and Sherman in turn defended Grant during moments of public and political doubt, particularly when Grant was accused of drunkenness or recklessness. Their trust was forged under fire at battles such as Shiloh, where Sherman held firm under surprise attack, and during the grueling Vicksburg Campaign, where Sherman helped execute complex maneuvers to trap the Confederate army.

Grant, quiet, modest, and emotionally reserved, was a steady and methodical commander. Sherman, fiery, intellectual, and prone to emotional outbursts, was a brilliant strategist and fierce believer in the war's moral imperative. The men had first met several years before the war, while both were serving in California. After Grant's victory at Vicksburg, Sherman publicly credited him, writing, *"Grant is not a showy man, but he is a fighter. He don't fret himself and he don't lose time."* Despite their differences, they became a perfect team, bound by mutual respect, shared hardship, and a deep understanding of total war's demands.

After Vicksburg, Sherman wrote of Grant: *"He stood by me when I was crazy, and I stood by him when he was drunk. Now we stand by each other always."* The rise of William Tecumseh Sherman is inseparable from his friendship and loyalty to Ulysses S. Grant. The two men, seemingly opposites in temperament, formed one of the most effective partnerships in American military history.

Grant trusted Sherman with operational freedom and valued his honesty. Sherman admired Grant's calm under pressure. Their mutual respect would become crucial as the war evolved. When Grant took over at Chattanooga, he called for reinforcements, including Sherman, whose army was marching from Vicksburg. Their plan was to break Bragg's siege on the city, drive the Confederates from the heights, and open the gateway into Georgia.

Breaking the Siege, Lookout Mountain and Missionary Ridge

On October 16, Grant had been given overall command of the Military Division of the Mississippi, which included all the Union armies in the western theater. With his new assignment Grant reorganized his forces and their commanders. He assigned Sherman's army to approach Chattanooga from the west. Hooker's forces were to hold the southern flank. Thomas's renewed Army of the Cumberland remained at the center, inside Chattanooga. The final confrontation with Bragg's Confederate forces was imminent.

On November 23, Grant wanted to confirm the positioning of Confederate forces and so ordered Thomas to conduct what was officially termed a *"reconnaissance in force."* The target was Orchard Knob, a small but strategic elevation of ground about halfway between Union-held Chattanooga and the Confederate line entrenched along Missionary Ridge. Though the operation was meant to feel out Confederate strength, Thomas, always true to his calm and deliberate nature, prepared with the precision of a full-scale assault.

Around 1:30 p.m., some 14,000 Union troops, primarily from Thomas's IV Corps under General Gordon Granger, stepped off in full view of both Union and Confederate lines. The lead brigades included those of Brigadier Generals Wood and Sheridan. What followed surprised everyone, including the brigade commanders and even Grant himself.

Across the open fields between Chattanooga and Orchard Knob, Union soldiers advanced in textbook formation, steady and swift. Confederate skirmishers from General Patrick Cleburne's division attempted to hold their ground, but with the shock and speed of the Union movement his division was quickly overwhelmed. Orchard Knob, previously little more than a forward picket post, was now the site of sharp fighting. The Confederate defenders were driven off quickly, and Union troops seized the knob and surrounding high ground within the hour.

What began as a reconnaissance had turned into a seizure of the center of the battlefield. Grant, observing the ease with which the knob was taken, quickly recognized the tactical value of this unexpected gain. Artillery was hauled up to the summit, and earthworks thrown together by the Union soldiers who now occupied it. Orchard Knob gave the Union a commanding view of both Missionary Ridge and the valley below. It would become Grant's command post for the remainder of the battle.

The sudden Union movement further depleted Bragg's already shaken confidence. From his headquarters on Missionary Ridge, Bragg had recently made the fateful decision to weaken his center, shifting reinforcements to guard against Sherman's arrival on the Confederate right. Now, with Union troops firmly lodged in the center of the field, his strategic gamble was starting to unravel.

For the Union soldiers on Orchard Knob, the day ended with the taste of a very easy victory. It was an uncommon feeling after the recent defeat at Chickamauga and the long siege that followed in Chattanooga. Their confidence was growing exponentially. That night, fires flickered atop the knob as officers met to plan their next moves. Below them, Bragg's army watched and waited, unsure whether the action they had just witnessed was the opening move of a massive assault or merely a feint. In truth, it was both. November 23 had shown that the initiative belonged to the Union now, and it marked the first decisive crack in Bragg's ring around Chattanooga.

November 24

In the morning of November 24, the hills surrounding Chattanooga were shrouded in a heavy fog. From the valley floor, Union soldiers could scarcely see the heights above. Lookout Mountain, steep and brooding, rose to the southwest like a fortress. Its upper slopes vanished into a low-hanging fog that clung to the ridge line and swirled between the trees.

The day's objective was to drive Confederate forces from Lookout Mountain and break their grip on the southern approaches to the city. The job fell to General Hooker, commanding a mixed force of approximately 10,000 men, including units from the XI and XII Corps and reinforcements from the Army of the Cumberland. Their attack would be directed against Brigadier General Stevenson's Confederate division, entrenched on the mountain's slopes.

From the peak of Lookout Mountain Confederate signalmen had been accustomed to watching every Union movement from their perch. The morning fog of November 24 completely obliterated any opportunity to see the movements of the enemy below. With reinforcements in place and the Cracker Line open and providing necessary supplies, Grant saw the opportunity to dislodge the Southern defenders and seize the mountain as a steppingstone to Missionary Ridge.

Hooker launched his attack around 10 a.m., advancing along the western base of the mountain with General Geary's division in the lead. The soldiers skirted the bank of the Tennessee River, using the natural cover of boulders and trees to approach the lower slopes. Confederate pickets opened fire, and the sound of musketry echoed in the canyons as the Union line pressed upward. These defenses were quickly overrun.

Rain the night before had turned the trails to mud, and the mountain itself was cloaked in fog so thick that the Union attackers could barely see a few yards ahead. Confederate defenders had very little idea what was about to befall them. What followed was a strange and surreal battle. Regiments advanced into the mist, fired blindly, and pushed through underbrush and stone outcroppings. Lines became jumbled. Officers lost track of units. But the advance continued, though somewhat chaotic.

By midday, Union troops had seized the Cravens House, a key position about halfway up the mountain's slope. This was Stevenson's main line of defense, a narrow shelf of ground that offered room for artillery and typically a sweeping view of the valley below. After bitter hand-to-hand fighting and sustained volleys of musket fire, the Confederates began falling back. Union flags now flew from the Cravens farmstead, visible through the fog to the soldiers cheering below.

From his new base camp on Orchard Knob, General Grant peered through the mist. At times he could see nothing; then, suddenly, the clouds would lift, revealing blue-coated troops advancing upward. Because of the eerie battle scene, with fog obscuring the battlefield from those watching from below. *"Battle Above the Clouds"* was coined for the encounter by observers of the attack. But to the men involved, it was a fight waged in a world apart, distant, gray, and otherworldly.

Stevenson's Confederates, outnumbered and increasingly isolated, withdrew during the night to rejoin Bragg's main force on Missionary Ridge. Lookout Mountain was abandoned, and the Union now held the western gateway to Chattanooga. The day ended in Union triumph. Men who had starved during the siege only weeks earlier now stood atop the enemy's high ground, looking down on the valley below. Hooker's men, soaked and mud-spattered, lit fires on the mountain's face. Below, Union pickets cheered. Confederate hopes were beginning to unravel.

November 25

The morning of November 25 was cold and clear. The fog that had engulfed Lookout Mountain had lifted, and for the first time in days, sunlight illuminated the ridges, valleys, and fields that would determine the fate of the Western Theater. The attention of all the Union forces turned to Missionary Ridge, a long, steep spine of land running north to south, occupied with Confederate earthworks and cannon. This was Bragg's final defensive line, a natural fortress defended with artillery and anchored by a seasoned fighting force.

Union commander Grant, now observing the field from Orchard Knob, had a bold, three-part plan. The main effort would be made by General Sherman, whose forces had crossed the Tennessee River days earlier and now faced the northern end of the ridge. Sherman's job was to attack the Confederate right and roll down the line. Meanwhile, Joseph Hooker, fresh off his success at Lookout Mountain, would push in from the south, flanking Bragg's left. At the center, General Thomas was set to stage a diversionary demonstration to pin down Confederate reserves.

By noon, Sherman's men were engaged on the northern flank, but progress was slow and costly. Sherman had misjudged the terrain. Instead of a single ridge, he faced a complex network of hills including Billy Goat Hill and Tunnel Hill, each stoutly defended by Cleburne's battle-hardened division. Confederate resistance was fierce, and by mid-afternoon it was clear that Sherman's assault had stalled.

Seeing the situation stalemate and concerned that Bragg might reinforce his right and crush Sherman, Grant ordered Thomas to proceed with his part of the plan. He was to seize the rifle pits at the base of Missionary Ridge. The order, issued around 3:30 p.m., was meant to be limited. But what happened next transformed another modest diversion into one of the most spectacular battlefield reversals of the war.

Some 20,000 Union troops, veterans of the siege and survivors of Chickamauga, stepped off across the open ground between Orchard Knob and the base of the ridge. The advance was orderly and determined, their lines stretching for miles. Under artillery fire and musketry, they reached the rifle pits and overran the first Confederate position. But then, something extraordinary happened, without orders, and against the expectations of their commanders, the men began to climb the ridge.

It was a spontaneous movement, driven by momentum, frustration, and perhaps a deep, unspoken resolve to erase the shame of their previous defeat. Officers tried to halt the charge, but the rank and file soldiers continued to press upward. They scrambled over rocks, roots, and fallen logs. They moved in clumps, dodging fire from above. Regimental flags appeared here and there, urging the men forward. The Confederate defenders, stunned by the audacity and scale of the attack, began to falter. Their second line was hastily manned and incomplete. Bragg, who had thinned his center to reinforce the flanks, now faced a collapse in the very heart of his line. At the top of the ridge, Union troops surged over the crest, driving the defenders back in confusion. Brigades broke. Cannons were abandoned. Soldiers fled. The Confederate center was shattered. Hooker's men were now pushing up from the south, and Sherman, though stymied, had held Cleburne in place. The entire Confederate position came undone.

By nightfall, the Army of Tennessee was in full retreat, streaming eastward toward Ringgold, Georgia. Missionary Ridge finally again belonged to the Union. Union victory was complete. Bragg's army retreated into Georgia. Chattanooga was saved. Grant wrote, *"It is a rare sight to witness such bravery. No orders could have inspired more spirit than the men already possessed."* Sherman, though disappointed by his own sector's performance, praised Thomas's men and acknowledged the stunning success. *"The assault of Thomas's troops at the center was one of the grandest military feats I have ever witnessed, and one of the most brilliant charges ever made in war."*

One officer wrote, *"It was as if the mountain itself rose up and our men rose with it."* Bragg's army broke under the pressure. Many Confederates abandoned their positions and fled. Entire brigades retreated in disorder.

The Gateway to Georgia

With the Confederate retreat from the area around Chattanooga, the Union had broken the Southern control in eastern Tennessee and opened a vital path into the Deep South. The mountains that had once formed a natural barrier were now in Union hands, and the railroads leading to Atlanta were within reach. President Lincoln, recognizing the magnitude of the victory, declared, *"Thank God, that all is well at Chattanooga!"* In Washington, confidence was often on a roller coaster, but now it surged. In Richmond, panic began to seep into government circles.

Sherman was left in command of operations in the region while Grant was promoted to general-in-chief of all Union armies. It was now up to Sherman to carry the war into Georgia. With a keen eye on Atlanta, the Confederacy's manufacturing and rail hub, he began preparing for a campaign unlike any yet seen in the war. The strategic objective was twofold: capture Atlanta and, by doing so, cripple Confederate logistics. But Sherman envisioned a broader goal, one rooted in total war. He believed that to end the conflict, the South's ability and will to continue the war must be destroyed. His operations in Georgia would soon reflect that belief.

Throughout the winter of 1863 and into 1864, Sherman's forces rested and refitted. Supply lines were improved. Plans were drawn. He coordinated with Grant, who would simultaneously press Lee in the East while Sherman advanced through the West. It was to be a pincer movement; one designed to crush the

Confederacy from both directions. And so, the stage was set for Sherman's Atlanta Campaign. The gateway was open. The march into the very heart of Dixie was about to begin.

Sherman's new command, the Military Division of the Mississippi, placed him in charge of a vast swath of Union armies across the West. The force under his control numbered over 100,000 men. It was divided among three principal armies: the Army of the Tennessee under James McPherson, the Army of the Cumberland under George Thomas, and the Army of the Ohio under John Schofield.

As the smoke cleared from the skies above Chattanooga in late November 1863, the United States stood at yet another pivotal threshold. The Union victory had broken the Confederate siege of the city and sent Braxton Bragg and his demoralized army retreating into the hills of northern Georgia. It was a defeat from which the Confederacy would never truly recover in the Western Theater. With Union forces now holding the strategic *"Gateway to the Deep South,"* the path lay open for further Union advances into Georgia, Alabama, and beyond.

The immediate aftermath of Chattanooga brought sweeping changes. Bragg, whose leadership had been questioned for months by his own subordinates, tendered his resignation on December 2. President Jefferson Davis accepted it, though he retained Bragg as a military advisor in Richmond, a decision that further soured Davis's relationship with other Confederate commanders. But Bragg had been a staunch political ally of Davis for a long time, so this was likely a political favor. To replace Bragg in the field, Davis turned to General Joseph Johnston, a seasoned officer known for his cautiousness. Johnston would spend the coming months trying to reforge the shattered remnants of the Army of Tennessee into a force capable of resisting the inevitable Union advance.

Meanwhile, Union leadership basked in the glow of another crucial victory. Grant's masterful orchestration of the Chattanooga campaign had not gone unnoticed. In Washington, murmurs began to grow louder that Grant might soon be called to oversee the entire Union war effort. General Sherman, Grant's trusted subordinate, also emerged from the campaign with an enhanced reputation and began preparing for winter operations that would ultimately point him toward Atlanta. Chattanooga was not merely a battlefield victory, it was a seismic strategic moment, shifting the balance of power permanently toward the Union in the West.

Even as Union forces secured Chattanooga, further east another drama was unfolding. In Knoxville, Tennessee, Union General Ambrose Burnside and his men had been besieged by Confederate forces under James Longstreet in Knoxville. Burnside had taken up a defensive position there.

Longstreet had been detached from Lee's army after Gettysburg and was now laying siege to Burnside's army. A major assault during the siege occurred on one of the city's significant defensive positions, Fort Sanders. That assault was thwarted by Burnside's defensive efforts, which were initially mocked in Washington. On December 4, with the news of the coming of Union reinforcements under Sherman, Longstreet abandoned the siege. His retreat into the rugged country of eastern Tennessee marked another strategic victory for the North. The Union had secured East Tennessee, a region rich in Unionist sentiment, and deprived the Confederacy of a vital corridor for troop movements and supplies.

Throughout December, the war's political dimensions sharpened. President Abraham Lincoln, ever mindful that battlefield victories alone would not secure the Union's future, delivered his annual message to Congress on December 8. In it, he emphasized the Union's recent military successes and the moral weight of the Emancipation Proclamation. *"The most remarkable feature in the military operations of the year is General Grant's campaign in Mississippi, resulting in the fall of Vicksburg, and the capture of one of the largest Confederate armies... Of those who were slaves at the beginning of the rebellion, full one hundred thousand are now in the United States military service... Numbers add strength to ourselves and weaken the enemy in equal proportions... The national resources, then, are unimpaired, and the national credit is greater than it ever has been... In giving freedom to the slave, we assure freedom to the free, honorable alike in what we give and what we preserve... A way is presented whereby the national authority may be re-established and the Union reconstituted... The dogmas of the quiet past are inadequate to the stormy present... As our case is new, so we must think anew, and act anew."*

Even as the war raged on the battlefields, President Abraham Lincoln turned his mind toward the war's end. He understood that victory on the battlefield would be incomplete without a plan for political reunification, a strategy to bring the Southern states back into the Union, and a way to heal a nation that had torn itself apart.

PART FIVE: FUTURE PREPARTION

CHAPTER 22
PROCLAMATION OF AMNESTY AND
RECONSTRUCTION

The victories at Gettysburg, Vicksburg and Chattanooga had begun to tilt the war in favor of the Union, but the path to peace was far from clear. The idea of slavery had been shattered in principle by the Emancipation Proclamation, yet in practice, the nation remained deeply fractured.

Fully understanding the challenges that lay ahead if the Union were to win the war, and the South would need to be folded back into the United States of America on December 8, 1863, Lincoln issued one of the most significant documents of his presidency: the Proclamation of Amnesty and Reconstruction

The proclamation offered a remarkably lenient path back to the Union for those who had participated in the rebellion. Under its terms, any Confederate, with notable exceptions for high-ranking political and military leaders, could receive a full pardon simply by swearing an oath of allegiance to the United States and agreeing to accept the end of slavery. Once ten percent of a state's voting population, based on the 1860 rolls, had taken the loyalty oath and established a new government, Lincoln promised to recognize it as the legitimate government of that state.

Lincoln's language was clear but hopeful: *"A way is presented whereby the national authority may be re-established and the Union reconstituted."*

This plan, often called the *"Ten Percent Plan,"* was amazingly moderate in a time of extremism. Rather than seeking retribution, Lincoln sought rehabilitation. He understood that the war's end would demand not only the laying down of arms, but the restoration of civil society. His offer of amnesty was not just a political tactic, it was a statement of national mercy, designed to shorten the war, undermine Confederate morale, and prepare the way for a lasting peace. Lincoln's design reflected both moral vision and political calculation. It attempted to peel away Southern moderates from the Confederacy, undermine the rebellion from within, and hasten the end of the war.

However, the plan had its critics. Many in Lincoln's own party, particularly the Radical Republicans who feared the plan would restore power to the elites and saw the overall scope of the Ten Percent Plan as far too lenient. Men like Senator Charles Sumner and Representative Thaddeus Stevens demanded harsher terms, believing the South needed to be punished and fundamentally reconstructed, politically, economically, and socially, before it could be trusted again. To them, Lincoln's offer of forgiveness seemed to betray the enormity of the war's bloodshed and the evil of slavery itself. However, to Lincoln, the Proclamation was not about punishment, it was about restoration of the Union. *"A house divided against itself cannot stand,"* he had said in 1858. By 1863, he was actively trying to rebuild that house, brick by brick, beginning with those willing to swear allegiance to the new order.

Lincoln, ever the political realist, anticipated opposition to his plan. He made clear that his plan did not exclude Congress from taking its own action on Reconstruction. His proclamation was an opening offer, not a final decree. *"This plan is presented not as a final measure, but as one suggested by the present condition of affairs."* He invited experimentation and refinement, provided the essential goals remained. The goals that had been set in place by the Declaration of Independence, Union and liberty. It firmly placed Lincoln's vision before the nation of a swift, merciful reunification based on loyalty and freedom, not vengeance.

Even among his allies, there were doubts about the proclamation. Could Southern whites truly accept emancipation? What would become of the newly freed Black population? Could Unionists trust the loyalty of former rebels? The Proclamation didn't answer these questions, but it raised them with urgency. For Lincoln, the Union could not wait for perfect answers. It needed to start healing now, in the shadow of war.

The Proclamation of Amnesty and Reconstruction was an act of courage and conciliation. It laid the foundation for Lincoln's evolving vision of post-war America: a vision not merely of reunification, but of a reborn nation committed to freedom and democracy. Though its full implementation would be delayed and reshaped by assassination, politics, and resistance, it signaled, unmistakably, that the war was not just to defeat the South. It was to rebuild the United States on a solid new foundation.

Importantly, the Proclamation tied the concept of national restoration to the abolition of slavery. No state could return to the Union without recognizing slavery would no longer exist, and that all current slaves are emancipated. By doing so, Lincoln ensured that the meaning of the war was not just to reunite the states into a cohesive group, but to establish that union that disallowed any slavery. It was his aim that sentiment would be embedded in whatever peace eventually came.

Few states would immediately take up Lincoln's offer in 1863. Louisiana, Tennessee, and Arkansas started the process. However, Congress rejected their constitutions and refused to seat delegates from these states. The war was still too hot and Confederate leaders were in no mood to contemplate surrender. Yet the proclamation sent a powerful message to both North and South, that the United States government did not seek the destruction of the Southern people, but rather their restoration within a nation remade in liberty.

It was, in many ways, one of Lincoln's boldest acts of leadership laying the political foundation for national healing even before the war was won.

The ink on Lincoln's Proclamation of Amnesty and Reconstruction had barely dried when sharp objections began to rise from within his party. Radical Republicans in Congress, long suspicious of Lincoln's moderate tendencies, viewed his Ten Percent Plan as dangerously lenient. They believed that it failed to fundamentally remake the South or ensure lasting protections for the newly freed Black population.

In early 1864, Congressional leaders crafted their own response. The Wade-Davis Bill was so named for its two primary architects, Senator Benjamin Wade of Ohio and Representative Henry Davis of Maryland. The bill proposed a far stricter approach to Reconstruction, one rooted in the belief that the former Confederate states had forfeited all their rights by rebellion and must now be treated almost as conquered provinces.

The Wade-Davis Bill demanded that at least fifty percent of a Southern state's white male citizens, not merely ten percent, take a stringent loyalty oath before any form of self-government could be reestablished. Furthermore, it insisted that only those who could swear they had never willingly supported the Confederacy would be allowed to vote or hold office. These were known as *"ironclad oaths,"* deliberately excluding almost the entire political leadership of the South.

Crucially, the bill made no immediate provisions for pardons or the restoration of political rights without an arduous legal process. In contrast to Lincoln's offer of swift amnesty, Wade and Davis envisioned a slow, punitive process designed to break the power structures that had led to southern secession in the first place.

The ideological divide between Lincoln and the Radical Republicans was more than a dispute over policy, it reflected two competing visions for the postwar United States. Lincoln, while personally abhorring slavery and committed to emancipation, prioritized the speedy restoration of the Union above all else. The Radicals, meanwhile, sought a complete social revolution in the South including the dismantling of the old planter aristocracy and the establishment of civil rights for freedmen that was enforced by federal authority.

When the Wade-Davis Bill passed Congress in July 1864, Lincoln chose not to sign it. Instead, he issued a "pocket veto," allowing the bill to expire without his signature by adjourning Congress. This quiet rejection infuriated Radical leaders. In retaliation, Wade and Davis issued the *"Wade-Davis Manifesto"* a scathing public statement accusing Lincoln of usurping Congressional powers and endangering the nation's future by offering forgiveness too easily. Despite the fury of his detractors, Lincoln held fast. He believed that flexibility and forgiveness were the keys to restoring the Union and avoiding a new cycle of resentment and rebellion.

In one of his characteristic turns of phrase, Lincoln remarked: *"I must keep some consciousness of being somewhere near right; I must stand with anybody that stands right; stand with him while he is right, and part with him when he goes wrong."*

Thus, the seeds of a fierce postwar struggle over the nature of Reconstruction were sown long before the guns had fallen silent. Lincoln's Proclamation of Amnesty had envisioned a merciful path home for the South, but whether the country would accept that path or demand harsher measures remained an open and bitter question as 1863 gave way to 1864.

Even as Union armies secured great victories on the fields of Chattanooga and Knoxville, another kind of battle was unfolding in the halls of Washington, a battle fought with proclamations, legislation, and deeply divided visions of what the reunited nation should become following the war. With the

Emancipation Proclamation, Lincoln had stood on high moral ground, but there were many in the north who did not agree that was the best course of action.

1863 Comes to an End

Smaller skirmishes and cavalry raids peppered the final weeks of 1863, particularly in Tennessee, Mississippi, and Arkansas. Death still occurred in significant numbers, just not as much as in the major battles of the year. Union forces began preparing for new campaigns deep into Confederate territory, with General Sherman eyeing an advance into Mississippi that would become the Meridian Campaign early in the new year. No grand battles unfolded before the year's end, but the movements and preparations hinted at the enormous campaigns that would define 1864.

As December faded into the harsh winter of January, the North stood with renewed hope. Though the cost had been terrible with more than 275,000 Americans dead and wounded over the course of the year, the Union could now realistically imagine the war's end. For the South, battered by significant losses, political discord, and economic ruin, the year closed with dark foreboding. The Confederate dream, born in the heat of secessionist passion, had begun to crumble under the relentless pressure of Northern arms, naval blockade, and internal decay caused by the incredibly oppressive war.

Thus, the year 1863 ended, with the Union triumphant on every major front, a president preparing the nation for peace and reconstruction, and a Confederacy staggering yet still determined to fight on. The blood of a generation had been spilled across the hills, valleys, and plains of America, but, at long last, there appeared a distant, flickering light of hope on the horizon. Chattanooga was the last major confrontation of the year.

America remained bloodied and divided but it was not yet totally broken. It had been a year of terrible suffering on the battlefields of North and South and in the homes that waited, prayed, and mourned. It was a year when Black Americans, after centuries of bondage, were at last given an important glimpse of freedom. The political climate in Washington had been forever reshaped. The financial foundation of the nation had been stabilized. There was still more dying, more hardship, and more sorrow to endure before the great conflict could end. But assuming no new catastrophe undid the hard-won progress of 1863, there now seemed, for the first time, a path forward for a Northern victory. A path toward peace at last. Thank God Almighty!

From the fields of Gettysburg to the fortress of Vicksburg, from the trenches around Chattanooga to the thickets of Chickamauga, the cost of the conflict had climbed beyond anything once imagined. 1863 was the bloodiest year of the war, it is estimated that about 275,000 soldiers had fallen dead, wounded, or missing during the campaigns of that single year. 130,000 men on the Union side and 145,000 men from the Confederacy. In homes across the divided country, grief became a second language; black crepe hung from doors, and empty chairs haunted family gatherings. Hope wavered even among the most determined.

1863 had not only been a year of loss it was also a year of profound transformation. With the Emancipation Proclamation, the Union cause expanded beyond mere preservation of the nation to include a new birth of freedom from those previously denied. Black soldiers, many of them once enslaved, now fought and died under the Union flag. A broader vision of America's future. one grounded in liberty, not just union, began to take shape through the death and sacrifice.

Leadership, too, had evolved. Abraham Lincoln, once hesitant, now moved forward with a firm moral compass, speaking of a *"new birth of freedom"* at Gettysburg. Ulysses S. Grant had risen from relative obscurity to command of the armies of the West and then of the entire Union Army with quiet, relentless effectiveness. Robert E. Lee, the South's greatest hope, had seen the limits of courage alone at Gettysburg, and would never again have the strength to carry the fight northward.

Still, victory for either side remained a difficult uncertainty. One of the lessons of the war was that there had been numerous twists and turns, wins and losses determined largely by the whims of fate. Though the Confederacy was increasingly battered and cornered, their resilience was palpable. The armies dug in for another winter of hardship, knowing that the next year's battles would be at least as desperate. In the fields, in the cities, and in the hearts of soldiers and civilians alike, 1863 ended not with triumph or defeat, but with exhaustion, grim determination, and the dim flicker of hope that the suffering might one day form a new nation with higher moral value.

To a certain extent America had been reborn by the proclamations of the President. It appeared to be headed again toward unification It was still bleeding, unsettled, and was staggering toward the threshold of an unknown future.

Here are some major 1863 battles and their individual casualty estimates (Union and Confederate combined casualties)

Stones River (January 1863)	~24,000
Chancellorsville (May 1863):	~30,500
Gettysburg (July 1863)	~51,000
Vicksburg Campaign (May to July 1863):	~37,000
Chickamauga (September 1863):	~34,600
Chattanooga Campaign (November 1863):	~12,500

Smaller battles (e.g., Fort Hindman, Port Hudson, Second Fort Wagner, Knoxville Campaign, etc.): ~50,000+

EPILOGUE
LINCOLN'S DESPAIR AND THE ELECTION OF 1864

As 1863 came to an end, Abraham Lincoln found himself perched on a very weak foundation. The Union had secured pivotal victories that hinted at the possibility of eventual success. More importantly, Lincoln had finally found a commander in Ulysses S. Grant who might be able carry the war to its desired conclusion. Yet the conflict would not be finished for a long time. The Confederacy, though battered and now divided geographically between east and west, remained fiercely determined. Their faith in Lee sustained their will to fight, and their unyielding commitment to their cause, defined as the preservation of their way of life, showed no signs of wavering. With each successive campaign, the toll in lives grew ever more staggering on both sides.

And in the North, the mood was darkening, there was near universal glee remaining over the victories of Vicksburg and Gettysburg. Many thought those two victories would quickly bring an end to fighting, but they did not. Lincoln's days were filled with telegrams and troop reports, but his thoughts were increasingly occupied by politics, and by fear. The presidential election of 1864 loomed, and Lincoln believed, without a significant advance toward a resounding victory, he would lose the election.

Lincoln had good reason to worry. The Emancipation Proclamation, while hailed by abolitionists, had alienated conservative Democrats and some moderate Republicans. The Union conscription of only certain white male citizens into the army, provoked riots and resentment. Inflation hit the working class harder than it did the gentry, causing a loss of confidence that the war was being issued judiciously, and there was an ever-widening gap between the wealth of the rich and the lack thereof of the poor. Even loyal Republican newspapers began publishing articles questioning Lincoln's competence.

By the winter of 1863, Lincolns popularity had plummeted. In a confidential letter, Gideon Welles, his own Secretary of the Navy, wrote: *"The President looks worn and broken... I fear he is losing not only the confidence of the people but his own confidence as well."*

The weight of war bore down on Lincoln, not just as president but as a man. The death of his son Willie the year before had plunged him into an ever-present shroud of grief. Mary Todd Lincoln, still inconsolable, turned to séances and mediums, which made her ridiculed in many circles. Lincoln himself was often seen wandering the halls of the White House at night long after most had turned into their beds. He had aged considerably in the last four years and now looked very gaunt and haunted. *"I am nothing,"* he once said, *"but sadness walking."*

But there was another source of his anxiety: the growing belief that the Democratic Party would nominate George McClellan; the very general Lincoln had once appointed to lead the Union armies and shortly thereafter fired for inaction. McClellan retained his popularity among soldiers and civilians alike. He was young, handsome, and carried the air of dignity that many Americans missed in the chaos of war. And for Lincoln, worst of all, McClellan was being positioned as the *"peace candidate,"* a man who could end the bloodshed, even if that meant recognizing the Confederacy.

Lincoln didn't just fear McClellan politically; he feared what McClellan's victory would mean for the country. *"If McClellan is elected,"* Lincoln told an aide, *"I shall not be able to preserve the Union. It will go down in blood and ruin."*

McClellan's Democratic platform emphasized ending the war and negotiating with the Confederacy. His stance suggested a willingness to compromise, which could have led to a peace agreement rather than the Union victory that would eventually occur. A peace agreement with the Confederacy would likely have resulted in a fragmented United States, with some Southern states achieving independence, whether independently or as a sovereign nation. It is also possible that the terms of any agreement would have included concessions that altered the territories of the remaining states. McClellan's stance on slavery was more nuanced than Lincoln's. While he supported the war effort, he later expressed a desire for gradual emancipation, suggesting he might have sought a peace agreement that included a plan for gradual or partial emancipation, potentially with provisions to protect slaveholders' rights.

Lincoln refused to compromise his message for any potential political gain. He would not rescind emancipation. He would not sue for peace. He would not promise victory without effort. He would tell the truth and trust the people to see it through. His cabinet was split. Some Republican leaders even floated the idea of replacing Lincoln on the ticket. *"Let him be remembered kindly,"* one party boss said, *"but let him be retired."*

In August 1864, Lincoln was so certain of defeat that he drafted a secret memorandum. He sealed it and had his cabinet sign the outside without reading it. *"This morning, as for some days past,"* the note read, *"it seems exceedingly probable that this Administration will not be re-elected. Then it will be my duty to so co-operate with the President-elect, as to save the Union between the election and the inauguration; as he will have secured his election on such ground that he cannot possibly save it afterward*s."

It was a chilling act of humility, and patriotism. Lincoln was preparing, even in political defeat, to hand off the nation intact, if he could. But fate and a few bold decisions were about to shift the winds.

The Rise of McClellan, Betrayal and Resolve

In the summer of 1864, the rumors became reality that George McClellan, the once-promising general Lincoln had relieved of command in 1862, was nominated as the Democratic Party's candidate for President. His running mate was George Pendleton of Ohio, a staunch Copperhead and vocal opponent of emancipation. The Democratic platform called for an immediate ceasefire and a negotiated peace, even if it meant disunion.

The Democratic Party was deeply divided between War Democrats and Peace Democrats (or Copperheads). They adopted a platform at their Chicago convention that called for an immediate ceasefire and negotiated peace with the Confederacy. This *"peace plank"* was authored by Copperhead leader Clement Vallandigham and reflected the sentiments of those opposing the war's continuation. However, McClellan, aligning more with the War Democrats, personally rejected this peace platform. He advocated for the continuation of the war to restore the Union but did not support the abolition of slavery, distinguishing his stance from President Lincoln's policies. This divergence between McClellan's views and his party's official platform led to inconsistencies in his campaign messaging.

McClellan believed the Civil War should be fought strictly to preserve the Union and not to abolish slavery. He thought making slavery the central issue of the war would divide the North, alienate border states like Kentucky and Missouri, and prolong the conflict. He opposed Lincoln's Emancipation Proclamation. While he personally disliked slavery, he did not believe in using the war as a means to end it. McClellan feared that emancipation would radicalize the war and make post-war reconciliation with the South more difficult. Though not a pro-slavery advocate in the mold of Southern Democrats, McClellan shared the racial attitudes common to many Northern moderates of his day, skeptical of full equality for Black Americans and resistant to any dramatic societal shift.

To Lincoln, the irony was bitter. McClellan had led the Army of the Potomac with caution and indecision, and sometimes a great reluctance to move at all. Lincoln had pleaded with him to pursue Lee's army, to strike boldly. *"If General McClellan does not want to use the army,"* Lincoln had once quipped, *"I would like to borrow it for a time."* Now, the general who once ignored his orders was seeking his office.

McClellan gained some traction during the summer of 1864, when Union war efforts seemed stalled, casualties were high, and there was growing dissatisfaction with Lincoln's leadership. Many in the North were tired of the war and hoped for a negotiated peace. McClellan's image as a former commanding general and a voice for moderation gave him some appeal, especially among urban voters and Democrats in the North.

But Lincoln, ever the master of discipline, chose not to attack McClellan personally. He would not accuse him of cowardice or betrayal. He knew the country was already divided. To stoke further animosity would only deepen the wound. Instead, Lincoln focused on clarity of contrast. He stood for Union, emancipation, and the fulfillment of democratic ideals. McClellan stood for conciliation, compromise and, as Lincoln feared, capitulation.

The Republican Party, in a move of both principle and pragmatism, rebranded itself as the National Union Party. This broadened the coalition to include War Democrats and independents who supported the Union cause but had no love for the old Republican label.

Lincoln also made a bold and risky political choice by dropping his sitting Vice President, Hannibal Hamlin of Maine, and selecting Andrew Johnson, a Democrat from Tennessee. Andrew Johnson was a slave holder who remained loyal to the Union, even after his state had seceded. After secession of Tennessee, Lincoln appointed Johnson military governor of the state. Johnson imposed Union control, earning a reputation for toughness as well as vindictiveness.

It was a striking symbol that a president of the North would choose a running mate from the South, staking his reelection not on party loyalty but on national unity. Still, the odds of a Lincoln win looked grim. As late as August, Lincoln still believed he would lose. The war, at times, seemed endless.

Grant's brutal campaign in Virginia had earned him the nickname *"the butcher."* Sherman was stalled outside Atlanta waiting for a breakthrough. Newspapers editorialized with negativity about the progress of the war. Copperheads declared that Lincoln had torn the country apart and delivered nothing but death. Leading up to the election, Democratic papers painted Lincoln as a failure who had mismanaged the war and the country. Papers such as the New York Journal of Commerce and The New York World editorialized in favor of George McClellan and accused Lincoln of corruption, incompetence, and war-mongering. Some editorialists attacked Lincoln's character, education, and even his family. He was caricatured in editorial cartoons and called a baboon, gorilla, and simpleton by hostile editors

Lincoln did not retreat. Instead, he sharpened his message: finish the work. Do not dishonor the dead by giving up. Do not surrender the cause when victory is so near. He met with soldiers, freedmen, religious leaders, and ordinary citizens. His speeches grew more grounded, more intimate. He appealed not to politics, but to the American conscience. *"I cannot say the country is entirely saved,"* he said, *"but I can say it is not entirely lost and I shall do nothing to make it so."*

Redemption Through Strategy and Spirit

And then just two months before the election came the battlefield victory for which Lincoln was waiting. Sherman captured Atlanta shortly after managing to cut their supply lines from the south. Sherman began his siege of Alanta on May 7, and on September 2, the Confederates evacuated the city, after a siege lasting 120 days.

The telegraph wires lit up across the country. Church bells rang. The stock market surged. And suddenly, Lincoln's political fortunes had reversed. Supporters who had grown silent found their voices again. Doubters reconsidered that maybe Lincoln could win the war after all. Soldiers, in letters and editorials, praised Lincoln's steadiness, even the newspaper editorials became a bit more positive. Momentum had shifted with the renewed positivism of the North. And with it, Lincoln began to allow hope back in for another term as president.

The tide that had once seemed ready to wash Abraham Lincoln from office now surged back in his favor. Not only had Atlanta fallen, but that event was soon followed up by other good news. Union victories in the Shenandoah Valley under General Philip Sheridan continued the good news for the President.

For the first time in months, the headlines were working with Lincoln instead of against him. Lincoln fully understood that battlefield victories alone wouldn't guarantee reelection. He still had to win hearts, minds and especially votes, in a country sick of war and divided by class, race, and region. So, he turned to the one strategy that had always defined his leadership. He told the truth told plainly and without fear.

Lincoln never claimed the war was easy, nor that peace was near. Instead, he made a moral appeal to perseverance. He asked the country to finish the job, to not *"swap horses in midstream,"* as one of his campaign slogans went. He explained to citizens, both weary and grieving, that to abandon the war effort now would render every sacrifice meaningless, that the blood spilled at Antietam, Vicksburg, and Gettysburg must not have been shed in vain. *"I know not how to aid you,"* he told a group of Illinois soldiers, *"except to say that I love you. I honor you. I trust you. And I shall stand by you as long as you stand by me."* These were not the words of a conqueror, but of a companion.

On November 8, 1864, the people spoke loudly and clearly. Lincoln won 55% of the popular vote and 212 of the 233 votes of the electoral college. McClellan carried only three states: Kentucky, Delaware, and New Jersey. It was a clear and decisive win for the president. Even Lincoln was stunned, he had been fearful of defeat until the result was announced. That night, in one of the sitting rooms of the White House, he told friends, *"I am thankful, profoundly thankful. God has been very good to us."*

The Soldier Vote

One of the most remarkable features of the 1864 election was the vote of the Union soldiers themselves. Over 150,000 union fighters cast ballots from the field, a logistical feat orchestrated through absentee voting legislation passed in several Northern states. Democrats believed many soldiers would vote for McClellan, their former commander. But Lincoln's quiet acts of compassion and steadfast leadership had not gone unnoticed. Soldiers remembered his visits to hospitals. They recalled his refusal to demonize the South. They admired his resolve. In the end, more than 75% of Union soldiers voted for Lincoln.

One Union private, writing to his family, explained: *"He has borne the whole weight of this war without flinching. He is the only one who has not tried to use it to his own advantage. That is why I trust him."*

Lincoln's celebration was tempered. He realized that he had the reins of power allowing him to reunite the national by conquering the South. Also, he knew the war was not over. He, as well as the public who elected him, now realized that victory should come soon. But thousands more would die. And the wounds, physical, political, and spiritual, would not close quickly.

By the close of 1864, Abraham Lincoln stood not as the same embattled politician of the year before, but as the renewed steward of the Union. The reelection had not only validated his policies, it had affirmed his vision, with the help of Generals Grant and Sherman that the war must end not in compromise, but in conscience fulfilled. And yet, the transformation of Lincoln was not merely political. It was personal, even spiritual. The man who had entered office with measured legality and careful moderation now spoke with the authority of moral conviction, though never with self-righteousness. He had been changed by grief, by duty, by doubt, by faith but mostly by the war between the states.

He wielded power, at times, almost reluctantly, and sometimes painfully. He dismissed calls for retribution against the South and his own deserters. He discouraged triumphalism. When Union victories came, he insisted on modesty. He believed that what the country needed most was healing, not vengeance.

His evolving philosophy of leadership, humble, principled, and patient, emerged in his words and in his face. Photographs from this period show deep lines carved into his cheeks, a sadness behind the eyes. One journalist noted, *"He looks more like a man bearing a cross than wearing a crown."*

He had become, in a real sense, the conscience of the Union. He spoke not just for the North, but for its better angels, the idea that the nation was worth preserving because of what it aspired to be, not simply what it had always been. *"Fellow citizens,"* he told an audience in late 1864, *"we cannot escape history. We of this Congress and this administration will be remembered in spite of ourselves."*

And indeed, he would be. Lincoln had walked through the valley of doubt and emerged with a deeper certainty not in himself, but in the possibility of a nation reborn. He had faced division without succumbing to it. He had faced hatred without mirroring it. And in 1863, he had stood on a battlefield and dared to suggest that a *"new birth of freedom"* might still be possible, not just for the nation, but for all its people.

The legacy of that year, forged in fire, sealed in ink, and carried in the hearts of soldiers, widows, freedmen, and factory workers, would follow him to his final days. But in that moment, at the turning of the war and the pivot of the nation's fate, Abraham Lincoln was no longer just the President of the United States. He was the soul of its second founding.

Who can say how profoundly the nation might have been shaped by four more years of Lincoln's leadership? His steady hand could have guided Reconstruction with greater unity, offered stronger protections for newly freed slaves, and perhaps tempered the lasting legacy of bigotry and division. The course of American history its progress, its wounds, its reconciliation might have looked very different had Lincoln lived to finish the work he began, at the very moment his presence was needed most.

REFERENCES

Chapter 1 A Nation Divided, The Road to 1863

Foner, Eric. *The Fiery Trial: Abraham Lincoln and American Slavery*. New York: W.W. Norton & Company, 2010.

Holzer, Harold. *Lincoln at Cooper Union: The Speech That Made Abraham Lincoln President*. New York: Simon & Schuster, 2004.

McPherson, James M. *Battle Cry of Freedom: The Civil War Era*. New York: Oxford University Press, 1988.

Potter, David M. *The Impending Crisis, 1848–1861*. Completed and edited by Don E. Fehrenbacher. New York: Harper & Row, 1976.

Walther, Eric H. *The Shattering of the Union: America in the 1850s*. Wilmington, DE: Scholarly Resources Inc., 2004.

Would you like to follow this with a few quotes from Lincoln or newspapers reacting to his election?

Boritt, Gabor S., ed. *The Lincoln Enigma: The Changing Faces of an American Icon*. New York: Oxford University Press, 2001.

Davis, William C. *Jefferson Davis: The Man and His Hour*. Baton Rouge: Louisiana State University Press, 1991.

Donald, David Herbert. *Lincoln*. New York: Simon & Schuster, 1995.

Foner, Eric. *The Fiery Trial: Abraham Lincoln and American Slavery*. New York: W. W. Norton & Company, 2010.

McPherson, James M. *Battle Cry of Freedom: The Civil War Era*. New York: Oxford University Press, 1988.

Potter, David M. *The Impending Crisis, 1848–1861*. Edited by Don E. Fehrenbacher. New York: Harper & Row, 1976.

Stephens, Alexander H. *A Constitutional View of the Late War Between the States*. Philadelphia: National Publishing Co., 1868.

Thomas, Emory M. *The Confederate Nation, 1861–1865*. New York: Harper & Row, 1979.

Chapter 2 Lincoln, Congress, Defining Federal Power

Blight, David W. *Race and Reunion: The Civil War in American Memory*. Cambridge: Harvard University Press, 2001.

Boritt, Gabor S., ed. *The Lincoln Enigma: The Changing Faces of an American Icon*. New York: Oxford University Press, 2001.

Current, Richard N. *The Lincoln Nobody Knows*. New York: Hill and Wang, 1958.

Donald, David Herbert. *Lincoln*. New York: Simon & Schuster, 1995.

Foner, Eric. *The Fiery Trial: Abraham Lincoln and American Slavery*. New York: W. W. Norton & Company, 2010.

Gallagher, Gary W. *The Confederate War.* Cambridge: Harvard University Press, 1997.

Gienapp, William E. *Abraham Lincoln and Civil War America: A Biography.* New York: Oxford University Press, 2002.

McPherson, James M. *Battle Cry of Freedom: The Civil War Era.* New York: Oxford University Press, 1988.

Neely, Mark E., Jr. *The Fate of Liberty: Abraham Lincoln and Civil Liberties.* New York: Oxford University Press, 1991.

Paludan, Phillip S. *The Presidency of Abraham Lincoln.* Lawrence: University Press of Kansas, 1994.

Perman, Michael. *Emancipation and Reconstruction, 1862–1879.* Wheeling, IL: Harlan Davidson, 1987.

Reid, Brian Holden. *The Origins of the American Civil War.* London: Longman, 1996.

Rhodes, James Ford. *History of the United States from the Compromise of 1850 to the McKinley-Bryan Campaign of 1896*, Vol. 3. New York: Macmillan, 1909.

Smith, Jean Edward. *Grant.* New York: Simon & Schuster, 2001.

Chase, Salmon P. *The Salmon P. Chase Papers.* Edited by John Niven. Kent, OH: Kent State University Press, 1993.

Donald, David Herbert. *Lincoln.* New York: Simon & Schuster, 1995.

Goodwin, Doris Kearns. *Team of Rivals: The Political Genius of Abraham Lincoln.* New York: Simon & Schuster, 2005.

McPherson, James M. *Battle Cry of Freedom: The Civil War Era.* New York: Oxford University Press, 1988.

Nicolay, John G., and John Hay. *Abraham Lincoln: A History.* 10 vols. New York: The Century Co., 1890.

Seward, William H. *The Works of William H. Seward.* Edited by George E. Baker. Boston: Houghton, Mifflin and Company, 1884.

Welles, Gideon. *The Diary of Gideon Welles, Secretary of the Navy Under Lincoln and Johnson.* Boston: Houghton Mifflin, 1911.

Current, Richard N. *The Lincoln Nobody Knows.* New York: McGraw-Hill, 1958.

Donald, David Herbert. *Lincoln.* New York: Simon & Schuster, 1995.

Goodwin, Doris Kearns. *Team of Rivals: The Political Genius of Abraham Lincoln.* New York: Simon & Schuster, 2005.

Nevins, Allan. *The War for the Union: The Organized War to Victory, 1863–1864.* New York: Charles Scribner's Sons, 1971.

Welles, Gideon. *Diary of Gideon Welles: Secretary of the Navy Under Lincoln and Johnson.* Edited by Harold C. Syrett. New York: W.W. Norton, 1960.

Belz, Herman. *Abraham Lincoln, Constitutionalism, and Equal Rights in the Civil War Era.* New York: Fordham University Press, 1998.

Burlingame, Michael. *Abraham Lincoln: A Life*. 2 vols. Baltimore: Johns Hopkins University Press, 2008.

Chase, Salmon P. *Inside Lincoln's Cabinet: The Civil War Diaries of Salmon P. Chase*. Edited by David Donald. New York: Longmans, Green & Co., 1954.

Chapter 3 Freedom Rings, The Emancipation Proclamation

Lincoln, Abraham. Collected Works of Abraham Lincoln. Edited by Roy P. Basler. 9 vols. New Brunswick, NJ: Rutgers University Press, 1953.

U.S. War Department. The War of the Rebellion: A Compilation of the Official Records of the Union and Confederate Armies. Washington, D.C.: Government Printing Office, 1880–1901.

Douglass, Frederick. Life and Times of Frederick Douglass. Boston: De Wolfe & Fiske, 1892.

Guelzo, Allen C. Lincoln's Emancipation Proclamation: The End of Slavery in America. New York: Simon & Schuster, 2004.

Holzer, Harold, ed. The Emancipation Proclamation: Three Views. Baton Rouge: Louisiana State University Press, 2006.

McPherson, James M. The Negro's Civil War: How American Blacks Felt and Acted During the War for the Union. New York: Pantheon Books, 1965.

Berlin, Ira, Joseph Reidy, and Leslie Rowland, eds. Freedom: A Documentary History of Emancipation, 1861–1867. Series I: The Destruction of Slavery. New York: Cambridge University Press, 1985.

Foner, Eric. The Fiery Trial: Abraham Lincoln and American Slavery. New York: W. W. Norton & Company, 2010.

McPherson, James M. Battle Cry of Freedom: The Civil War Era. New York: Oxford University Press, 1988.

Neely, Mark E. Jr. The Last Best Hope of Earth: Abraham Lincoln and the Promise of America. Cambridge, MA: Harvard University Press, 1993.

Donald, David Herbert. Lincoln. New York: Simon & Schuster, 1995.

Blight, David W. Race and Reunion: The Civil War in American Memory. Cambridge, MA: Harvard University Press, 2001.

Chapter 4 Robert E. Lee, Duty or State Allegiance

Boritt, Gabor S., ed. *The Gettysburg Gospel: The Lincoln Speech That Nobody Knows*. New York: Simon & Schuster, 2006.

Coddington, Edwin B. *The Gettysburg Campaign: A Study in Command*. New York: Charles Scribner's Sons, 1968.

Connelly, Thomas L. *The Marble Man: Robert E. Lee and His Image in American Society*. Baton Rouge: Louisiana State University Press, 1977.

Davis, William C. *Look Away! A History of the Confederate States of America*. New York: Free Press, 2002.

Draper, Theodore. *A Struggle for Power: The American Revolution*. New York: Times Books, 1996.

Freeman, Douglas Southall. *Lee's Lieutenants: A Study in Command*, Vol. II: *Cedar Mountain to Chancellorsville*. New York: Scribner, 1943.

Freeman, Douglas Southall. *R. E. Lee: A Biography*, Vol. III. New York: Charles Scribner's Sons, 1935.

Gallagher, Gary W. *Lee and His Generals in War and Memory*. Baton Rouge: Louisiana State University Press, 1998.

Gallagher, Gary W. *The Confederate War*. Cambridge: Harvard University Press, 1997.

McPherson, James M. *Battle Cry of Freedom: The Civil War Era*. New York: Oxford University Press, 1988.

Thomas, Emory M. *Robert E. Lee: A Biography*. New York: W. W. Norton & Company, 1995.

Blight, David W. *Race and Reunion: The Civil War in American Memory*. Cambridge, MA: Harvard University Press, 2001.

Dowdey, Clifford. *Lee*. Boston: Little, Brown and Company, 1965.

Freeman, Douglas Southall. *R. E. Lee: A Biography*. 4 vols. New York: Charles Scribner's Sons, 1934–1935.

Norris, Wesley. "Testimony of Wesley Norris, Late a Slave of Gen. R.E. Lee." *National Anti-Slavery Standard*, April 14, 1866.

Pryor, Elizabeth Brown. *Reading the Man: A Portrait of Robert E. Lee Through His Private Letters*. New York: Viking, 2007.

Thomas, Emory M. *Robert E. Lee: A Biography*. New York: W. W. Norton & Company, 1995.

Giovannetti, Justin. "Robert E. Lee's Views on Slavery." *Smithsonian Magazine*, August 12, 2020.

Janney, Caroline E. *Remembering the Civil War: Reunion and the Limits of Reconciliation*. Chapel Hill: University of North Carolina Press, 2013.

Kornblith, Gary J., and Carol Lasser. *Elusive Utopia: The Struggle for Racial Equality in Oberlin, Ohio*. Baton Rouge: Louisiana State University Press, 2018.

Vandiver, Frank E. *Mighty Stonewall*. College Station: Texas A&M University Press, 1957.

Freeman, Douglas Southall. *R. E. Lee: A Biography*. 4 vols. New York: Charles Scribner's Sons, 1934–1935.

Thomas, Emory M. *Robert E. Lee: A Biography*. New York: W. W. Norton & Company, 1995.

Gallagher, Gary W. *Lee and His Army in Confederate History*. Chapel Hill: University of North Carolina Press, 2001.

Chapter 5 Frustrations of Union Command

McPherson, James M. *Battle Cry of Freedom: The Civil War Era*. New York: Oxford University Press, 1988.

Sears, Stephen W. *George B. McClellan: The Young Napoleon*. Boston: Ticknor & Fields, 1988.

Hattaway, Herman, and Archer Jones. *How the North Won: A Military History of the Civil War*. Urbana: University of Illinois Press, 1983.

Williams, T. Harry. *Lincoln and His Generals*. New York: Alfred A. Knopf, 1952.

Simpson, Brooks D. Ulysses S. Grant: Triumph over Adversity, 1822–1865. Boston: Houghton Mifflin, 2000.

Thomas, Benjamin P. Abraham Lincoln: A Biography. New York: Alfred A. Knopf, 1952.

Grant, Ulysses S. Personal Memoirs of U. S. Grant. New York: Charles L. Webster & Co., 1885.

Sherman, William T. Memoirs of General William T. Sherman. 2 vols. New York: D. Appleton and Company, 1875.

McClellan, George B. McClellan's Own Story: The War for the Union. New York: Charles L. Webster & Co., 1887.

Lincoln, Abraham. Collected Works of Abraham Lincoln. Edited by Roy P. Basler. 9 vols. New Brunswick, NJ: Rutgers University Press, 1953.

Williams, T. Harry. Lincoln and His Generals. New York: Alfred A. Knopf, 1952.

McPherson, James M. Tried by War: Abraham Lincoln as Commander in Chief. New York: Penguin Press, 2008.

Guelzo, Allen C. Fateful Lightning: A New History of the Civil War and Reconstruction. New York: Oxford University Press, 2012.

Bonekemper, Edward H. McClellan and Failure: A Study of Civil War Fear, Incompetence, and Politics. Jefferson, NC: McFarland & Company, 2007.

Simpson, Brooks D. Ulysses S. Grant: Triumph over Adversity, 1822–1865. Boston: Houghton Mifflin, 2000.

Wert, Jeffry D. General James Longstreet: The Confederacy's Most Controversial Soldier. New York: Simon & Schuster, 1993.

Sears, Stephen W. George B. McClellan: The Young Napoleon. New York: Ticknor & Fields, 1988.

Cooling, Benjamin Franklin. Joseph Hooker: Fighting Joe. Hamden, CT: Archon Books, 1994.

Eicher, John H., and David J. Eicher. Civil War High Commands. Stanford, CA: Stanford University Press, 2001.

Trudeau, Noah Andre. The Last Citadel: Petersburg, Virginia, June 1864–April 1865. Baton Rouge: Louisiana State University Press, 1991.

Chapter 6 Grant and Lee

Bonekemper, Edward H. *Ulysses S. Grant: A Victor, Not a Butcher*. Washington, D.C.: Regnery History, 2014.

Coddington, Edwin B. *The Gettysburg Campaign: A Study in Command*. New York: Charles Scribner's Sons, 1968.

Freeman, Douglas Southall. *R. E. Lee: A Biography*, Vol. III and IV. New York: Charles Scribner's Sons, 1935.

Freeman, Douglas Southall. *Lee's Lieutenants: A Study in Command*, Vol. II and III. New York: Scribner, 1943.

Gallagher, Gary W. *Lee and His Generals in War and Memory*. Baton Rouge: Louisiana State University Press, 1998.

Grant, Ulysses S. *Personal Memoirs of U.S. Grant*. New York: Charles L. Webster & Company, 1885.

McFeely, William S. *Grant: A Biography*. New York: W. W. Norton & Company, 1981.

McPherson, James M. *Battle Cry of Freedom: The Civil War Era*. New York: Oxford University Press, 1988.

Thomas, Emory M. *Robert E. Lee: A Biography*. New York: W. W. Norton & Company, 1995.

White, Ronald C. *American Ulysses: A Life of Ulysses S. Grant*. New York: Random House, 2016.

Bonekemper, Edward H. *Grant and Lee: Victorious American and Vanquished Virginian*. Washington, D.C.: Regnery Publishing, 2007.

Simpson, Brooks D. *Ulysses S. Grant: Triumph over Adversity, 1822–1865*. New York: Houghton Mifflin, 2000.

Davis, William C. *Crucible of Command: Ulysses S. Grant and Robert E. Lee — The War They Fought, the Peace They Forged*. Boston: Da Capo Press, 2014.

Chapter 7, Daily Life in a War-Torn Nation

Alcott, Louisa May. *Hospital Sketches*. Boston: James Redpath, 1863.

Barton, Clara. *Clara Barton: Professional Angel*. By Elizabeth Brown Pryor. Philadelphia: University of Pennsylvania Press, 1987.

Douglass, Frederick. *The Life and Times of Frederick Douglass*. Boston: De Wolfe & Fiske Co., 1892.

Faust, Drew Gilpin. *This Republic of Suffering: Death and the American Civil War*. New York: Alfred A. Knopf, 2008.

Foster, Stephen. *Hard Times Come Again No More*. New York: Firth, Pond & Co., 1854.

Giesberg, Judith. *Army at Home: Women and the Civil War on the Northern Home Front*. Chapel Hill: University of North Carolina Press, 2009.

Grant, Susan-Mary. *The War for a Nation: The American Civil War*. London: Routledge, 2006.

Ken Burns. *The Civil War*. PBS Documentary Series. Washington, D.C.: Florentine Films, 1990.

McWhirter, Christian. *Battle Hymns: The Power and Popularity of Music in the Civil War*. Chapel Hill: University of North Carolina Press, 2012.

Silber, Irwin, ed. *Songs of the Civil War*. New York: Columbia University Press, 1960.

Stowe, Harriet Beecher. *A Key to Uncle Tom's Cabin*. Boston: Jewett and Company, 1853.

Twain, Mark. *Roughing It*. Hartford: American Publishing Company, 1872.

Whitman, Walt. *Drum-Taps*. New York: 1865.

Wiley, Bell Irvin. *The Life of Billy Yank: The Common Soldier of the Union*. Baton Rouge: Louisiana State University Press, 1952.

Wiley, Bell Irvin. *The Life of Johnny Reb: The Common Soldier of the Confederacy*. Baton Rouge: Louisiana State University Press, 1943.

Wilson, Charles Reagan. *Baptized in Blood: The Religion of the Lost Cause, 1865–1920*. Athens: University of Georgia Press, 1980.

Douglass, Frederick. *Selected Speeches and Writings*. Chicago: University of Chicago Press, 1999.

McPherson, James. *Battle Cry of Freedom: The Civil War Era*. New York: Oxford University Press, 1988.

Levine, Bruce. *Confederate Emancipation: Southern Plans to Free and Arm Slaves during the Civil War*. Oxford University Press, 2006.

Faust, Drew Gilpin. *This Republic of Suffering: Death and the American Civil War*. New York: Vintage, 2008.

Kornblith, Gary J., ed. *The American People in the Civil War Era*. Boston: Bedford/St. Martin's, 2003.

The *Anglo-African*, January–March 1863 editions.

U.S. Congressional Records, 1863.

Confederate Congressional Debates, 1863.

Carney, William H. Personal Accounts and Medal of Honor Citation

Chapter 8 Legislation and Desertion – Struggles in Congress and Camp

Congressional Globe. 37th and 38th Congresses, 1863. Washington, D.C.: Government Printing Office.

Lincoln, Abraham. Collected Works of Abraham Lincoln. Edited by Roy P. Basler. 9 vols. New Brunswick, NJ: Rutgers University Press, 1953.

Confederate States of America. Statutes at Large of the Provisional Government of the Confederate States of America. Richmond: R. M. Smith, 1864.

U.S. War Department. The War of the Rebellion: A Compilation of the Official Records of the Union and Confederate Armies. Washington, D.C.: Government Printing Office, 1880–1901.

Neely, Mark E. Jr. The Fate of Liberty: Abraham Lincoln and Civil Liberties. New York: Oxford University Press, 1991.

Patrick, Rembert W. Jefferson Davis and His Cabinet. Baton Rouge: Louisiana State University Press, 1944.

Harris, William C. Lincoln and the Union Governors. Carbondale: Southern Illinois University Press, 2012.

Arnold, James R. The Civil War: A Soldier's Life. New York: Facts on File, 2004.

McPherson, James M. What They Fought For, 1861–1865. Baton Rouge: Louisiana State University Press, 1994.

Linderman, Gerald F. Embattled Courage: The Experience of Combat in the American Civil War. New York: Free Press, 1987.

Escott, Paul D. After Secession: Jefferson Davis and the Failure of Confederate Nationalism. Baton Rouge: Louisiana State University Press, 1978.

Berlin, Ira, ed. Freedom: A Documentary History of Emancipation, 1861–1867. New York: Cambridge University Press, 1982.

Hearn, Chester G. When the Devil Came Down to Dixie: Ben Butler in New Orleans. Baton Rouge: Louisiana State University Press, 1997.

McPherson, James M. Battle Cry of Freedom: The Civil War Era. New York: Oxford University Press, 1988.

Trefousse, Hans L. The Radical Republicans: Lincoln's Vanguard for Racial Justice. New York: Knopf, 1969.

Chapter 9 The Indian Wars

"The Indian War in Minnesota." St. Paul Pioneer, July–August 1863.

"Further Engagements with the Sioux." The Minnesota State News, July 24, 1863.

"The War with the Navajo." Santa Fe New Mexican, October 1863.

"General Watie's Success in the Indian Territory." Richmond Examiner, August 12, 1863.

"News from the Indian Country." New York Times, July 27, 1863.

"Operations Against the Indians." Harper's Weekly, August 15, 1863.

Bailey, Lynn R. Indian Slave Trade in the Southwest: A Study of Slavery in the Borderlands. Los Angeles: Westernlore Press, 1966.

Clodfelter, Micheal. The Dakota War: The United States Army Versus the Sioux, 1862–1865. Jefferson, NC: McFarland & Company, 1998.

Dunlay, Thomas W. Wolves for the Blue Soldiers: Indian Scouts and Auxiliaries with the United States Army, 1860–90. Lincoln: University of Nebraska Press, 1982.

Hoig, Stan. The Peace Chiefs of the Cheyennes. Norman: University of Oklahoma Press, 1980.

Meyer, Roy W. History of the Santee Sioux: United States Indian Policy on Trial. Lincoln: University of Nebraska Press, 1967.

Sweeney, Edwin R. Cochise: Chiricahua Apache Chief. Norman: University of Oklahoma Press, 1995.

Thrapp, Dan L. *The Conquest of Apacheria*. Norman: University of Oklahoma Press, 1967.

Utley, Robert M. *Cochise: Apache Warrior and Statesman*. New Haven: Yale University Press, 2012.

Utley, Robert M. *Frontiersmen in Blue: The United States Army and the Indian, 1848–1865*. Lincoln: University of Nebraska Press, 1981.

White, Richard. *"It's Your Misfortune and None of My Own": A History of the American West*. Norman: University of Oklahoma Press, 1991.

Wilkins, Thurman. *The Chickasaws: A History*. Norman: University of Oklahoma Press, 1983.

"The Indian Tribes and the War." *Chicago Tribune*, October 4, 1863.

Abel, Annie Heloise. *The American Indian as Slaveholder and Secessionist*. Cleveland: Arthur H. Clark Company, 1915.

Bailey, Garrick Alan. *The Osage and the Invisible World: From the Works of Francis La Flesche*. Norman: University of Oklahoma Press, 1995.

Bailey, Richard. *Neither Carpetbaggers Nor Scalawags: Black Officeholders During the Reconstruction of Alabama, 1867–1878*. Montgomery: Black Belt Press, 1999.

Carley, Kenneth. *The Dakota War of 1862: Minnesota's Other Civil War*. St. Paul: Minnesota Historical Society Press, 2001.

Dunlay, Thomas W. *Kit Carson and the Indians*. Lincoln: University of Nebraska Press, 2000.

Ehle, John. *Trail of Tears: The Rise and Fall of the Cherokee Nation*. New York: Anchor Books, 1988.

Iverson, Peter. *When Indians Became Cowboys: Native Peoples and Cattle Ranching in the American West*. Norman: University of Oklahoma Press, 1994.

Kvasnicka, Robert M., and Herman J. Viola. *The Commissioners of Indian Affairs, 1824–1977*. Lincoln: University of Nebraska Press, 1979.

McCaslin, Richard B. *Portraits of Conflict: A Photographic History of Texas in the Civil War*. Fayetteville: University of Arkansas Press, 1998.

Roberts, David. *The Long Walk: The Forced Navajo Exile*. New York: W.W. Norton & Company, 1993.

Stremlau, Rose. *Sustaining the Cherokee Family: Kinship and the Allotment of an Indigenous Nation*. Chapel Hill: University of North Carolina Press, 2011.

Thrush, Coll. *Indigenous London: Native Travelers at the Heart of Empire*. New Haven: Yale University Press, 2016.

Utley, Robert M. *Frontiersmen in Blue: The United States Army and the Indian, 1848–1865*. New York: Macmillan, 1967.

West, Elliott. *The Last Indian War: The Nez Perce Story*. New York: Oxford University Press, 2009.

Carson, Christopher. *Memoirs of Kit Carson: The Great Western Pathfinder*. Edited by Charles Burdett. Philadelphia: J.W. Bradley, 1860.

U.S. War Department. *Official Records of the Union and Confederate Armies in the War of the Rebellion*, Series I, Volume XXXIV, Part II. Washington: Government Printing Office, 1891.

Santa Fe New Mexican. "Col. Carson's Campaign Against the Navajo." October–December 1863.

Dunlay, Thomas W. *Kit Carson and the Indians*. Lincoln: University of Nebraska Press, 2000.

Roberts, David. *The Long Walk: The Forced Navajo Exile*. New York: W.W. Norton & Company, 1993.

Utley, Robert M. *Frontiersmen in Blue: The United States Army and the Indian, 1848–1865*. New York: Macmillan, 1967.

Hafen, LeRoy R. *Kit Carson: A Pattern for Heroes*. Lincoln: University of Nebraska Press, 1993.

Thrush, Coll. *Native Seattle: Histories from the Crossing-Over Place*. Seattle: University of Washington Press, 2007.

Sides, Hampton. *Blood and Thunder: The Epic Story of Kit Carson and the Conquest of the American West*. New York: Doubleday, 2006.

Chapter 10 Blood, Bandages, Medicine, and Mortality

Adams, George Worthington. *Doctors in Blue: The Medical History of the Union Army in the Civil War*. Baton Rouge: Louisiana State University Press, 1952.

Bollet, Alfred J. *Civil War Medicine: Challenges and Triumphs*. Tucson: Galen Press, 2002.

Cunningham, Horace H. *Doctors in Gray: The Confederate Medical Service*. Baton Rouge: Louisiana State University Press, 1958.

Freemon, Frank R. *Gangrene and Glory: Medical Care during the American Civil War*. Urbana: University of Illinois Press, 1998.

Garrison, Fielding H. *An Introduction to the History of Medicine*. Philadelphia: W.B. Saunders, 1929.

Hartzell, Joseph C. *Camp Life in the Union Army*. Cincinnati: Hitchcock and Walden, 1864.

Letterman, Jonathan. *Medical Recollections of the Army of the Potomac*. New York: D. Appleton and Company, 1866.

Schultz, Jane E. *Women at the Front: Hospital Workers in Civil War America*. Chapel Hill: University of North Carolina Press, 2004.

Schultz, Jane E. *This Birth Place of Souls: The Civil War Nursing Diary of Harriet Eaton*. New York: Oxford University Press, 2010.

Styple, William B. *"The Little Bugler": The True Story of a Twelve-Year-Old Boy in the Civil War*. Kearny, NJ: Belle Grove Publishing, 1998.

United States Sanitary Commission. *Documents Relating to the Sanitary Commission*. Washington, D.C., 1861–1865.

Vaughan, C.G. *Reminiscences of a Confederate Surgeon*. Nashville: Publishing House of the M.E. Church, South, 1900.

Adams, George Worthington. *Doctors in Blue: The Medical History of the Union Army in the Civil War*. Baton Rouge: Louisiana State University Press, 1952.

Bollet, Alfred J. *Civil War Medicine: Challenges and Triumphs*. Tucson: Galen Press, 2002.

Cunningham, Horace H. *Doctors in Gray: The Confederate Medical Service*. Baton Rouge: Louisiana State University Press, 1958.

Freemon, Frank R. *Gangrene and Glory: Medical Care during the American Civil War*. Urbana: University of Illinois Press, 1998.

Garrison, Fielding H. *An Introduction to the History of Medicine*. Philadelphia: W.B. Saunders, 1929.

Hartzell, Joseph C. *Camp Life in the Union Army*. Cincinnati: Hitchcock and Walden, 1864.

Letterman, Jonathan. *Medical Recollections of the Army of the Potomac*. New York: D. Appleton and Company, 1866.

Schultz, Jane E. *Women at the Front: Hospital Workers in Civil War America*. Chapel Hill: University of North Carolina Press, 2004.

Schultz, Jane E. *This Birth Place of Souls: The Civil War Nursing Diary of Harriet Eaton*. New York: Oxford University Press, 2010.

Styple, William B. *"The Little Bugler": The True Story of a Twelve-Year-Old Boy in the Civil War*. Kearny, NJ: Belle Grove Publishing, 1998.

United States Sanitary Commission. *Documents Relating to the Sanitary Commission*. Washington, D.C., 1861–1865.

Vaughan, C.G. *Reminiscences of a Confederate Surgeon*. Nashville: Publishing House of the M.E. Church, South, 1900.

Chapter 11 Confederacy Abroad

Crook, D. P. *The North, the South, and the Powers 1861–1865*. New York: John Wiley & Sons, 1974.

Hubbell, John T. *The Confederate Diplomats: The South's Agents in Europe, 1861–1865*. Baton Rouge: Louisiana State University Press, 1976.

Jones, Howard. *Union in Peril: The Crisis Over British Intervention in the Civil War*. Chapel Hill: University of North Carolina Press, 1992.

McPherson, James M. *Battle Cry of Freedom: The Civil War Era*. New York: Oxford University Press, 1988.

Seward, William H. *The Diplomatic Correspondence of the United States During the Civil War*. Washington, D.C.: Government Printing Office, 1862–1865.

Stampp, Kenneth M. *America in 1857: A Nation on the Brink*. New York: Oxford University Press, 1990.

Foreman, Amanda. *A World on Fire: Britain's Crucial Role in the American Civil War*. New York: Random House, 2010.

Blackburn, George M. *French Newspaper Opinion on the American Civil War*. Westport, CT: Greenwood Press, 1997.

Crook, D. P. *The North, the South, and the Powers 1861–1865*. New York: John Wiley & Sons, 1974.

Foreman, Amanda. *A World on Fire: Britain's Crucial Role in the American Civil War*. New York: Random House, 2010.

Hubbell, John T. *The Confederate Diplomats: The South's Agents in Europe, 1861–1865*. Baton Rouge: Louisiana State University Press, 1976.

Jones, Howard. *Blue and Gray Diplomacy: A History of Union and Confederate Foreign Relations*. Chapel Hill: University of North Carolina Press, 2010.

McPherson, James M. *Battle Cry of Freedom: The Civil War Era*. New York: Oxford University Press, 1988.

Owsley, Frank L. *King Cotton Diplomacy: Foreign Relations of the Confederate States of America*. Chicago: University of Chicago Press, 1931.

Adams, Ephraim Douglass. *Great Britain and the American Civil War*. 2 vols. New York: Russell & Russell, 1958.

Crook, D. P. *The North, the South, and the Powers, 1861–1865*. New York: Wiley, 1974.

Doyle, Don H. *The Cause of All Nations: An International History of the American Civil War*. New York: Basic Books, 2015.

Ferris, Norman B. *The Trent Affair: A Diplomatic Crisis*. Knoxville: University of Tennessee Press, 1977.

Foreman, Amanda. *A World on Fire: Britain's Crucial Role in the American Civil War*. New York: Random House, 2010.

Seward, William H. *The Diplomatic History of the War for the Union*. Edited by William H. Seward Jr. New York: G.P. Putnam's Sons, 1877.

Chapter 12 New York Draft Riots

James McPherson (*Battle Cry of Freedom*)

Leslie M. Harris, in *In the Shadow of Slavery*, suggests the real death toll was almost certainly higher, especially among Black victims.

The *New York Tribune* and *New York Times* both noted gruesome scenes of widespread violence and mob brutality.

Bernstein, Iver. *The New York City Draft Riots: Their Significance for American Society and Politics in the Age of the Civil War*.

McPherson, James. *Battle Cry of Freedom: The Civil War Era*.

Harper's Weekly Archives, July 1863

Douglass, Frederick. *Selected Speeches and Writings*.

New York Times, July 13–16, 1863 Reports

Chapter 13 Freedom and the 54th Massachusetts

Douglass, Frederick. *Selected Speeches and Writings*. Chicago: University of Chicago Press, 1999.

McPherson, James. *Battle Cry of Freedom: The Civil War Era*. New York: Oxford University Press, 1988.

Levine, Bruce. *Confederate Emancipation: Southern Plans to Free and Arm Slaves during the Civil War*. Oxford University Press, 2006.

Faust, Drew Gilpin. *This Republic of Suffering: Death and the American Civil War*. New York: Vintage, 2008.

Kornblith, Gary J., ed. *The American People in the Civil War Era*. Boston: Bedford/St. Martin's, 2003.

The *Anglo-African*, January–March 1863 editions.

U.S. Congressional Records, 1863.

Lincoln, Abraham. Collected Works of Abraham Lincoln. Edited by Roy P. Basler. 9 vols. New Brunswick, NJ: Rutgers University Press, 1953.

Emilio, Luis F. A Brave Black Regiment: The History of the Fifty-Fourth Regiment of Massachusetts Volunteer Infantry, 1863–1865. Boston: Boston Book Company, 1894.

Douglass, Frederick. Life and Times of Frederick Douglass. Boston: De Wolfe & Fiske, 1892.

U.S. War Department. The War of the Rebellion: A Compilation of the Official Records of the Union and Confederate Armies. Washington, D.C.: Government Printing Office, 1880–1901.

Cornish, Dudley Taylor. The Sable Arm: Black Troops in the Union Army, 1861–1865. Lawrence: University Press of Kansas, 1987.

Trudeau, Noah Andre. Like Men of War: Black Troops in the Civil War, 1862–1865. Boston: Little, Brown and Company, 1998.

Duncan, Russell. Where Death and Glory Meet: Colonel Robert Gould Shaw and the 54th Massachusetts Infantry. Athens: University of Georgia Press, 1999.

Berlin, Ira, Joseph Reidy, and Leslie Rowland, eds. Freedom: A Documentary History of Emancipation, 1861–1867. Series II, The Black Military Experience. New York: Cambridge University Press, 1982.

Blight, David W. Race and Reunion: The Civil War in American Memory. Cambridge, MA: Harvard University Press, 2001.

Holzer, Harold, ed. The Emancipation Proclamation: Three Views. Baton Rouge: Louisiana State University Press, 2006.

Guelzo, Allen C. Lincoln's Emancipation Proclamation: The End of Slavery in America. New York: Simon & Schuster, 2004.

Washington, Bryan. "Glory and Historical Representation." Journal of Popular Film and Television 18, no. 1 (1990): 30–38.

Carney, William H. Personal Accounts and Medal of Honor Citation.

Chapter 14 The Battle of Stones River

Cozzens, Peter. *No Better Place to Die: The Battle of Stones River*. Urbana: University of Illinois Press, 1990.

Daniel, Larry J. *Battle of Stones River: The Forgotten Conflict Between the Confederate Army of Tennessee and the Union Army of the Cumberland*. Baton Rouge: Louisiana State University Press, 2012.

Hazen, William B. *A Narrative of Military Service*. Boston: Ticknor and Company, 1885. (Especially see Chapter 5: "The Defense of the Round Forest.")

Horn, Stanley F. *The Army of Tennessee*. Norman: University of Oklahoma Press, 1941.

McDonough, James L. *War in Kentucky: From Shiloh to Perryville*. Knoxville: University of Tennessee Press, 1994.

National Park Service. *Stones River National Battlefield*. U.S. Department of the Interior. Accessed May 22, 2025.

U.S. War Department. *The War of the Rebellion: A Compilation of the Official Records of the Union and Confederate Armies*. Series I, Volume XX, Part I. Washington, D.C.: Government Printing Office, 1887.

Chapter 15 Chancellorsville, Triumph and Tragedy in the Wilderness

American Battlefield Trust. "Chancellorsville Campaign Maps."

Holt, David. *A Mississippi Rebel in the Army of Northern Virginia*.

Freeman, Douglas Southall. *Lee's Lieutenants: A Study in Command*.

National Park Service. "Chancellorsville Battlefield Guide."

McPherson, James. *Battle Cry of Freedom: The Civil War Era*.

Gallagher, Gary W. *Chancellorsville: The Battle and Its Aftermath*. Chapel Hill: University of North Carolina Press, 1996.

Sears, Stephen W. *Chancellorsville*. Boston: Houghton Mifflin, 1996.

Freeman, Douglas Southall. *Lee's Lieutenants: A Study in Command, Vol. II – Cedar Mountain to Chancellorsville*. New York: Scribner, 1943.

Wert, Jeffry D. *General James Longstreet: The Confederacy's Most Controversial Soldier*. New York: Simon & Schuster, 1993.

Chapter 16 Gettysburg, Turning the Tide

American Battlefield Trust. "Gettysburg Campaign Maps."

Wainwright, Charles. *A Diary of Battle: The Personal Journals of Colonel Charles S. Wainwright*.

Rhodes, Elisha Hunt. *All For the Union: The Civil War Diary and Letters of Elisha Hunt Rhodes*.

National Park Service. "Gettysburg Maps and Troop Positions.

McPherson, James. *Battle Cry of Freedom: The Civil War Era*.

Pickering, George E. *Letters from the Front, 1863*.

Wilkes, Nathan. *Private Papers of the Army of Northern Virginia*.

Catton, Bruce, *The Army of the Potomac: Glory Road*. Garden City, NY: Doubleday & Co., Inc., 1952.

Clark, Champ, *Gettysburg: The Confederate High Tide*. Alexandria, VA: Time-Life Books, 1983.

Donald, David Herbert, *Lincoln*. New York: Simon & Schuster, (Kindle Edition), 2011.

Foote, Shelby, *The Civil War, A Narrative: Fredericksburg to Meridian*. New York: Vintage Civil War Library, Knopf Doubleday Publishing Group (Kindle Edition), 2011.

Long, E.B. with Long, Barbara, *The Civil War Day by Day*. New York: Da Capo Press, Inc., 1971.

McPherson, James M., *Battle Cry of Freedom: The Civil War Era*. Oxford History of the United States Book 6, Oxford University Press (Kindle Edition), 1988.

Rhodes, James Ford, *History of the Civil War, 1861-1865*. New York: The MacMillan Company (Kindle Edition, Reservoir House, 2016), 1917.

Sears, Stephen W., *Gettysburg*. New York: Houghton Mifflin Harcourt Publishing Company (Kindle Edition), 2003.

Sears, Stephen W., *Lincoln's Lieutenants: The High Command of the Army of the Potomac*. Boston, New York: Houghton Mifflin Harcourt Books, (Kindle Edition), 2017.

Welles, Gideon, *Diary of Gideon Welles Volumes I & II*. Kindle Edition. Abridged, Annotated.

Wert, Jeffry D. (Patricia L. Faust ed.), *Historical Times Illustrated Encyclopedia of the Civil War*. New York: Harper & Row, 1986.

Coddington, Edwin B. *The Gettysburg Campaign: A Study in Command*. New York: Scribner, 1968.

Shaara, Michael. *The Killer Angels*. New York: Ballantine Books, 1974.

Pfanz, Harry W. *Gettysburg: The Second Day*. Chapel Hill: University of North Carolina Press, 1987.

Chamberlain, Joshua Lawrence. *The Passing of the Armies: An Account of the Final Campaign of the Army of the Potomac*. New York: G.P. Putnam's Sons, 1915.

Chapter 17 Lincoln at Gettysburg, the Speech

Everett, Edward. *Oration Delivered on the Battlefield of Gettysburg, Nov. 19, 1863, at the Consecration of the Cemetery*. Boston: Little, Brown and Company, 1863.

Garry Wills. *Lincoln at Gettysburg: The Words That Remade America*. New York: Simon & Schuster, 1992.

Poynter Institute. "Today in Media History: Reporters Describe Lincoln's 1863 Gettysburg Address." Last modified November 19, 2014.

Springfield Republican. "Gettysburg Address Commentary." November 1863. Quoted in Wills, *Lincoln at Gettysburg*.

Chicago Times. "Editorial on the Gettysburg Address." November 20, 1863. Quoted in Sandburg, Carl. *Abraham Lincoln: The War Years*, Vol. 2. New York: Harcourt, Brace & Company, 1939.

Philadelphia Evening Bulletin. Editorial on the Gettysburg Address. November 1863. Quoted in Poynter Institute, "Today in Media History."

The New York Times. "The Gettysburg Ceremony." November 20, 1863. Accessed via New York Times archives.

Sandburg, Carl. *Abraham Lincoln: The War Years.* 4 vols. New York: Harcourt, Brace & Company, 1939.

Vanity Fair. "In 1863, the New York Times Did Not Care for the 'Business-Like' Gettysburg Address." Published November 18, 2013.

Chapter 18 Victory at Vicksburg, Dividing the Confederacy

American Battlefield Trust. "Vicksburg Campaign Maps."

Grant, Ulysses S. *Personal Memoirs of U.S. Grant.*

McPherson, James. *Battle Cry of Freedom: The Civil War Era.*

Smithsonian Civil War Diaries Archive

National Park Service: Vicksburg National Military Park

Lincoln, Abraham. Collected Works. University of Michigan Digital Library.

Bearss, Edwin C. *The Vicksburg Campaign.* 3 vols. Dayton, OH: Morningside Bookshop, 1986.

Ballard, Michael B. *Vicksburg: The Campaign That Opened the Mississippi.* Chapel Hill: University of North Carolina Press, 2004.

Grant, Ulysses S. *Personal Memoirs of U.S. Grant.* Edited by Mark Twain. New York: Charles L. Webster & Company, 1885–86.

Shea, William L., and Terrence J. Winschel. *Vicksburg Is the Key: The Struggle for the Mississippi River.* Lincoln: University of Nebraska Press, 2003.

Simon, John Y., ed. *The Papers of Ulysses S. Grant.* 31 vols. Carbondale: Southern Illinois University Press, 1967–2009.

Smith, Timothy B. *Champion Hill: Decisive Battle for Vicksburg.* El Dorado Hills, CA: Savas Beatie, 2004.

Tucker, Phillip Thomas. *The Siege of Vicksburg: Climax of the Campaign to Open the Mississippi River, May 23–July 4, 1863.* Mechanicsburg, PA: Stackpole Books, 1999.

U.S. War Department. *The War of the Rebellion: A Compilation of the Official Records of the Union and Confederate Armies.* Series I, Vol. XXIV, Parts I–III. Washington: Government Printing Office, 1889.

Winschel, Terrence J. *Triumph & Defeat: The Vicksburg Campaign.* Campbell, CA: Savas Publishing, 1999.

Chapter 19 Port Hudson, Controlling the Mississippi River

Banks, Nathaniel P. *Official Report of the Siege and Reduction of Port Hudson.* Washington, D.C.: Government Printing Office, 1863.

Bearss, Edwin C. *The Campaign for Port Hudson.* 3 vols. Baton Rouge: Louisiana State University Press, 1957.

Bergeron, Arthur W. Jr. *Port Hudson: Confederate Bastion on the Mississippi.* Baton Rouge: Louisiana State University Press, 1981.

Cornish, Dudley Taylor. *The Sable Arm: Negro Troops in the Union Army, 1861–1865*. New York: W.W. Norton & Company, 1966.

Hearn, Chester G. *The Capture of Port Hudson: The Union Army and Navy Finally Break the Confederate Stronghold on the Mississippi River*. Baton Rouge: Louisiana State University Press, 1995.

Hollandsworth, James G. Jr. *The Louisiana Native Guards: The Black Military Experience During the Civil War*. Baton Rouge: Louisiana State University Press, 1995.

Official Records of the War of the Rebellion. Series I, Vol. XXVI, Part I. Washington: Government Printing Office, 1889.

Smith, John David. *Black Soldiers in Blue: African American Troops in the Civil War Era*. Chapel Hill: University of North Carolina Press, 2002.

Winters, John D. *The Civil War in Louisiana*. Baton Rouge: Louisiana State University Press, 1963.

Chapter 20 Chickamauga, a Stream of Death

Cozzens, Peter. *This Terrible Sound: The Battle of Chickamauga*.

McPherson, James. *Battle Cry of Freedom*.

National Park Service: Chickamauga and Chattanooga National Military Park

Official Records of the War of the Rebellion

Eyewitness letters from the 21st Ohio and 58th Indiana Infantry

Cozzens, Peter. *This Terrible Sound: The Battle of Chickamauga*. Urbana: University of Illinois Press, 1992.

Cozzens, Peter. *The Shipwreck of Their Hopes: The Battles for Chattanooga*. Urbana: University of Illinois Press, 1994.

Daniel, Larry J. *Battle of Chickamauga: A Soldier's View*. Shippensburg, PA: White Mane Publishing, 1989.

McDonough, James L. *Chattanooga—A Death Grip on the Confederacy*. Knoxville: University of Tennessee Press, 1984.

Robertson, William Glenn. *River of Death—The Chickamauga Campaign*. Chapel Hill: University of North Carolina Press, 2018.

U.S. War Department. *The War of the Rebellion: A Compilation of the Official Records of the Union and Confederate Armies*. Washington, D.C.: Government Printing Office, 1880–1901. Series I, Vol. 30 (Chickamauga), Vol. 31 (Chattanooga).

Woodworth, Steven E. *Six Armies in Tennessee: The Chickamauga and Chattanooga Campaigns*. Lincoln: University of Nebraska Press, 1998.

Chapter 21 Chattanooga and the Ascendance of Sherman

Grant, Ulysses S. Personal Memoirs of U. S. Grant. New York: Charles L. Webster & Co., 1885. (See especially Chapter 40–42 for Grant's account of Chattanooga and Sherman's role.)

Sherman, William T. Memoirs of General William T. Sherman. 2 vols. New York: D. Appleton and Company, 1875.

U.S. War Department. The War of the Rebellion: A Compilation of the Official Records of the Union and Confederate Armies. Washington, D.C.: Government Printing Office, 1880–1901. (Series I, Vols. 30 and 31, for official reports on the Chattanooga Campaign.)

Cozzens, Peter. The Shipwreck of Their Hopes: The Battles for Chattanooga. Urbana: University of Illinois Press, 1994.

McDonough, James Lee. Chattanooga: A Death Grip on the Confederacy. Knoxville: University of Tennessee Press, 1984.

Woodworth, Steven E. Six Armies in Tennessee: The Chickamauga and Chattanooga Campaigns. Lincoln: University of Nebraska Press, 1998.

Esposito, Vincent J. West Point Atlas of American Wars: Volume I, 1689–1900. New York: Frederick A. Praeger, 1959.

Marszalek, John F. Sherman: A Soldier's Passion for Order. Carbondale: Southern Illinois University Press, 1993.

Liddell Hart, B. H. Sherman: Soldier, Realist, American. New York: Dodd, Mead & Company, 1929.

McPherson, James M. Battle Cry of Freedom: The Civil War Era. New York: Oxford University Press, 1988. (Especially chapters covering late 1863 and Union command transitions.)

Simpson, Brooks D. Ulysses S. Grant: Triumph over Adversity, 1822–1865. Boston: Houghton Mifflin, 2000.

Williams, T. Harry. Lincoln and His Generals. New York: Alfred A. Knopf, 1952.

Chapter 22 Proclamation of Amnesty and Reconstruction

Lincoln, Abraham. Collected Works of Abraham Lincoln. Edited by Roy P. Basler. 9 vols. New Brunswick, NJ: Rutgers University Press, 1953.

U.S. War Department. The War of the Rebellion: A Compilation of the Official Records of the Union and Confederate Armies. Washington, D.C.: Government Printing Office, 1880–1901.

Belz, Herman. Reconstructing the Union: Theory and Policy during the Civil War. Ithaca, NY: Cornell University Press, 1969.

Foner, Eric. Reconstruction: America's Unfinished Revolution, 1863–1877. New York: Harper & Row, 1988.

Guelzo, Allen C. Lincoln's Emancipation Proclamation: The End of Slavery in America. New York: Simon & Schuster, 2004.

Harris, William C. With Charity for All: Lincoln and the Restoration of the Union. Lexington: University Press of Kentucky, 1997.

Trefousse, Hans L. Historical Dictionary of Reconstruction. Westport, CT: Greenwood Press, 1991.

Randall, James G., and Richard N. Current. Lincoln the President: Midstream to the Last Full Measure. 2 vols. New York: Dodd, Mead, 1955.

Vorenberg, Michael. Final Freedom: The Civil War, the Abolition of Slavery, and the Thirteenth Amendment. New York: Cambridge University Press, 2001.

Donald, David Herbert. Lincoln. New York: Simon & Schuster, 1995.

Epilogue Lincoln's Despair and the Election of 1864

Lincoln, Abraham. Collected Works of Abraham Lincoln. Edited by Roy P. Basler. 9 vols. New Brunswick, NJ: Rutgers University Press, 1953.

U.S. War Department. The War of the Rebellion: A Compilation of the Official Records of the Union and Confederate Armies. Washington, D.C.: Government Printing Office, 1880–1901.

Goodwin, Doris Kearns. Team of Rivals: The Political Genius of Abraham Lincoln. New York: Simon & Schuster, 2005.

Foner, Eric. The Fiery Trial: Abraham Lincoln and American Slavery. New York: W. W. Norton & Company, 2010.

McPherson, James M. Battle Cry of Freedom: The Civil War Era. New York: Oxford University Press, 1988.

Shenk, Joshua Wolf. Lincoln's Melancholy: How Depression Challenged a President and Fueled His Greatness. Boston: Houghton Mifflin, 2005.

Flood, Charles Bracelen. 1864: Lincoln at the Gates of History. New York: Simon & Schuster, 2009.

Guelzo, Allen C. "The 'Blind Memorandum' of August 23, 1864." Friends of the Lincoln Collection, accessed May 30, 2025.

Bernstein, Iver. The New York City Draft Riots: Their Significance for American Society and Politics in the Age of the Civil War. New York: Oxford University Press, 1990.

Sandburg, Carl. Abraham Lincoln: The War Years. 4 vols. New York: Harcourt, Brace & Company, 1939.

Leech, Margaret. *Reveille in Washington, 1860–1865*. New York: Harper & Brothers, 1941.

www.ingramcontent.com/pod-product-compliance
Lightning Source LLC
La Vergne TN
LVHW052016080426
835513LV00018B/2051